Copyright © 1994 by Louis Goldblatt.

All rights reserved. No part
of this manuscript may be
copied in any form without
permission of the author.

Photographs from the author's collection.

Book layout and production by CarrDESIGN

Cover design by Timothy Carr

Jacket coordinator John Sisson

Manufactured in the United States of America

Printed by Edwards Brothers Incorporated

Library of Congress Catalogue Card Number: 95-94045
ISBN: 0-9645331-0-3

Dedication

To my wife Bobbie . . . the dream I never dared. If love is God's highest meaning for the world, then the reward of our love and life together is itself my thankful prayer in return. No pain can withstand your glow. We have together built and cherished everything there is that's worthwhile. I am eternally grateful — eternally loving you.

Lou

Biography

Louis Goldblatt, born in Stachov, Poland in 1903, came to the United States as a young child with his parent who, upon migrating to this country, settled in Chicago. His retail career began at an early age when he worked for his brothers after school in a small dry goods store opened in 1914 that grew into a chain of 47 Goldblatt's department store throughout the midwest.

In his teens, he traveled to New York alone on buying trips. In 1934, Goldblatt was named a vice president. He held the posts of General Advertising Manager; subsequently, General Merchandising Manager. Following military service, he was named Executive Vice President and Secretary-Treasurer of the then 10-unit company.

Diversely experienced in all areas of retailing, Goldblatt contributed significantly to the growth of Goldblatt's, particularly since becoming President and Chief Executive Officer in 1964. During the following years, until his retirement in 1979, the company reached record highs in both sales and net earnings.

Louis Goldblatt's concept of management has been to afford

Life is a game, play to win!

opportunity to all and to find developable qualities in people and growth potential in conditions. He has been Trustee of the Goldblatt Bros. Foundation; President of the Heart Research Foundation; Director of the Gastro-Intestinal Research Foundation; Director, Chicago Better Business Bureau; Director, Civic Center Bank and Trust Co.; and Director, State Street Council. Also, member, Executive Service Corps of Chicago; Guarantor, Lyric Opera of Chicago. Recipient: Medal, Italian Knighthood of Merit; Silver Plaque Award, National Conference of Christians and Jews; Order of Lincoln Medallion, Lincoln Academy of Illinois; and Retailer of the Year Award, Brand Names Foundation. Also, Goldblatt is listed in Who's Who in America. In 1989—special commendation by resolution of the Eighty-Fifth General Assembly of the State of Illinois—for accomplishments exemplified by dedication, ambition and hard work.

Louis Goldblatt resides with his wife, Bobbie, in Wilmette, Illinois, where they raised three sons.

Louis Goldblatt

Table of Contents

Preface

Chapter I:
Exodus: From Strachov to Chicago   5

Chapter II:
Life Behind the Goldblatt's Polska Skalp   21

Chapter III:
Initial Forays into the Wider World   40

Chapter IV:
The Goldblatt's Get into the Dry Goods Business   50

Chapter V:
Bar Mitzvah Boy Becomes Merchant   62

Chapter VI:
Joining My Brothers in Business   73

Chapter VII:
Merchandising Mania   88

Chapter VIII:
From Dry Goods to Department Store   105

Life is a game, play to win!

Chapter IX:
One Store Becomes Four   124

Chapter X:
Growing Through the Depression   143

Chapter XI:
Goldblatts Gets to State Street   171

Chapter XII:
Lt. Louis at War with the U.S. Army   195

Chapter XIII:
Coming Home to New Challenges   228

Chapter XIV:
Goldblatt's Goes Establishment   260

Chapter XV:
The Sixth Sense of Retailing   282

Chapter XVI:
Taking Charge   299

Chapter XVII:
Disengaging   331

Afterward   343

Appendices:
Texts of Speeches   346

Louis Goldblatt

Life is a game, play to win!

Preface

Never could I have predicted that the day would come in my 91st year that I would publish a book about so many of my memories of a lifetime. Ever since I was a child, I have made both mental and written notes of stories my parents, brothers, and sisters used to tell. Over these many years, I saved all these notes, clippings, letters and kept them sort of like a diary. I spent most of my life in the department store business, and when I retired at age 75, I sorted out all my memorabilia into large envelopes and filed them according to years.

I have often wondered at what age a person begins remembering certain events, and I believe it's around the age of five or six. Some of the first things I remember are watching Momma and Poppa sitting at a table drinking a *glass* of tea and biting off a piece of *lump* sugar with each sip.

I also remember one exceptionally cold day when I started kindergarten and was sent off to school bundled in an ankle-length Cossack-style coat that one of my parents had brought from Poland. It had silk-braided loop frogs instead of buttons and buttonholes and a host of other grotesquely comical features — a glaring invitation to ridicule by the other kids. I was mortified with embarrassment as I found myself heading into a group who, at the sight of me, loosed a fusillade of denunciations, choice among which were *"Staro Kraj Zyo,"* meaning old world Jew.

Depending on the neighborhood they came from, these kids called each other pollack, sheenee, or dago and were never at a loss to articulate their wrath or abuse toward new fellow Americans. Oh, how I despised that coat.

As I grew older, I remembered stories my family used to tell of their life in Europe and how they finally arrived in America. I was so enthralled listening to these stories that most often I wrote them down and saved them, just like some kids would save the cards of famous movie actors that were enclosed in packages of cigarettes. Later, during my business, army, and private life experiences, I continued making notes of these memories.

Now at last, I've permitted my mind to wander and record in writing many of them. Like all human beings, I've had my share of good and bad experiences, of joy and sorrow. All in all, I must say the angels have watched over me, because at 90 years of age, I'm healthy, happy, and give thanks to God for my wonderful family: my wife Bobbie (I'm not sure whether it was her or the angels that watched over me) and our three loving sons Gary, Stuart, and David. It is possible that I'm so fortunate because I don't permit disagreeable memories to linger in my mind.

Some years ago, I was asked to give my philosophy of life to the publisher of *Who's Who in America* and I responded with the following:

> *Only some see through the disguises of oppor-*
> *tunity. The disguise might appear as a problem, even*
> *a misfortune. But within every dark cloud, the cre-*

ative mind can find opportunity. Find it and feed it with the fierce perseverance that will make opportunity real. Play to win. You can only lose by limiting your dream and your own part in it. Limits are man-made. Focus on the satisfaction of accomplishment. It is the great reward; all else will follow.

People, like opportunity, often come disguised, but within the seemingly inept may lie a large potential of expertise. Find it! Fuse an idea to the best potential of everyone on the team, and then build faith with all your might. Accomplishment compounds, like stepping stones. You buy the future with the present.

Do not accept on face value. There is a deeper meaning to everything and everyone. Blind acceptance is self-deception set to routine, while curiosity and innovation are the spearhead of growth and progress.

The body and mind and soul of man are tuned to service. Let life be waste-free, free of time waste above all else. Therein lies the key to good health, happiness, and fruitful long life. Time and all you do with it is an investment in the future. And the future is where you spend the rest of your life. Nothing is spontaneous, not even an accident. Everything happens because.

I believe in all this just as fervently as I did when I wrote it.

How could I ever forget the day I retired from

Goldblatt's chain of department stores after I'd spent more than 60 years in that business. It was September 14, 1979, and it was Bobbie's birthday. This was fitting because we always had some pranks, if not craziness, going on between us on our birthdays — stunts like gifts, cards, and notes in unexpected places. Surprise parties and a repeat, perhaps, of a not-too-threadbare antic I had pulled off across the years. I was known for insane capers, like one I pulled on a cold, wintery day when I left the office to come home to the Drake Hotel where I had lived for 25 years, the last five of which I had been married to Bobbie. I managed to let myself in, unseen, and spied her ironing at the far end of the suite. I crept in and took off all my clothes, except for my shoes, socks, overcoat, and hat. I went out into the outside corridor and just rang the door bell. After a moment she opened the door. I went in and removed my overcoat. Lo and behold, there I stood, *stark naked!* "Hi Sweetheart! What's for dinner?" I asked.

If I live to be a thousand, I'll never forget her shriek, then the endless laughter between us. It was just that laughter that branded the memory of it on the two of us. Laughter, optimism, and sentiment have imprinted many other memories of a long and fortunate life, a life that began on Christmas Day, 1903, in a small city in southern Poland.

Life is a game, play to win!

Chapter I
Exodus: From Stachov to Chicago

A huddled trio was about to join the huddled masses back in 1903. On a dark and early morning in July, Shimon Youna Goldblatt had traveled the road and river from Stachov, Poland, to Cracow; a few days later, he was joined by two of his six children. Alex, the eldest at 16, and Sarah, third eldest at 12, would leave Stachov two days later to catch up with their father and together sail for America. By not having set out from their home together, Shimon felt there was less risk in raising any suspicion. The timing was not without provocation. Alex had come of age for impending army service, but that was only one of many reasons that led to Shimon's decision to flee Poland and later to send for the family that stayed behind.

There could be no rest for the father until they were all out and safe, away from the pogroms so frequent near the Russian border. The exodus bore no heroics. In fact, the opposite was true. It was thought shameful by many within the community for Shimon and his two children to flee, leaving behind his wife Hencha, four months pregnant with their seventh child. I was that child. In appearance, Shimon's action smacked of desertion and the community was not apt to make a judgment that allowed the benefit of any doubt.

Cracow was a day away by wagon and boat from the

Chapter I   Exodus: From Stachov to Chicago

small medieval city of Stachov in south central Poland. It sat on the banks of the Visyula River in the shadow of the Capathian Mountains, near what has since become the Polish/ Slovakian border. As arranged, the children met with their poppa and all three were soon watching the shoreline disappear from the packed deck of the liner *Peace*. Fourteen days later, fatigued and worn, they disembarked at Halifax, Canada. From there they traveled first to Toronto, where they lived and worked for some months before moving to Chicago, their final destination. The year before, Orville and Wilbur Wright had pioneered the first successful flight at Kitty Hawk, North Carolina. Events in the world were to move very quickly in the next few decades, but for Shimon and the children then, it might just as well have been a thousand years ago.

Shimon worked long and hard at odd jobs and was able to save the money to send for Anna, then 15 and second eldest. Back in Stachov, Shimon's father, a well- known rabbi in the community, decided to will a large apartment house he owned to his daughter–in–law, Hencha, whom he loved dearly.

The fateful morning of Shimon's departure was for many in their small community an unforgettable breach of devotion. The father of a half–dozen children, he had just slipped away without the knowledge of his neighbors or even some of his relatives. But secrecy was vital in the strategy of escape, and Shimon could afford no undue risk. In his heart he felt that God would judge his action by his motive: his determination to get his family away safely. This, to him, was more important than propriety.

Shimon had been obsessed with visions of the land across the sea, where the streets were paved with gold and the Goldblatt family would no longer fear the Cossacks. One day, after he had been in America for nearly two years, he received a letter from Hencha telling him of the death of his father, the rabbi. She also wrote that, having inherited the apartment building, she sold it and would use part of the money to bring the rest of the family to America. A mixed blessing, Shimon thought. Although he grieved his father's death, his joy knew no bounds when he learned that the family was on its way. Otherwise, it would have taken years for them to be reunited. The pain of separation was to be no more.

Hencha at 34 was a fine-looking woman; her plump figure was none the worse for having borne seven children. She adjusted her *scheitel*, the wig traditionally worn as head covering by women of the Orthodox belief, then she gathered up the children and all the belongings they could carry and embarked for America.

It had been two years since Hencha and the children saw husband and father. The joy of the voyage's meaning was nearly more than she could bear, but the reunion was not to be without impediment. Just about the time they were to board the ship, Maurice, the fourth-eldest child, was detained in Cracow due to an eye infection. It would be some months before he would be permitted to sail.

The sea voyage for Hencha and the children was a nightmare. Three-year- old Rose, 12-year-old Nathan, and myself at not quite two, took turns at excruciating sickness. The discomfort was incessant, but Hencha was strong and healthy and endured her children's misery. They were on their way and that was all that mattered. The ocean voyage wasn't forever, but there would never have been an end to the Cossacks.

Hencha felt she should have slept better than she did. She was beset with thoughts of her life and lay awake thinking

Chapter I   Exodus: From Stachov to Chicago

about her past, her own childhood, friends and relatives left behind. She thought how she and Shimon would no longer be working in their tiny shop making boots for Cossacks. Her mind traveled back to the *shiddach*, or match, their parents had arranged when she was in her teens. She thought how very shy she was when she first met her future father–in–law, the famous rabbi of Stachov who would come to love her so dearly.

Tradition! First the *shiddach* and then the dowry, always negotiation up to the end and not without anxiety. The couple could only wait. The principals sat together behind closed doors sipping tea, philosophizing, and from time to time getting back to her father's list of the small dowry. It seemed endless, but by comparison with many other marriages at that time, it was brief.

Settled! Hencha and Shimon were to be wed; she was 17, and he two years her senior. Bashful and blushing, she fell in love at once with the handsome young man, sinewy and six–feet tall, with a faint wisp of a moustache he had been cultivating and which she was never to forget.

She was likewise amused by the vision of her mother sitting in her rocking chair, clutching at her cane and puffing away on her pipe. Hencha was proud of her stock and marveled at her own endurance. Large families were hard work and most women suffered in appearance and stamina.

In America, Shimon Youna had come to be known as Simon. His preparation for the family included acquiring a larger third–floor walkup tenement flat on Milwaukee Avenue, known then as Polish Broadway. The intersection of Milwaukee and Chicago avenues was the pilgrimage route for Chicago's burgeoning Polish community; several Polish neighborhoods all converged at that one intersection. This corner remained the focal point of the Polish population in Chicago, the center of Polish development. It provided a noble genesis, a port of entry for tens of thousands of Polish immigrants who sought haven and a place to build productive lives. Here was a fount of strength for Chicago and for America, right in that neighborhood. I could imagine no greater synergism than between it and my family.

Back then, most of the people there did not speak, read, or write anything but Polish. They wore European–style clothing and ankle–length overcoats; the men wore fur Cossack hats; the women covered their heads with *schalles* and wore high– laced shoes. They made no conscious effort to alter their outward appearance, and their strangeness exacted its own penalties from the rowdies and hate mongers. In Chicago, the Polish Broadway neighborhoods were but a scene in the drama of immigration being enacted in major cites across the country. In retrospect, their integration only seemed to be slow; actually, events were to move rapidly. As a people, they were a force that would become a factor. What they wore hardly related to what they were.

In their apartment, Simon had covered the three flights of stairs with white muslin sheeting he bought at Wieboldt's Dry Goods Store on Milwaukee Avenue. Since then, whenever I hear of a red–carpet treatment, I can't help but think of Poppa's ingenuity back at the turn of the century. With some good public relations, his gesture might have become the white–muslin treatment for all time. In his heart he meant the same majesty for this beloved family. He scattered rose petals on the stairs leading to the flat.

Time and time again, he had collected Alex, Anna, and Sarah to rehearse the welcome they had prepared together. It

Chapter I   Exodus: From Stachov to Chicago

concluded with *My Country 'tis of Thee*, the music for which was provided by a phonograph record. He would carefully place it on the Victrola, which he cranked up to play repeatedly in the ecstasy of his anticipation. Simon danced with his daughters, and he danced alone, singing *America the Golden Land*, the highlight of the program. Finally, the great day arrived. Dressed in a new suit, with handlebar mustache properly waxed, Simon was ready.

Face to face, the reunion was earsplitting, with everyone talking, hugging, kissing, even screaming all at once, then stopping and starting again. Giggles, shrieks, and fleshy pinches, too, evidence of their good health and weight. It was probably the greatest outpouring of family affection anyone could ever hope to witness. There was wine and the wonderment that comes from the blessing of being together. For a long while, Hencha stood motionless with her mouth agape and tears streaming down the sides of her face. Simon explained to her that in America the name Hencha was called Hannah, and that she became.

Precious, this culmination of dreams, risk, prayer, hard work, separation, and sacrifice. It was a day that was never to fade in our memory. Together, the family would confront the challenges of a new land. Maurice's detention was disheartening, but at least he would be coming and the rest were here already. Simon thanked God for such bounty.

They celebrated deep into the night, talking nonstop, relating experiences during the separation. Eventually, they wound down, tired and exhausted from long hours and inadequate sleep; one by one, they retired.

The practice of taking in boarders was nearly essential to the economy of existence; the family settled down in a still larger apartment, but took in several Polish immigrants who helped pay for food and rent. Life was hard, but as there were no options, hardship was the only accepted route. It was the given by which Simon, Hannah, and the children plodded through the weeks and months almost without pause, without even the luxury of the dubious relief of self pity. Every day was a crowded countdown of necessities. Invariably, there were surprises and, not infrequently, emergencies. The home was a scene of closely managed yet rocky emotional terrain. Hannah struggled for order by maintaining a routine that at times made her abrupt, shrill, and uncompromising. Digression only made for chaos; chores left undone stressed the race against time all the more.

Momma's no–nonsense love and devotion was all the greater for her herculean labors and the methodical existence she imposed on the rest of us. There was marvelous clockmanship to the sounds of Momma, each one a pealing call to action. By her rules, no question, hesitation, or backtalk was tolerated. The kids would only wince. "It's two o'clock!" Her shout came off like a starter's gun to whomever was primed to that particular bellow. "Sarah, peel the potatoes, now!" She went on without stopping, "Nathan, pick up the chicken from the butcher and come straight home! Alex, bring over Rose to the bathtub." She was sergeant, dispatcher, cook, laundress, banker, shoelace–tyer, and nose wiper. "Here Rose, blow!" With a pinch of her handkerchief secured by three powerful fingers she would screw the child's nose with what seemed half a turn, then back with what seemed only a quarter turn.

Words such as drudgery and sweat of the brow were never thought, let alone uttered. They never are during the period of ordeal itself. There was no room for platitudes in the serious business of a family getting on with living and growth.

Chapter I   Exodus: From Stachov to Chicago

That's the way it was. There was a majesty, not just a garden-variety dignity, that Momma was to represent across the decades.

Simon went to work before sunrise, leaving Hannah besieged in the home. From early dawn, her inexplicable sense of where the children were and what they were doing functioned at a high rate; her sixth sense was never dulled by her burdens. Uncanny. I could never to attempt to understand it, nor would I have wanted to pierce its mystery.

Her personal pleasure was as unique as her gusto and drive. Hannah took snuff. What's more, she satisfied her double-edged craving by smoking strong, dark Turkish cigarettes, besides. Regularly, Simon prepared quantities for her every Tuesday night by cranking the small, tarnished hand roller that she had carted all the way from Stachov. I so looked forward to the thump-thump-squeak, thump- thump-squeak of the little machine; fast, then slow, then quickening again. I would listen in my tiny room with my head on my pillow to the rhythm that was searching for a tune. I derived joy knowing it would bring her pleasure. The acrid traces of smoke permeated my room with the pungent signal that Momma was resting. I recall how it heightened my sense of her love and nearness before I fell off to sleep.

There are treasured things other than a legendary, overwhelmingly loving mother with which the handiwork of God can bless us, but not too many. In the edifice of her family, Hannah was the bricks and mortar. Simon was more like a river. Constant, unswerving, he was a man for all seasons, a listener who scanned words and experience for the birth of a small notion.

Hannah and Simon were in full accord on what the children could or could not overhear. As a rule, they spoke Yiddish and continued to do so until the language of America became second nature and Yiddish faded in accordance with the law of disuse. Polish, however, was spontaneously called upon in the event of an immediate private exchange when we were around, a then and now urgency. In fact, they often spoke Polish no matter who was near, whatever their age. The mother tongue was reserved to cloak a sensitive topic, frustrating our curiosity about what they were saying. Hannah and Simon were rarely in accord on anything else. Mostly, it was Simon who came around.

    They loved each other without a shred of symbolism. No perfume or packaged adoration. They never kissed or hugged. Occasionally, only when close enough, a pat; never two pats, but one. By then they had produced seven children, but their public display was nil. I wondered in later years how their love took form. From whence did it spring? How did they know and feel that it existed in the first place? Then I came to realize that it existed outside the two of them. It was in the orbiting entities of their common concerns and gratifications, more than between them as a romance. It was a love sustained by their contentment with the God– given wholesomeness and vitality of their healthy children, by the tastes and aroma of delicious food, by the satisfaction of putting a few dollars away from time to time and watching it grow, by the peace of their precious freedom from fear in America, by the niche they found and the promise!

    Unmistakably, it was the intensity with which they coped with their problems, together. They had suffered too much and worked too hard for ritual and the games people play. Theirs was not second best. Rather, in spite of an everyday bluntness, their

Chapter I   Exodus: From Stachov to Chicago

love had risen to a no–frills level that too few achieve. Oneness by guardianship, by trial, by living completely for each other and bound by the fiber of family well–being. Their love was for a thousand reasons, but invisible to the naked eye — or ear, for that matter. They fought like hell! We, their children, were thus exposed, either to reflect these influences, or to grow away toward change and difference.

Furthermore, common influences will bear disparate stamps where there are many children. To be considered is the period, place, and time of the child's upbringing in the home as well as relative age within the group. Certainly, a diverse combination of tangible and intangible factors come into play. Out of this chemistry were formed the traces of a most unusual family.

As it happened, Alex was the most disadvantaged because he was the oldest. Already a young man when he arrived in America, he immediately set out to work and was never to have any schooling here. He was amenable, easygoing, content not to reach beyond his grasp nor crave education. If he excelled at all, it was in lethargy. A result of this was his classic distortion of English; at times, he mutilated the language beyond recognition. Further, he had a Polish Yiddish accent, and his abilities in those languages was hardly accomplished as well. Ordinarily, most people improve at what they do with time and experience. It always confounded me that Alex's bad English appeared to be worsening as he aged.

The good news was that he was considerate and obliging. Everyone who knew him loved him. The bad news was that he was only to reach a lamentable level of a young man's prime. Alex was Alex; he was most distant from the influences, parental and sibling, that were to affect the rest of us.

Anna was physically stocky, five feet five and dark complected, after Poppa. She was shrewd, and in many ways possessed characteristics of both her parents. Like Momma, she was assertive and domineering; she played the boss throughout her life. Like Poppa, she was argumentative but dependable. We knew when Anna was near. The first opinion on any subject was hers, and it generally came on strong. The last opinion to change, of course, was Anna's, and most of the time, it exploded in defiance with her added warning, "O.K., but wait, you'll all see!" Long on argument, short on fuse, down deep she was kind, but since she played the boss, her kindness was from the top down, never across.

Simon's six–foot stature was not the sign of the patriarch. Considering the heights of his children, a geneticist might have said that his height was recessive. A sociologist would have added that Simon himself was recessive, that he no more sought to captain his ship than Hannah would ever dream of relinquishing her crown. Like with the bees, there could be only one queen. Nor was Poppa's handlebar moustache to be mistaken for an emblem of authority. It barely weathered the second–in–command role he complacently endured, and eventually it eroded to a Charlie Chaplin smudge. Though physically imposing, Simon could become vague. In addition to his six–foot–one–inch height, he had a long, oval face, protruding cheek bones, black curly hair, and penetrating black eyes. Neither outgoing nor social, he was the perfect extra for an Arabian movie, a lone figure silhouetted in the desert away from the throng, poised to listen for sounds.

Nevertheless, he maintained a facade, portraying the role of breadwinner and father. Simon was strict and demanded respect from his wife and children, which was, indeed, unquestioningly given. We didn't dare cross Poppa. Thrifty was a generous understatement in describing Simon; stingy would be more accurate. Although his father had been a rabbi, and he was reared in Orthodox Judaism, he later adopted the Conservative belief. It was not altogether sad for Simon. Although his life was diluted as a man, as a father, and in a sense, even as a Jew, he compensated well with his undiluted love for his wife and children. Not demonstrative, beneath his brashness and regrettable temper, there love was always.

I do not deny the man, who otherwise lacked in daring, his moment of towering courage. It was Shimon Goldblatt who spearheaded the exodus, so fraught with danger and challenge, that brought the family to America. His powerful instinct for his family's survival led him in the direction of America. No wonder his daring left him after that. It ran dry, bless him. Who is to know? Perhaps his flight and the promise of America was his own boyhood dream, deferred.

Hannah's appearance was illusory. She was heavier than her plump size 20_ revealed. Whatever advantage that provided was offset by her appearing even shorter than her actual five foot three. It mattered little, as she was richly endowed with a radiant angel face and sparkling blue eyes that in only a matter of minutes would calm distraught children and adults alike. That was her gift. Hannah's advice was sought by all who knew her. Her counseling apparatus included tea and sympathy at the huge kitchen table, a soothing, hushed conversation, and deep personal concern.

As a child I was, naturally, the object of ten thousand of Momma's touches and the miracles performed by her short stubby fingers out of the labors of love. Her stocky frame was refuted by her gentleness. Her tiny feet belied her girth. She wore her hair swept off her neck up on her head in a fusion of curls. Hers was a totally loving personality, capped by the virtues of charity and generosity. By the same token, she would never shrink, nor would she have any of her children sidestep where self–assertiveness was required. She was daring, too, and when Hannah dared, her eyes blazed when she reached the action end of a decision.

The years were not uneventful. They couldn't be for our size family, or for a nation well into the early years of the century of progress. Alex married a girl named Ida. Anna and Sarah married two brothers, Kay and Jake Handelsman. At the time, Kay worked in a piano factory and Jake in a cigar factory.

In 1903, the United States took possession of the Panama Canal Zone in a plan to link the Atlantic and Pacific oceans, one of the earliest abbreviations of time and space in a century that would see the world's size contract immeasurably. A year later, faces of children everywhere would have a new reason to light up: the ice cream cone, a major contribution to civilized fun and nutrition, was invented by Charles E. Menches. Four years later, the face of the world itself was due for upheaval with Henry Ford's introduction of the Model T. In 1905, the first Nickelodeon theater in the world opened outside of Pittsburgh. It was so popular that there were 5,000 Nickelodeons in the country by 1907.

Back in our town, Chicago's last cable car made its final run on Cottage Grove Avenue in 1906. The following year the U.S. flag acquired its 46th star, the sooner state of Oklahoma. My brother, Joseph or Joe, later to be called Joel, was born in 1907; a few years later, in a leap of courage and imagination, our parents were to make another acquisition of their own.

Chapter I   Exodus: From Stachov to Chicago

My family in 1906, only a year after Hannah had arrived with five of her children, joining Simon, who had come from Poland two years earlier with oldest brother Alex and third eldest Sarah. Momma is holding the youngest brother Joe (3 mos.); to her left are my sisters Rose (age 5) and Anna (age 19); to her right are Poppa, me (the little boy in the white, age 3), brothers Nathan (then 13) and Maurice (age 15). Standing behind Rose and Anna are sister Sarah (age 17) and Anna's husband Kay Handlesman; Alex (age 21) is standing between Momma and Poppa.

Life is a game, play to win!

At age 5, I posed for a serious formal portrait.

Chapter I Exodus: From Stachov to Chicago

Hannah (behind the counter at left) and Simon Goldblatt in their Polska Sklap at Chicago and Milwaukee avenues, the center of Chicago's Polonia, In 1910. An aunt stands next to Poppa; a cousin (with hair bow) sits with sister Rose at right; behind them is our buther, whose name was Ludvak. We lived in a small apartment behind the store.

Life is a game, play to win!

Chapter II
Life behind the Goldblatt's Polska Skalp

It was in 1910 that my father and mother had saved enough money to open their Polska Skalp at 1148 West Chicago, near Milwaukee Avenue, selling groceries, produce, meats, and sundries. I never saw a census of the neighborhood, but if any of its residents weren't greenhorns, the popular label given Polish immigrants, they were darn few and far between. The dictionary on my desk defines greenhorn as "an inexperienced person, especially one easily fooled." I quite believe that, at the time, it was a proper designation for that particular segment of the population. But our store was snug and glowing; my parents operated it for six years.

After my elder sisters, Anna and Sarah, and oldest brother Alex were married, there remained a family that consisted of Momma and Poppa, Maurice, Nathan, Rose, Joseph, and myself. We all lived in a four–room flat in the back of the grocery store. The toilet, which we shared with two other families, was out in the backyard. It was a fact of life. We just knew it was there and was all we had. I took no naturalist's delight in the fiery eyes of stray cats when I made my way out back, an inconsolably desolate trek on a cold night.

The store itself was 80–feet deep by 20–feet wide, with a dirt–floor basement that flooded when it rained and turned to mud. The basement was harsh in its dankness and housed a large built-in oven on which Poppa cooked and smoked quantities of kielbasa, the Polish sausage — a highly odiferous, although uncomplicated, culinary process. The pungency of Poppa's output, mixing with the suffocating smell of earth and evaporating stale rainwater, produced an ungodly grievous smell, battering to the senses. Poppa hung the sausages, which were 21- inches long and an inch and a half thick, over a long rod that he had fitted from wall to wall. With cooking and smoking completed, he brought it up and placed it on the butcher counter for sale. Kielbasa, resembling an oversized horseshoe, was both the staple and a delicacy of our Polish neighbors and the Goldblatt clientele.

Hannah and Simon's store was not off limits to the infestation of rats in the neighborhood. My sole recollection of any special aptitude of Poppa's was his assiduous study about and creation of a better rat trap, a contraption that easily exceeded in inventiveness the proverbial better mouse trap. He filled a large barrel with water and balanced the lid precariously over a wood bar across its diameter, then proceeded to bait the lid with cheese. The greenhorn rat, inexperienced and easily fooled, would alight on any part of the lid, only to have it tilt under his weight. Then the victim plummeted down into the waiting water and drowned, gone from the neighborhood forever.

Came morning, the first thing Poppa did was to fish out the deceased rats and start a new day with a fresh batch of kielbasa. Quite obviously, in the scene of sunless dirt floors, mud, rodents and Rube Goldberg devices to catch them with, the era of the food inspector had not yet been ushered in, nor fortunately was it exactly around the corner. Nevertheless, life and commerce went on, and the Polska Skalp, with its growing customer base, was none the worse for it as far as I knew.

Electric lighting was rare. The store and most homes in the neighborhood were lit by gas or kerosene lamps, which were started by lighting the wick inside a glass chimney. Wall–hanging lamps were of extra–functional design, having the added feature of a reflector mirror spreading the light over a larger area. The store did a steady business in kerosene and kept it in ample supply down in the basement. When customers came in carrying empty gallon cans for a fill up, we children took turns groping our way by dim lamplight down the dark stairway into the asphyxiating assault of the basement's smell. We'd fill the empty can and, charged with repugnance, scurry back up, often tripping over the steps, frantic to return to the world of light, air, and voices. At sundown, street lamps were illuminated by lamp-lighters, who ignited the gas mantels with their long poles. Such was the Dickensian setting of Chicago, the stuff that pretty Christmas cards are made of today, ignoring the travail and inconvenience those ancient lighting devices represented.

The huge breadbox in the store's entranceway offered tender drama to the rites of the morning, starting with the arrival of the bakery wagon at precisely 4:30 A.M. to load the box with fresh bread for the day. To my still–unfaded wonder, Momma's shaggy dog, Daisy, upon hearing the clatter, would bark and scamper through the flat, jump up on her bed and pull away the *piezyna* or feather comforter. Though rude as awakenings go, Daisy was as reliable as Big Ben. She never failed in her mission, and although not a key employee of the store, she was every day the first. Not surprisingly, Momma was never startled by the pounce, and she was always certain to pat Daisy on the nose in gratitude, saying, "*A gezunt, tiera,*" or bless you, dear one. Then it happened. One sorrowful day, Daisy ran

Chapter II Life behind the Goldblatt's Polska Skalp

into the street and was struck and killed by a streetcar. We were all devastated. Momma was inconsolable and worked the rest of that day with tearful eyes. When the streetcar snuffed out Daisy's life, we were all doubly stuck. It was the family's first loss.

Poppa was up at four in the morning. He went to the barn out in back, hitched up the horse and wagon, and headed for South Water Street Market to buy the needs for the day. Examining the offerings with closest scrutiny, squeezing here, smelling there, rejecting this, accepting that and wincing at the prices, he loaded the wagon with poultry, meat, dairy products, fruit, vegetables, and canned goods. Many more items he bought and sold in bulk, such as beans, oatmeal, rice, prunes, and raisins. He had to shoulder it all, besides, over to his waiting rig and pitch it in with some accuracy in consideration of distribution of weight.

Very little was packaged or branded. Even the coffee, such as Bogota Santa or Peaberry, was sold out of large burlap bags and ground at the time of purchase by a hand–cranked grinder. When Poppa wasn't buying and hauling or making kielbasa, he was at the butcher end of the store. Momma was mostly in groceries. Perhaps in self–defense, the customers preferred Momma to wait on them, as Poppa was argumentative. He stood determinedly over the scale, focusing for the longest time on the quivering indicator so as to make reading precise to the smallest fraction and charge it into the purchase. In contrast, Momma's handling of customers with purchases was swift.

I grew up in the city of stockyards loathing the slaughter of animals. To the child that I was, Poppa's workday in the store, and his appearance as well, ran a course of harrowing sights and sounds. Oblivious to the blood oozing from the butchered carcasses, he was continuously cleaving sections, hacking parts, slitting meat, paring fat, and chopping and slicing to the customer's requirement. Poppa made this an ever–diminishing process, taking the hunks of meat from large to small. He had come to master it through to his picayune manner of weighing, wrapping, and cash taking, down even to the customer's departure. What an innocent opener to the day's carnage was his scattering of the sawdust–like flower petals on to the floor behind the butcher counter. They floated down in lithesome contrast to the gory halves of animals hanging high on hooks above.

Were the next customer to want a fresh cut of mutton, Poppa would clear the chopping block with a swipe or two of the edge of his cleaver. Then he would lift the poor lamb's carcass up off its hook and, swaying wildly under the weight, thrust it down on the block. Poppa would seem to strike the pose of a diamond cutter targeting a most difficult point of impact, before hacking away to produce the requested weight. His white butcher apron, freshly laundered each day, was a gory specter of blood by midday and a stinking, grimy abomination by the store's closing time when he would go set the barrel rat trap downstairs.

I anxiously awaited the days Poppa would take me to the market with him, which he did every so often. It was the height of adventure for me, leaving the few blocks that were my world. I loved sitting beside him, high in the front of the wagon feeling his strong frame close to me and enjoying his command of the rig while he navigated his route through the crowded streets. Besides, what would a youngster prize more than the joy of pretending he was actually doing the buying. The reality was a

Chapter II   Life behind the Goldblatt's Polska Skalp

horse and wagon under the spell of a trip with Poppa. He was kind and considerate when he wasn't brusque, and even more so when we were alone.

"Louis, tomorrow you go the market with me so you go to sleep early tonight," Poppa would say. The command invitation electrified me.

"We're gonna have a long day, and we'll be working hard together. We gotta pick up a whole lot of everything." He knew how good it made me feel to become his working partner, sharing his responsibilities. I knew he, too, got a kick out of making out that the work I was required to do was difficult and held special challenges for a young boy.

I took a deep breath of excitement. I wish I knew why he elected one day out of all the others. Or was it that he was more the psychologist than I gave him credit for? Perhaps lately I had been morose or appeared noticeably neglected. At any rate, I was up in the morning with no need to be awakened, soon ready without any urging, awaiting him out in the barn.

After we got started, Poppa steered the horse right on to the streetcar tracks, where once securely on course, he might drop off into a catnap without offering any apparent resistance, only to be startled awake by the clang of the streetcar behind us. We moved out of its path, letting the menace pass at its own snail's pace, then steered back on to the tracks, only to repeat the process four or five times before reaching our destination. I never feared for our well-being, though we were in the center of a busy thoroughfare with Poppa half the time asleep at the reins, while I watched behind for the next streetcar and wondered what the next intersection would bring.

I always knew when Sunday came around. I could hear the neighbors at their concertinas and accordions singing popular Polish songs. In their limited program, these came in two varieties: Polish patriotic and risque. There was nothing in between. Why on earth, I wondered, would a family so compellingly obliged to depart their homeland, cross an ocean, travel to middle America, then settle here, only to arrive and sing songs like "*Jeszcze Polska Nie Zginela*" or "May Poland Live Forever?" If it were satire, it wasn't so delivered in their favored rendition. Or, rising to their height of musical passion, my neighbors would draw a selection from their more–than–ample repertoire of the risque, songs like "*Wczoraj ona chciala to na podlodze, Dzisiaj ona chce to na kanapie*," or "Yesterday She Wanted It on the Floor, Today She Wants It on the Couch."

    There was a religious and ceremonial side to Sunday, too. Most of the community was deeply religious. Every Sunday the people would dress in all their finery, sometimes almost beyond easy recognition, and parade to church . At Easter they were especially resplendent, and all the more inspired by the spirit as well as the season of the holiday. They carried colorful straw baskets filled with candy, foods, and colored eggs, nested in shredded green paper. Ours was an entirely relocated community; its members had suffered in different and similar ways to get here. They deserved renewal in their lives, and the Easter holiday observance, a celebration of resurrection, held special meaning for them and inspired considerable enthusiasm.

    I was still learning how I was supposed to feel about many things, and plainly, Easter was not our holiday. We were not into its frills and certainly not into its spiritual meaning. For a long while I had mixed signals. Denied the holiday's color and joy, I felt the sense of exclusion. Yet, I could share in

Chapter II   Life behind the Goldblatt's Polska Skalp

the neighborhood's excitement, the spectacle of the people in their celebration. My own pride began to bloom, as it does when one is a spectator at a parade of a group one admires. These were our friends as well as our neighbors and customers, and I enjoyed seeing our friends happy. My feeling was reinforced by Momma, and the enormous respect she enjoyed within the community. It transcended religious differences; more poignantly, her love and kindness supplanted them.

Matka, or mother, Goldblatt was called upon frequently for counsel and advice by the many of her customers who became her friends. They came with a litany of family matters, such as ongoing squabbles through to situations of a drunken husband who beat his wife and children, to matters of illness, destitution, and crime in the family. They knew of Matka's goodness where such goodness, to most of them, was tantamount to piety. Perceiving her as close to God, they asked for her prayers when a family member was very sick. What mattered Easter when such affection existed between the Goldblatt's and the Catholic community!

Momma was often greeted with "Matka darling, I need prunes and oatmeal and, darling, when can we sit? My daughter Sophie's man finally came home last night. It was terrible. Matka, when can we sit down?"

"You'll come by late tonight, after closing. The children will be sleeping. We'll sit quiet. I'll make tea and we'll talk. In the meantime, don't burn your chickens behind you. The world will still be here." I sometimes think that although a psychiatrist defined catharsis, Momma perfected it.

Momma kept a huge ledger at the store in which she listed each customer's record of purchases. She entered date of purchase, date payment promised, and a record of payments made.

Not an unusual ledger, except instead of titling the accounts with the customer's name, Momma mercilessly wrote in the customer's most vividly identifiable physical characteristics. "Fat woman with chin wart bought groceries April 16 for $2.16 and now owes a total of $12.44." In the absence of a wart or an extremely long nose, she might have noted, "woman with seven children," or "drunken husband."

Our neighbors were an honorable group. They were religious and responsible. Sooner or later they were bound to pay their debts. Momma's accounts receivable always peaked on pay day. "You see, the one with the big behind and piano legs, she came in today and paid three dollars and a quarter," she would say. They were so determined to repay their obligations that, long after Hannah and Simon shut down the store and retired, debtor customers looked them up as much as 20 years later to make still additional or final payments. Not infrequently, they sent their money in an envelope unidentified by a return address, attributing the delay to matters of illness or other severe problems.

There were times Hannah even had collection assistance from providence itself. When misfortune befell a customer's family, it tended to sensitize an already religious predisposition and motivate a special visit to church and confession. This clearing of one's conscience while seeking solace often motivated a cleaning of one's slate and settling a bill with Matka, even if the payment had to be mailed from another city in the event the debtor had moved.

Hannah often sent money to poor relatives in Poland, and frequently without Simon's knowledge. Simon had given her a gold pendant watch and chain as a wedding gift and one day he asked, "Hannah, how come I don't see you wearing the

Chapter II   Life behind the Goldblatt's Polska Skalp

gold pendant watch and chain?"

"I must have misplaced it, or maybe I lost it somewhere. I looked and can't find it."

The vague, glib reply infuriated Simon. He called her names like "*shmoder*," or slob. "*Gey zu cholera*," or go to hell, he would say. That was their way. Although their language was horrendous, it was intended more to relieve the angered than to devastate the victim. Their ties were unshakable, and recrimination under such emotionally charged circumstances was par for the course. Hannah knew only too well the whereabouts of the gold jewelry, but was never to tell Simon. She only hoped it did as much good back in Poland as she had prayed for it to do.

#

Winter had a way of dredging the depths of our endurance. Yet in their innocence, children invariably find innovative ways to couple ordeal with diversion. In a room in back of the store was a parlor stove with isinglass panels. Coal was costly and the half ton stored in the basement was seldom used. Instead we burned paper, cardboard, and wood from cartons and crates of the trade. Then, too, the streets were laid with wood blocks paved over with tar. Though it was against the law, we children went out and dug up some of the blocks and took them home for firewood to stay warm on cold nights. Of course, the trail of the resultant street cavities presented a hazard, but that was never given so much as a thought.

In addition to providing wood for family warmth, these adventures offered the sheer delight of tearing away and chomping like chewing gum on pieces of tar torn up right off the streets. We often did the same with tar off of roofs.

Though now buses and trains are as well heated as homes, back then many streetcars were open sided and passengers were exposed to the brunt of the worst cold Chicago had to offer. The one or two penny cost of a transfer by which one could travel to most any part of the city offered little consolation on these cold jaunts.

Amazing, how during those early days I wasn't more seriously injured than I was, or even killed. Momma and Poppa were always so busy waiting on customers; it was impossible for them to watch after me as closely as I no doubt deserved. One day, I tripped and fell down the cement steps leading to the basement and split my head wide open. I was rushed to the hospital and, fortunately, escaped what might have been a tragedy. After that I was duly warned in no uncertain terms to be more careful, but as with all children, that warning went largely unheeded.

It wasn't long before I reverted to my own carelessness and jeopardies, and sure enough, I did it again! This time, down the same steps, again causing a wide– open head wound, and again, the mad, hysterical rush to the hospital to "save" me. I came away from both accidents scarred for life, both on my forehead and over an ear. If, truly, an angel watches over little children, that angel watched over me twice!

Though the chariots were missing, the horse was as fundamental to civilization in Chicago at the time as it had been in the days of ancient Rome. Streetcars were drawn by two horses. Police patrol wagons (known as paddy wagons after the Irish given name Patrick, as most policemen at that time were Irish) were also drawn by two–horse teams, while steam fire wagons were powered by a superb team of four, sometimes six, horses. They went hurtling through the streets. At full gallop,

Chapter II Life behind the Goldblatt's Polska Skalp

in summer, we kids ran after the horse–drawn ice wagon, which was easy to catch up to; we would grab off the pieces of ice that had broken from the big blocks headed for iceboxes in the homes. No one who as a child ever chased and so "burglarized" an ice wagon could forget the luscious, cold sensation of sloshing a great big chip of ice around in one's mouth on a swelteringly hot day.

Chasing ice wagons was perhaps one of our safer adventures, but accidents could happen even during the most innocent play. It was a hot September day in 1911 when an accident occurred that leaves me still with a scar on my ankle over four–score years later. I was eight years old and in third grade at the Motley School on the 1400 block of Chicago Avenue, two and a half blocks from our store. While playing a game of kick–the–can during recess, I backed up at running speed into an oncoming, fully loaded, four–horse–drawn tar wagon. Before I realized what happened, I was trampled on and my ankle was crushed under the wagon's front wheel. Then, seeing that a rear wheel was about to run me over, I reacted instantaneously, with a backward somersault. That was all I remembered.

I came to in excruciating pain, and that's when I saw my severely lacerated ankle. The hullabaloo had drawn a large crowd of adults and children from every direction, including my sister Rose, who was in fifth grade at the same school. She immediately became hysterical at the sight of her brother laying prostrate in the gutter. Once more I lapsed into unconsciousness, and this time when I came to I was back in our living room with the doctor holding my foot down in near boiling water for fear of infection. The agony of my hell did not prevent Poppa from scolding me. "And you had to go play in the street with those hoodlums with nothing better to do but go crazy and not even see such a wagon that it should run over you. We send a kid to school to learn something and he winds up with a broken foot under a wagon in the gutter." In delivering his tirade, he scarcely took a breath.

When her turn finally came around, Momma was crying so hysterically I could barely make out what she was saying. "Darling Louis, you might have been killed by such a wagon. You're home now, my darling, and your Momma will take care of you. Thank God, thank God, you rolled away from the wheels just in time."

Alternately, they continued for hours, going out of the room, coming back and starting again. Momma professed love, care, and gratitude to God; Poppa, with only varying inflection, sustained his harangue practically word for word.

I was bedridden for months. The doctor came to visit every week, peeling away the ugly dead flesh and monitoring the healing process. I began to get around only with the help of crutches. At that stage of recovery, the doctor stopped coming. I found myself happily anticipating my weekly visits to his office, mostly because Poppa carried me in his arms all the way from my bed to the doctor's examining table. Each such excursion I prized as a pronouncement of his love. Those episodes when a father of eight became a father of one were rare, an ironic consequence of my temporarily useless ankle. It was as though the harangues never happened. I said, "When I grow up, I will carry you, Poppa, and take care of you." I owned a piece of sunshine when the cradle that was his arms suddenly tightened, and Poppa hugged me. I must have grown an inch, too, by Poppa's lesson that loving means touching.

The poor driver of the tar wagon, although full of

remorse, had neither insurance nor money to pay the doctor bills, so instead he gave Poppa one of his horses.

#

Apart from Hannah's closeness to the people of the neighborhood, her customers and friends, the rest of the family was far too busy with hard work and routine to get involved socially in the community. That is, except for Nathan, who occasionally paid a beer–drinking visit to the policemen at the stationhouse a block from the grocery store. In a relatively few years, how completely changed had Simon's attitude toward authorities become, from fear of the Cossacks back in Stachov to his son's friendship with the local police here in Chicago. But certainly Simon himself wasn't inclined in the slightest to extend his circle beyond work and family. It was not his way.

As it happened, Momma did gravitate to a special activity, but only one, outside the store. Hers, though, was not diversion at all. Appropriately, it was business. Just across from the grocery store was a dance hall. Occasionally, she was summoned to do the catering for the weddings held there. Without exception, the main course was chicken. Whenever I learned that Momma was to do a wedding, a cold sweat came over me in expectation of the carnage to be presided over and performed by Poppa. My earliest hint of the forthcoming mass murder was seeing him hone his special ax to razor sharpness, preparing for the slaughter about to be committed in the basement of the grocery store.

For years afterward, my knee–jerk response to the word wedding was dread — I so disliked this ghastly specter of flying feathers and spurting blood, the gleam on the raised ax before its dreadful thud, the cackling pandemonium of the doomed. In enacting the nightmare, Poppa was not without flair. He was able to chop off a chicken's head, while at the same instant, through extending the downward blow to a sidesweep, fling the severed head into one barrel and toss the rest of the poor chicken into another. Thus he gave life to the old cliche. There was no doubt about it, when Poppa missed the second barrel and his prey went on to the floor, they did indeed run around like chickens with their heads cut off. Then, as if they hadn't lost enough dignity, Momma was standing by to throw them into scalding hot water, loosening their feathers so they could easily be plucked out. In less than a minute, they were transformed from flowering chickenhood to naked oblivion, save for the wedding feast ahead.

In a sense, Hannah's chickens helped augment the wedding gifts. The guests ate the chickens, which energized their dancing of mazurkas and *oberiks*. They would whirl at breakneck speed past the huge base drum placed in the center of the floor. As they passed, the dancers would fling their silver dollar wedding gifts onto the drum. The more energetically they danced, the more silver dollars they would hurl onto the barrel. The dancing was delightful, the mazurkas rocked the room. The *oberiks,* close cousin to the square dance, caught most of the celebrants doing their own beat. You couldn't help but hear the thumping drum sounds of the striking coins punctuating the festivities all night long.

In our neighborhood, the people found joy in celebrating every holiday, however inexplicable in origin or remote from mainstream religion. One such event was the day following Easter, called *smigus dingus*, or switching day, by the children. To commemorate Christ's suffering, or so we were told, the boys would take flexible branches from a tree, strip them of leaves, then switch *across* the legs of any girls who passed by. This habit, understandably, caused for a conspicuous absence of girls on the streets when the boys went prowling in search of likely young prey.

Even smaller children proved the unsuppressible passion for toys and playthings that exists in children of every generation. For two pennies, they could buy a multicolor–striped pop-corn–filled lunchbag that included a surprise lead toy. These they collected and exchanged with each other with much pride of ownership. Otherwise, very few toys were available except for those we made ourselves. For example, we would take an empty box used to hold spools of sewing thread, then through affixing milk–bottle caps for wheels, change these into the toy wagons. The wonder about a toy is what it does for the imagination; even a mere small box can give it flight. George Bernard Shaw said, "You imagine what you desire; you will what you imagine; and at last you create what you will."

There were exploits, too, laced with the excitement of forbidden fruit, matters of crime and punishment. While working in the grocery store, Momma always wore an apron and carried loose coins in the pocket to make change. Pretending it was necessary to talk to her, I intermittently pressed close to her so as to seize a chance to dip my fingers into the pocket and lift out a few coins. It was much later that I realized she knew what I was up to. Were she to allow herself to catch me, she would be obliged to punish me; or worse, she feared Poppa would learn of it. She tried to discourage me, but I would not be dissuaded. "Louis, tell me already, but you don't have to whisper and stand so close." "It's too hot." "Louis, you're pushing me." "Stand straight. Momma can hear you even though I think I heard the same thing already three times."

Though lacking in skill, I had the patience of a highwayman. My determination to pull off the heist was unswerving. "Momma, you don't understand. Bend over. I don't want anyone to hear. It's a secret, so you gotta stand close and I gotta whisper." All the while my eyes were shut tight with tension, and my fingertips darted frantically between the folds of her apron, flittering about for contact and extrication.

Punishment from Poppa was a consequence to be avoided, more so by us kids directly than by Momma's reluctance to let him do it. There were two good reasons. First, there was Poppa's temper. Second, the implement he chose, which was, oddly enough, inadvertently provided by Momma. She had been accustomed to breaking down the egg crates by pulling away the light boards from which they were made. Eggs were packed 12 dozen to the crate with cardboard dividers. The boards and the cardboard were stored for the stove with the isinglass panels, except for those determined to be suitable for paddling. When Poppa was especially angry with me or Joe, he would strike us by gripping the board with the edge pointing out; down it would come, causing a terribly painful sting. There was as well the nauseating anxiety of not knowing where the next blow might fall, what with his helter–skelter flailing.

Punishment from Momma was rare, only occasioned when our misbehavior was beyond even her tolerance, or when paddling from her would preempt paddling from Poppa. Never did she hit us with the edge of the board. That was Poppa's prerogative. Momma not only used the flat side, but she knew the flat side was weakened and frayed, its strength thus dissipated. The time being about three quarters of a century too early for any ruckus over child abuse, Poppa had airtight immunity. It

Chapter II   Life behind the Goldblatt's Polska Skalp

was almost a pleasure and unquestionably a relief to be punished by Momma; although, in a manner of speaking, the latter was all too infrequent.

It wasn't really stealing, lifting those few coins out of her apron pocket, not from Momma and not when it was so as to buy marbles, my fixation at the time. Larger marbles, called aggies, were made of glass with deep swirls of color; they were far superior to the clay kind called migs, which sold 10 for a penny. Second only to marbles was my love for spinning tops, which I selected from a variety of styles and colors. One of the competitive games with tops consisted of a couple of kids flinging their tops into a chalk–marked circle on the sidewalk. When one bumped another, the bumpee would be captured — and forfeit the game.

One afternoon at a fever pitch of excitement, I wound the string around my top as tightly as I could and flung it with all my might — only to see it whirl away at incredible speed and shatter the window of the tailor shop down at the corner. Upon hearing the crashing glass, I ran away and hid as fast and as far away as my legs would carry me. The tailor, not knowing which boy had broken his window, went about calling on all the families in the area who had boys. Finally, he reached the home of Simon Goldblatt.

The tailor's visit was unusual enough, but his low tone and serious stare upset Simon, who couldn't imagine his reason for being there. "Goldblatt, I'm coming over to talk wherever lives a boy who smashed a window from my shop. Like with a rock, a boy threw in a top, smashed by me the window and missed me in the eye by inches, I tell you." His plaint had already been well rehearsed at a dozen homes.

Poppa's denial was vehement. He behaved as though the

very idea that his son might have done such a thing was preposterous. To Simon, the tailor not only was in the wrong place, but was crazy, too. The tailor insisted on speaking to me personally. Poppa called me and asked directly, "Louis, you didn't break anybody's window. And tell him you didn't."

I replied, "Poppa, I did break the tailor's window and I ran away because I was afraid."

Poppa had to pay for a new plate glass window, and I paid with an especially painful thrashing beneath the edge of the egg–crate board. In no way could I defer the punishment to Momma. However, the incident of the broken window was a milestone. Right there and then, I either was seized by scruples or otherwise impelled to the unvarnished side of the truth. I had brought down Poppa's wrath, but the hell or highwater admission, to me, was without alternative. Obviously, my own perception of the difference between Momma's apron coins and the tailor's broken window was entirely subjective. Whether it was just plain noble, which I doubt, or a demon more to be feared than Poppa, I don't know. I do know, as for principle, if that's what emerged then, I am stuck with it. Galvanized!

Chapter III
Initial Forays into the Wider World

Momma had her hands full working in the store and taking care of us children. Often we would do things she wouldn't want to know about. For example, Rose and I would get punks (long pencil–thin weeds that could stay lit for hours and were used to light firecrackers) from the Chinese laundry, wrap them tightly in newspaper, and when nobody was around smoke them like cigarettes. Smoking held great appeal for me at the age of nine. I picked cigarette butts off the street and hid them away inside a cave under the sidewalk, to smoke them later.

Repeatedly, I ran away from home. Once, I even stayed out overnight. The consequence for that was being stripped naked and tied to the bedpost in a locked room. From that I broke loose and climbed down naked from the window, only to be brought back by some neighbors and punished even more severely. In endless cycle, mischief provoked punishment and punishment provoked mischief. Things were so turbulent that I was even punished for reasons I didn't understand and no amount of time will dim them in my memory.

After playing with a boy in the street, I had no more than walked through the doorway when Poppa gave me a crushing, wide–open–handed slap across my ear and head. Stunned, I felt as though I'd hit a wall. For a while I was deaf.

When I regained my senses, I heard Momma and Poppa hollering at each other. It turned out that Poppa had had a fist fight with his nephew, who also happened to be our neighbor. When he saw me playing with David Gold, the neighbor's son and my cousin, he completely lost control of himself and let me have it. In time, I came to realize that his real anger was aimed at Momma for letting me play with the boy, and he had just vented it on me. Ever after, my feeling for Poppa harbored a dark pocket of hatred for that incident.

Momma had a woman come in who helped with the housework and also looked after the children. Extremely tall, husky, and strong, she had the personality of a ditchdigger and the appearance of a stevedore. Emily (we never bothered to learn her last name) spoke with a thick German accent, worked hard and well, and was willing to take on any job whatsoever.

Before bedtime, she undressed Joe and myself and put us into pajamas; in so doing, she bent at angles so acute that I could not help but catch skittish glimpses of her bare breasts. Then, in complete contradiction with Emily the barbarian, she would set aside a few moments to adoringly caress my penis, from which I derived strange but pleasant sensations. I so looked forward to her putting me to bed. That was our secret, mine and Emily's, which I faithfully and most willingly kept from Momma.

Joe was an obstinate child, even at the age of five. When he didn't get his way, he whimpered and cried by the hour. When Poppa, who was not tolerant of such behavior, failed to quiet him, Joe was spanked frequently, which only made him cry louder. After hours of exhaustion, Joe would quiet down and fall asleep.

It seemed every day spawned renewed mayhem, a tangled skein of lawlessness, bedevilment, and uproar. A circus master would have done well to catch the spirit.

#

Meals in our life brought us together with the many facets of family existence, such as the exchanges by which we influenced each other, situations by which we either grew a little or regressed as developing personalities. At mealtimes, there was religion, the reaffirmation of the parental role, and the provision of a battleground. Momma, of course, did all the cooking. In those days, it was all from scratch. Preparation of meals was, for her, another way of expressing love. Her enjoyment never waned. We sat at a long, makeshift dinner table. In terms of frequency, not necessarily demand, boiled chicken was the specialty of the house. Uppermost on the unwanted list were always the wings, gizzard, and liver, which traditionally were pitched over to Poppa because no one else would eat them. Variety included boiled beef, or *flanken*, and a kind of hamburger, called *kottlets*, made from beef, bread crumbs, eggs, and onions.

There was chicken noodle soup, always chicken noodle soup! The making of Mamma's *logshins* (very thin) noodles never failed to capture my most concentrated attention. I would never cease to marvel how, after flattening the dough and cutting it into the thin, long strips, she would so rapidly and exquisitely proceed to chop, chop, chop, back up from the end of the collection, making it into finely cut bits as would defy the efficiency of any machine today. My eyes stayed glued at her two hands, each in perfect coordination with the other, moving, moving, moving along, as the knife sped along its seemingly automatic course.

Only the Sabbath meal on Friday nights was special and exciting; sometimes it was even the scene of a good fight. The prevailing risk was in the kind of dual ceremony the dinner entailed. On the one hand, the ceremony was gastronomical, even if this was confined only to Poppa's schnapps and schmaltz herring. Momma, on the other hand, would perform the religious ritual of lighting the Sabbath prayer candles, or *benshing licht*. Her angelic face would become fancifully aglow with the darting candlelight. Her head was covered in black lace; her hands, in spiritual grace, wafted above and around the meaning and the mystery of the quivering flames. Then we ate, though there were times when we didn't, as even the Sabbath meal couldn't always quell Poppa's temperament. And every so often, Hannah overcooked the food. Simon, in his inimitable way, would swear and throw his plate, schmaltz herring and all, across the room. He would call Hannah names, using his temper as his sword.

"Kush mir en tuchas" (kiss my ass!), Hannah sputtered as her perennial put down. Father never intended to be cruel, only audacious. He also laid claim to being the presiding authority at the Sabbath meal, at least. At any rate, after Momma's retort, the sword would go back into its scabbard and the dinner would be back on course.

My favorite snack was toast heavily smeared with chicken fat, or *schmaltz*. Momma would put a thick slice of rye bread on the cover plate of the coal and wood–burning stove. Then, she put her flat iron on top of the bread, on one side first, then the other. When the toast was done, she spread on the schmaltz, salted it, and handed it over to me, saying, *"Ess, ess mein lachtika kindt,"* or eat, eat, my loving child.

Ranking with that stovetop delicacy was the most deli-

Chapter III   Initial Forays into the Wider World

cious tasty treat, a kosher frankfurter. This was an extravagance that Momma and Poppa bought for Joe and me off a peddler's cart. I salivated at the thought of it. They weren't called hot dogs then. Momma called it *schmeckle*, an endearing term for little penis. Gorging oneself on a kosher frankfurter off a cart was high living, a gluttonous wide–open–mouth feast in itself, and the glutton had only to bite down on to the plump casing to release a burst of intermingling juices and flavors so divine as to be worthy of the poet. Stuffing down a frankfurter was without style or pretense and all the more enjoyed.

Polish Gentiles had different fare. The staple was *pierogi*, dumplings filled with sauerkraut and cheese, or frequently, fruit such as plums, cherries, or blueberries. They ate much sausage, plus *kartofel* or potatoes, and *kapusta* and *grochen*, kielbasa with sauerkraut and split peas. There was also stuffed cabbage and *bigos,* a hunter's stew made from fresh cabbage, sauerkraut, and four kinds of meat.

It is interesting how one's conditioning as a child can influence one's food likes, or dislikes, for a lifetime. In my desire to head off Momma and Poppa's arguments over a food that she may have burned, I would always pop up saying, "I'll take that." In the case of burned bread, for example, I would say, "I like it that way, burned!" Consequently, the bread or whatever the burned dish was at the time would never reach Poppa's plate, and there would be peace, until the next time. A result of that sacrifice, which turned out to be no sacrifice at all, I came to prefer burned bread, dark and very dark toast, or anything, for that matter, that was cooked over and beyond the call of duty.

In our neighborhood, there was a saloon on almost every corner. On a hot summer's night while Momma,

Poppa, Maurice, and Nathan played pinochle, I was sent with a quart-size coverless pail to fetch beer for a nickel. On the way back, show off that I was, I would ham it up and swing the pail a full circle up over my head without spilling a drop. Considering the near fatal risk I ran with Poppa had I let go of the pail, the penny tip I got wasn't nearly enough.

#

1912 and the years surrounding it were exciting and crowded with events that sensationalized the atmosphere. If not directly, then indirectly, they changed everyone's lives. New Mexico and Arizona were admitted as the 47th and 48th states. The *Titanic* struck an iceberg on its maiden voyage, going down with 1,513 of the more than 2,200 souls on board. The year before had marked the opening of the Everleigh Club, one of the world's most famous and opulent brothels, located at 2131 South Dearborn Street, only to be closed a few years later by Mayor Carter Harrison. That same year, Ronald Reagan was born. In 1913, Gideon Sundbach patented his separable fastener, which would come to be known as the zipper. The German invasion of France, Belgium, and Luxembourg in 1914 and the start of World War I gave Americans a reason to be thankful for not being on that forlorn continent. That same year, the Panama Canal officially opened to traffic, and Henry Ford's first auto assembly line was put in operation. In 1915, the steamboat *Eastland* sank in the Chicago River. Of the 2,000 Western Electric employees on board, 812 were lost.

The Chicago Municipal Pier (later renamed Navy Pier) was opened in 1912, providing dancing, band music, food for every taste, ice cream, popcorn, all kinds of entertainment including extravagant water shows, boat excursions, and a continuum of festivities that attracted the largest summer crowds Chicago had ever seen.

Joseph and I adored our older sister Sarah, and she would occasionally take us for a day's outing at the pier. She had boundless energy and was dedicated to living life to the hilt. Life to Sarah was not for the fainthearted. She was strong, a clone of Momma down to her identical features and exact size. Her small, even gentle, appearance was in complete contradiction to the fearlessness with which she would take on a challenge. Adventure to Sarah was an uplift, even a visit to the Municipal Pier. No sexist would have long survived in her company. Both she and Momma were proof that one should never equate size with tenacity and grit. (As I wrote these memories, my sister Sarah was about to celebrate her 103rd year. She died in 1993.)

At the pier, all the children were given free milk and the overall excitement was so intoxicating, we just couldn't wait for Sarah's next invitation. We were similarly thrilled when Momma sent us to spend the summer at Sarah's place, where she and Jake ran a grocery store on 26th Street and lived in a three-room flat above the store.

Though these greenhorn shopkeepers already had enough to cope with, their humble little world wasn't immune from the plundering of organized crime; as retailers, they felt especially threatened. I became aware of this threat while making mischief one rainy day — isn't that what rainy days are for? On this day, my playing had me bouncing on Jake and Sarah's bed; there I found a revolver under the pillow. Holding the handle between my thumb and index finger, I experienced feelings of both perplexity and intense excitement. Slowly, I raised the weapon up directly in front of my face. I turned my wrist for still closer inspection, tilted my head to look directly into the barrel, and proceeded to settle the grip into my palm. By then, simply captivated by heroics, I started to stretch my index finger onto the trigger.

Beginning to get accustomed to the gun's feel and weight, and the ease with which I was able to point it at the wall, the window, and the lamp, I took aim at the doorknob when the door suddenly sprung open. I was startled, frightened, paralyzed, with my arm outstretched and rigid. Sarah screamed. Jake stampeded to the doorway. I began to pee.

"Sarah! Sarah! What, what . . . oh my God! Louis, no! No Louis!" Jake thundered in utter panic.

I stood frozen with my finger on the trigger. Sarah was transfixed. Jake shoved her aside with such force as to send her crashing across the hallway onto the floor; then he stood to the side of the door, out of the direct line of fire. I didn't take a breath. If I did, I felt the gun would go off.

"Now Louis, put it down! Just put it down on the bed. By the handle, Louis, by the handle. Put the gun on the mattress and walk away." Jake's enunciation was sickeningly slow and precise, yet commanding in its tone. Sarah was huddled into a corner, gasping convulsively as though with the whooping cough to a rhythm unmistakably reserved for only the most horrified. I did as I was told. I also breathed again.

It seems Jake and Sarah kept the gun handy because they had found a Black Hand letter shoved under their door. The Black Hand, so called because its demands for money were delivered via a black-inked outline of a life-size hand, warned them not to report the threat to the police. If they did so, their

Chapter III   Initial Forays into the Wider World

store and home would be bombed. Sarah, however, did tell the police, who warned her that the letter came from the Mafia and that she and Jake should be on guard. Thank God, nothing ever come of it — except almost by my doing. Nevertheless, it was Sarah who had gotten the gun and was ready for the fight.

I don't think I missed a single bump that growing up in our neighborhood had to offer. The street gang then, no less than in years to come, was a means of identity. Peer pressure convinced young boys to join. Membership was a given; the gang was a society of the streets. I was the only Jewish member of the gang known as the Pollacks. My name was an oddity among its membership. In fact, for the longest time after the local phone directory came into being, we were the only Goldblatt listed.

As a gang, our most important function was to roam the streets. And why not, we owned them! We were sworn to "protect" them from the Italian gangs who had similarly vowed to protect their streets from the "pestilence" that was the Pollacks. I suppose from such carousing and mischief making, there eventually arose the gang version of turf. We used wop or dago as terms of reference for the enemy, our targets. Not only was such deprecation appropriate to our mission, but it aided our generating anger and hate, thus appeasing the hormones boiling over in us and providing us the will to strike.

No one ever won. Down deep we wanted it that way, with no victor. How else could we continue to vent our aggression!

Center Avenue, Grand Avenue, Superior, Huron, Ohio streets, and sometimes even Division Street were all our not–so–make–believe battlefields, upon which our individual performance came to be a measurement of loyalty, guts, and even resistance to pain.

It had always been a trivial mystery to me how a strangely simple and unrelated cause can sometimes, in the way things line up, squiggle across to have a most unexpected effect. How else might I rationalize Momma's innocently contributing her laundry to gang warfare — Momma, an armament supplier! There were few homemakers' conveniences then, and the demands of housework, including laundry, stretched women to the edge of their endurance. They did their wash in a boiler, a high, oval–shaped, tin vessel with a copper bottom that held about 10 gallons of water. It had a full cover and handle — an ideal shield to protect a young warrior from the rocks thrown at him.

Battles took place at night in the total darkness we created through throwing rocks at the gas mantels of the street lamps. When the lights went out, the war was on, and they often became really ugly. Momma never knew that, on more occasions than I care to remember, it was her wash–boiler cover that virtually kept me alive. Some of the boys, on both sides, carried pocket knives. Never guns. So that, in order to survive, one needed a wash–boiler cover — as well as a Polish, Italian, or Jewish good luck star up in heaven watching over.

Chapter IV
The Goldblatts Get into the Dry Goods Business

In 1913, my brother Alex and his wife Ida opened their store at 1444 West Chicago Avenue. I was not quite 10 years old and worked at the store Saturdays and Sundays when there was no school. Hannah and Simon referred to Ida as the *galitziana*, which connoted for them a significant cultural difference. Her family was from Galicia, a region in east central Europe, north of the Carpathian Mountains, that had been a part of Poland, then Austria, then Poland again, since the 14th century.

The store was a lot of hard work. Every day except Sunday, Alex and Ida prepared a variety of merchandise to be shown out in front of the store. They loaded it all into the wood cases that the shoe deliveries came in. Back then, shoes were packed three-dozen pair to the case, so the cases were rather large. We dragged them, loaded up with other merchandise, out to the sidewalk each morning, then back inside again at night after closing. The street was a stage — spectacular, noisy, colorful, and hectic. This composite of street strewn, awning hung, scrawly signed merchandise perfectly befitted the pulse of the community and the myriad needs of the bargain-hunting Polish consumer, who were our chief customers at the time.

Monday in the neighborhood was wash day. Thus, goods that Alex and Ida put on display were related to laundry, such as unbleached muslin, ticking, visor caps, boys' and girls' stockings, girls' bloomers, felt house–slippers and many more. Retail know–how was not taught in schools back then. It grew out of "wantmanship," that is, from the merchant's wanting to do business badly enough for ideas to come naturally. The idea behind everything we did was getting people to stop, to buy, and to buy more. Putting merchandise out on the sidewalk brought it closer to passing customers; it induced them to come inside to pay for what they had already selected and to find more of the same kind of bargains. The sidewalk provided the store more selling space, an opportunity no smart store owner would pass up.

Thus, the bait item, or loss leader, came into existence. Alex and Ida created their's, whatever was appropriate at the time. Such items were irresistibly priced, even if the price meant a loss to the store owner. These goods were designed to induce the customer to stop, make a purchase, and while still in a buying mood, make selections from the more profitable merchandise displayed inside with overwhelming prominence.

One such leader was laundry soap. It was my job to prepare it in huge quantities of 10–bar packages and mark it at a price well below the cost Alex had paid to buy it. At that, it was sold only when accompanying another purchase, so as to assure a profit mix and a larger sale. This came to be known as a tie–in sale.
Thus I had to haul hundreds of cartons of soap down to the basement, wrap 10–bar quantities up in newspaper, tie them with string, and then lug them all back up, ready to be dumped

Chapter IV   The Goldblatts Get into the Dry Goods Business

into cases to go out on the sidewalk. Even then, the variety of soaps was considerable. There were Fels Naptha, American Family, U.S. Mail (a name that couldn't go wrong), and Amber soap. Prophetic, it now seems, that as a child my first job was on the promotional slope of the retail mountain. It was the start of a courtship.

The nickel wasn't so lowly a piece of change then, and it happened to be the wage for my two–day–a–week job. A soap maven I had become. But my wage had buying power, too; for my nickel, I could go to any one of several picture shows, later to be called movies, and take along other kids as well. The vigor of the emerging motion picture industry showed itself almost immediately in fierce competitiveness. The Schindler Picture Show on Milwaukee Avenue near Chicago, for example, charged a nickel for six children. Picture shows were an earthshaking development. The acceptance they were accorded sent forth an onrush of heroes and heroines, victims and villains, all devised to lift an audience to the loftiest heights of imagination. Further, they expanded the experience of the greenhorn. Movies meant sharing other lives.

There was a star for every taste in excitement; one such was James Corbett. After becoming world heavyweight champion by knocking out John L. Sullivan in 1892, Corbett lost his title to Bob Fitzsimmons in 1897, then decided to take up a film career. I remember the movie he appeared in, called *The Midnight Man.* Crowd–drawing western stars at the time were Harry Carey, William S. Hart, and William Boyd, Hopalong Cassidy, Charles Ray, and Tom Mix. There were obsessive romantics like Rudolph Valentino; hilarious comedians like Ben Turpin, Charley Chaplin, and the Keystone Cops; plus there was Harold Clayton Lloyd, the naive buffoon, forever teetering

Life is a game, play to win!

on the brink of disaster. In real drama, there were stars like Pearl White, Mary Pickford, Douglas Fairbanks, and Helen Hayes. I especially enjoyed the incredible Harry Houdini in a movie called *The Iron Man*.

Even more incredible was that my nickels, and millions like them, paid for the start of a revolution.

Alex's store had a pricing policy, as many did at the time. Caveat emptor, let the buyer beware, predominated on the retail scene. Harry G. Selfridge, as president of Marshall Field & Company, was the first major retailer to establish a one-price policy; after that, some other retailers, seeing this the trend of the future, began to sell goods at set prices rather than bargain with customers about them. One particularly profitable item for Alex was the so-called pussy willow pure silk shirt, which came in brightly colored woven Roman stripes and was worn with a Van Heusen celluloid collar. At Christmastime, we were sure to suggest that customers might want an individually boxed silk tie along with the shirt, and we'd sell it at a price that depended solely on whether the customer was drunk or sober. Field's decision that goods should be sold at a set price wasn't apt to earn the silk-tie award in our end of town.

One day I cheated a customer, and that's when a line was drawn, if only a terms of the truth ethic, between Alex and myself. Back then content labeling on apparel was not required, and a customer had asked me whether a sweater she intended to buy was pure wool. Naturally, I asked Alex, who replied that it was and she bought it. After she left the store, Alex chuckled and said, "You know, Louis, that vas a good sweater sale you made unt a profitable vun, too. It vasn't even vool. It vas a hoondred parcent cotton, it vas." He continued with his voice pitched higher, emphasizing "hoondred parcent cotton," while at

Chapter IV   The Goldblatts Get into the Dry Goods Business

the brink of exploding in laughter, a sardonic grin came over his face in mockery of the customer.

I felt very badly and said to him, "Alex, it just doesn't seem right that a lady pays you good money for a sweater and when she asks a question she should be told the truth." At the threshold of an argument, I added, "She didn't pay any less for the sweater. It seems to me that she should get what I told her it was. Why not?"

"You know why not." Alex sputtered in reply. "Because a fool you are and a kid, too, mit a lot to learn unt I don't have time to learn you."

In the pit of my stomach, I could feel the same demon at work that had forced me to tell Poppa that it was I who broke the tailor's window. An alarm went off inside me that made me want to right the wrong, to run and find the customer, and holler, "You didn't buy what you thought." What was worse, I knew that eventually she would learn the truth and have my face in front of her when she did. To me, honesty with customers had no alternative; this was my earliest retail conviction. A customer is to be pleased, not angered. The whole idea was to get her to want to come back to buy more.

#

During summer vacations, I worked long hours everyday, beginning at a salary of $6 for a six-week day. Everyday was the start of an exciting new game. In the morning, before store-opening time, I would set a sales goal for myself, and with such first-clenching determination to beat my record of the day before that I didn't even allow myself time for lunch. Instead, I bought a pound of salted peanuts and popped them into my mouth a few at a time, munching while racing around the store waiting on customers. I figured I had to average so much in sales per hour over so many hours to the day. I was pitted against time. Selling then included measuring yard goods, weighing out bulk, counting small items, suggesting additional ones, plus replenishing stocks, making exchanges, and all the while noting what items the stock was getting low on so I would tell Alex to reorder them.

In contrast, Alex turned lover, seemingly at the drop of a hat. He and Ida left me alone in the store to go across the street where they lived, grabbing a matinee for themselves. When smitten with such urges, Alex's signal to his beloved was a quick motion of the head toward the door, the general direction of the intended tryst. In response, Ida coyly shrugged her shoulders, as if to say, "Well, I don't know."

"Louis, take care on the store. We'll be back," he shouted. Then they left, while under my breath I hummed the tune to "Yesterday She Wanted It on the Floor, Today She Wants It on the Couch." Be that as it may, their departure was a special learning opportunity for me. But I had to run even twice as fast, if that were possible.

Alex's dry goods store was 50–feet wide and 100–feet deep on two floors. From floor to ceiling were shelves stuffed with merchandise; counters ran the perimeter of the store. In the center were a few tables and some crates, which also brimmed with merchandise. Money was kept in a cash drawer that had finger levers at the bottom. A combination known only to the user released the drawer with the ring of a bell. The drawer was located beneath a counter in the front corner of the store, right next to a high showcase used to display men's ties.

Ida was an attractive and well–built woman. In the sum-

Chapter IV   The Goldblatts Get into the Dry Goods Business

mer she wore a housedress with absolutely nothing underneath it. When she had to reach for an item uppermost on the shelves behind her, she put one foot up on the showcase and the other on one of the shelves. By so doing, she straddled the narrow aisle at an irresistibly inviting angle. I always saw my opportunity coming. Whenever I spied Ida staring up at the topmost shelf, I would dart across the store at precisely the right moment. With all my juices churning, I made it my business to use the cash drawer and behold the view between the legs of the wife of my brother and boss, but for no longer than was safe. The depravity of the circumstances added to the excitement!

#

In the meantime, the laws of change were in force. The Goldblatt family had made its way of the greenhorn stage. These were the years that were to set our future course. The hardworking and sensible brothers, Maurice and Nathan, saved as much money as they could from their earnings, so as to gain a foothold of their own in the dynamic opportunities of the neighborhood.

Maurice had worked for a dry goods store on Milwaukee Avenue called Iverson's; Nathan, at Salk's, a men's clothing store also on Milwaukee. The year was 1914. Maurice was 21 and Nathan 19 when they combined their savings with a loan from Momma and Poppa. With a total capital of $500, they rented a store at 1617 West Chicago Avenue near Ashland and called it the Goldblatt Bros. Dry Goods Store.

While he worked at Iverson's, Maurice attended night school in order to learn what was called showcard writing. After school, often very late at night, he could be found hard at work —

making the signs, creating special displays, even building his ideas into make-believe show windows that he improvised in the back of the grocery store where he and Nathan lived.

Nathan, when he worked at Salk's, would position himself out on the sidewalk in the path of the passersby, hawking the leader items as well as the other "unbelievable" bargains inside the store. He sold even while on the sidewalk and virtually led customers physically, nudging them along to the inside of the store. His talent was his unfailing ability to push higher-cost items, thus earning extra commissions for himself.

Later, operating their own store, each of them would demonstrate their distinctive abilities and preferences and thus carve out separate dominions for themselves. They were superbly matched, however. They had an infinite capacity for hard work, sacrifice, and such long hours that, often, they slept in a back stockroom where they were frequently awakened by rats. They shared in the buying. Nathan bought shoes, men's and boys furnishings, underwear, and laundry soap. Maurice bought the curtains, yard goods, hosiery, ladies' and girls' apparel, plus feathers, a popular accessory at the time. Additionally, Nathan took on the operations side, meaning all the nonmerchandising duties required to run a store. Maurice made all the signs that were needed, trimmed the show windows, and handled the bookkeeping and banking.

They worked together harmoniously with mutual respect and devotion. They shared in everything, having even a joint bank account. Unquestionably successful, before too long they prevailed upon Momma and Poppa to close the grocery store, retire, and move across the street from the Goldblatt Bros. Dry Goods Store on Chicago Avenue. Simon and Hannah, indeed, craved their well-deserved new status. No one could question

Chapter IV   The Goldblatts Get into the Dry Goods Business

their dedication to running the grocery store and raising their family. When Nathan and Maurice opened their store, it had been barely five years since our parents acquired their U.S. citizenship on March 31, 1911. Having once described themselves as former subjects of czarist Imperial Russia, they would live in leisure as citizens of America.

Maurice was the supreme materialist. The acquisition of wealth was the well-spring of his incredible drive. He was lean, five feet five inches tall, and had piercing blue eyes, brown hair, and clear, sharp features.

Actually, he was a rather good-looking, dynamic young man. He was restless, seething with powerful ambition, and yearning for advancement in life. His direction was honed with singular, if not fanatical, purpose, but it was frustrated by his incurable inability to express himself, or more significantly to persuade others. Tirelessly persistent, he strained and argued to make his poorly expressed point. He would block his adversary's right of expression, dispute the other's reasoning every way he could. Often likened to a tool, Maurice was actually two tools: hammer and pincer. His aggressiveness, however, was not physical; he had no interest in sports. Nor was he interested in religion, or pets, and certainly not in art, as they all required time and energy with no monetary gain. He was quite outspoken about choosing friends, his sole criteria being how he might profit by them. While he was caustic and wouldn't hesitate to make empty promises, socially he was charm itself.

Maurice was gifted, and it showed at an early age. He saw potential where others didn't. He was forever seeking inroads to opportunities and predicting new worlds in years to come that required preparation now.

Nathan could have easily passed as a featherweight

fighter. He was one–of–a– kind, resembling no one else in the family — five feet two, flat faced, and pug nosed. If he were a boxer, likely he would have been the challenger. A tough guy, he looked the part. With Nathan, small and ferocious were not opposites. Actually, he was a good–hearted fellow with a flip side, a stubborn streak that had few peers. He collected his grudges and let them smolder. Whatever Maurice lacked in outside interests, Nathan more than compensated for with his avid enthusiasms about sports, animals, and art. But he shared Maurice's lack of interest in religion. Sam Goldwyn's famous quip about faith, "Gentleman, include me out," was eclipsed by Nathan's "as for religion, I can take it or leave it."

Nathan had guts and a brand of daring that showed from the start. Besides, he had luck on his side. Nathan would bet on almost everything and never ran from a fight, even when he should have. More than just street smarts, he possessed a unique mental agility. His ability to instantly comprehend and get to the heart of the matter with a merchant's perspective was brilliant. Indisputably, Nathan was a natural. In thorough command of the broad view, he abhorred detail and shunned study. When people got to know him, they loved him; some even adored him. Nathan saw an emerging merchant movement and, with grandiose determination, cast his future as a leader in it.

And so their store was in place along with and because of many circumstances of family and geography. Exposure to one another can create unusual combinations of allies, even with brothers. Like planets in the right orbit, they were people with ideas who came of age by putting ambition and loyalty to work for them right where they were. Their staging area was a small Polish neighborhood in the large city of Chicago. I always trace

Chapter IV The Goldblatts Get into the Dry Goods Business

the real beginning of the family business, the genie itself that got us going, back to the decision made by our parents in Stachov. They would trash their impotence by fleeing Europe and, by coming here, reinvigorate the potential of a family.

Storekeeping and the family seemed inseparable. My sister Anna Handelsman and her husband Kay started a dry goods store where Momma and Poppa had had their grocery. Later Sarah and Jake sold the grocery store they had on 26th Street to open a dry goods store also on Chicago Avenue, but much further west and out of the neighborhood, in an area called Austin. Joe, at the age of 10, began working for Maurice and Nathan after school and all day weekends.

Maurice and Nathan were passionate in striving to improve themselves toward improving their store. Joe was not immune from their disapproval nor excepted from their tutelage when he erred. He was not even spared object lessons if they upgraded the operation of the store.

Right inside the front entrance to the store was a high-traffic table that was always merchandised with especially good buys. Its purpose was to produce large sales volume, particularly on Saturdays, the biggest sales day of the week. Frequently, it was loaded with the fruit items that were in season. One day, Nathan sent Joseph to the market alone. "Joe, here's $100. Let the driver take you in the wagon and go to the market. Buy the best load of fruit you can find that we can sell at a crazy low price, but remember you've got to make a really good buy."

In a remarkably short time, Joe was back and running into the store to tell Nathan about the buy he made in strawberries. "Come out Nathan, and see for yourself!"

Nathan, naturally happy and excited, went outside

behind the store with his kid brother to look over the fruit and help with the unloading. He grew even more excited at the plump, high-quality fruit he saw, but then he realized that was only the topmost layer of each of the baskets. Dumping them, one, then two at a time, Nathan grew furious. "Just look at the shit you bought for a $100. It's rotten and crushed! Don't you look at what you're buying? They showed you their window trimming, and you handed over the money without even looking at what they were palming off. Haven't you learned anything working here? I wouldn't put that crap out at any price. You couldn't pay anyone enough to take it away. My brother, the sucker! They sure saw you coming." He continued the tongue lashing without stop. However, it was not Nathan's way to harbor hostility. He knew that was the worst buy the kid would ever make. Joe, head bent, just stood there fighting back the tears.

    The very next day, Nathan gave him another $100 and sent him to the market with the instruction not to come back if he got taken again. Joe's lesson was never to be forgotten.

Chapter V
Bar Mitzvah Boy Becomes Merchant

In 1916, Joe and I were still attending school, while also serving our separate apprenticeships under different teachers. The three-year difference in our ages thus imposed first on me the obligation of preparing for bar mitzvah, Hebrew for son of the commandment, the ceremony that marks a boy's coming of age at his 13th birthday.

How absurd was the preparation, which demanded blind obedience to an ordeal of tedious ritual. The countdown was via twice-a-week Hebrew school classes, held at the rabbi's home in the company of seven other young captives. The rabbi's only concern was the number of pages of the text that we read each session. There was drilling, always drilling, to the incessant beat of his stick against the side of a table. All in all, it was a daunting amount of reading and pronunciation, none of which I understood.

What a shame there was no way to get across to me the significance of the Hebrew scripture or the beauty of the ritual that lay ahead of me. Though I had the advantage of loving, well-meaning parents, the unfortunate result of their good intentions was a loveless ceremony that fell far short of the goal. There just was no intention on anyone's part, including my own, to arouse in me a relationship with God. There was, however, profound residual benefit that no one had planned on. My bar mitzvah turned out to be a high point in my development.

Over the months, it was Poppa who made me see it through. The ceremony would consist of my reading in Hebrew from the Torah, the first five books of the Bible kept in the ark of every synagogue, then reading in English a speech written for me by yet another rabbi.

Bar mitzvah, the day of my release, finally came! The misery of the training notwithstanding, I couldn't help but feel a sense of triumph at the sight of the sanctuary packed with all our friends and Momma and Poppa in the front row. The preliminaries came off as planned. I moved front and center on the platform and did my reading from the Torah. Then I began to feel like someone else's messenger. There I stood, Louis Goldblatt, poised to address a waiting world with a speech that belonged to someone else. Wearing my new blue serge suit, I stood motionless, red–faced, and wracked with nervousness. My sense of dishonesty was so acute I felt I could have glowed in the dark. It was that demon again, right in the pit of my stomach. It made me imagine everyone was whispering, "It's not his speech, it's not his speech." I had cramps, too! I wanted to go to the bathroom. There was just no way out. All I could think of was that Poppa did this to me and even Momma couldn't help me now.

I tried to speak several times, but my mouth just dropped open with nothing coming out. Finally, with my eyes closed I stammered out the line, "Today, I am a man!" I could speak no more. My mind went blank. My tongue curled and the palms of my hands grew cold and moist while I shifted from one foot to the other. Then, in desperation, I looked across to Momma and in a sudden burst cried out, "I was taught to memorize a speech

Chapter V   Bar Mitzvah Boy Becomes Merchant

but forgot what I was to say because the rabbi wrote it and it wouldn't be from my heart and I would sound like a parrot and I'm nobody's parrot."

I paused for an emotionally charged moment, swallowed hard, and gazed at both my parents. Slowly, meaningfully, I began to speak. I told them how grateful I was for all they had done for me. I asked their forgiveness for all the grief I caused them. For a full 15 minutes I continued an outpouring of affection and gratitude as only could be inspired by heartfelt spontaneity. Momma and Poppa's faces were contorted with tearful joy. I saw white handkerchiefs flashing everywhere. I heard noses blowing. During each pause there was such quiet, I could hear a pin drop. When I finished, the room was awash in sentiment and admiration. Momma and Poppa were aglow with pride. I could tell that even the rabbi took some pride in his rebel. Well, as an off-the-cuff bar mitzvah speech, it was probably a first!

My performance hadn't caused any job displacement because Poppa paid rabbi number two anyway. Besides, he could save the speech for his next victim. To this day, I never approach a podium without reflecting on that boy in the blue serge suit that day and the lesson learned apart from the scripture, not from within it. If ever you have anything to say and you want it heard, really heard, be certain it's truthful and sincere. Otherwise you're just a parrot and nobody believes a parrot. The rabbis hadn't planned this, but by causing me to throw off my shackles and forcing my own initiative, they had filled me with the independence that enabled me to say in echoing tones, "Today, I am a man!" Forever more, I had learned how to speak so people would listen!

I was feeling great. No more cramps. I drank wine, ate Momma's sponge cake, and fully enjoyed the celebration in the basement synagogue after the service. Momma and Poppa presented me with a solid gold watch and chain, which I treasured as more than a bar mitzvah gift. In 1966, I gave it to my eldest son, Gary, for his bar mitzvah. My other gifts included the proverbial fountain pens, pocket knives, books and baseballs, but most treasured was the sweet freedom from Hebrew lessons.

That same year, 1917, I endeavored to prove that 13 was, indeed, an unlucky number for me. I was struck with an acute attack of a burst appendix. The only doctor Poppa could find in the neighborhood who wasn't away in military service was one of our local drunkards. From time to time, we had seen him in the street, stumbling, almost going down. We would say, "There goes the doctor who could never freeze." In fact, we always had our doubts about whether he really was a doctor. But not this time. The laughing stock of the neighborhood became my only ministering angel.

I was rushed to the hospital and placed on the operating table, screaming in excruciating pain while still fully clothed. I managed a glance at the instrument the good doctor was waving about, first from head to toe, then from side to side. A short, curved knife; it resembled a linoleum cutter's tool we used at Alex's store when we cut off a nine–by–12 piece from the big roll in the back. Poppa remained in the operating room watching the trembling physician, now a surgeon, too. He proceeded to lower the menacing blade like a swinging pendulum and, in a few quick thrusts, succeeded in cutting away my clothing.

Soon the doctor was administering chloroform and, while not yet under it, I was able to see the horror on Poppa's face while watching his Louis's face turn blue. In my last few seconds of consciousness, I knew the doctor was incising my belly.

Chapter V Bar Mitzvah Boy Becomes Merchant

I can still feel it.

When it was all over, I was left with a 10-inch scar as a memento. The ordeal involved 10 days of draining the wound as well as other complications, and it was totally miraculous that I hadn't died for want of a proper doctor. Poppa said my survival was God's bar mitzvah gift to me. Well, then why send me this scourge in the first place? I asked. No appendicitis at all would have been a still better gift. More than likely, that swoop of misfortune was to teach me the lesson that my complaining about Hebrew lessons was blasphemous.

And why send a drunken doctor with a linoleum knife? No. God should have sent a doctor who looked like a great professor with gleaming instruments — and had sweet-smelling breath. It was no use. After that, I was to be a cantankerous believer at best, and even Poppa couldn't have prevented that from happening.

At this time, I was still working for Alex. School let out at 3:15, and I would arrive at the store by 3:30. There I would find salesmen from jobbing houses waiting to sell me various housewares items, for I was the buyer of them. I bought paring knives, Mason jars, water glasses, dishes, and can openers. All the time I was learning Polish because most of my customers spoke only that language.

Polish was alive for me, and the more I learned of it, the more it crowded out whatever Hebrew I was supposed to retain. In spite of the rabbi's lessons, now gratefully long since behind me, I still had to contend with Poppa and his ideas on observance. He lived a highly self-examined religious life that transcended his own faith and customs. He also demanded our observance as well. Any instance of religious disobedience on our part became a sticking point for him and an agony for us.

As early as I can remember, going back to shortly after the family first arrived here, Momma and Poppa observed Orthodox Judaism. They practiced strict adherence to ritual and custom and every Saturday went to the synagogue. As the years went by, their strict observance came into conflict with the demands of family and work. The requirements of their earlier devotion slowly faded. At the time of Joe's bar mitzvah and my own, their orthodoxy was at the brink of vanishing. Poppa continued to decree that we must, at least, attend Saturday services. Though he could no longer get Maurice and Nathan, who were already into young manhood, to go to services, when Joe and I resisted, he frequently pulled us by the ear. With my ear outstretched to near detachment, I screeched, "No, Poppa, I don't want to go. No, no, I won't go! I don't understand the Hebrew. Why should I go to just sit there? It isn't right!"

My resistance only quickened his pace and intensified the tug. "It's enough that God understands Hebrew. People are put on earth to produce, to leave something behind after they die. It's a sin not to produce. We must pray and give thanks for all the Lord has provided. When we work hard producing for six days, we must pray and give thanks on the seventh day by going to the synagogue."

No power could convince me. With my ear practically out of my head, with all the courage I could muster, I persisted, "It's your sin Poppa. You're committing a sin by going to synagogue on Saturday. Then you aren't working, you aren't producing, you're just sitting there. A man is just as good a Jew when he's a good citizen praying from his heart at home."

If anything, I managed to achieve a bumpy victory. As Joe and I grew older, time alone would transform Poppa's earlier outrage about our attitude to ongoing but subdued imperti-

Chapter V Bar Mitzvah Boy Becomes Merchant

nence. There is some sense, after all, to the imbalance of age and youth. As Poppa's influence became scorched and powerless, our sensibilities came of age. Joe and I always went to the synagogue on the high holy days out of respect for our parents, who had derived inordinate pleasure from the precious family events these days were to be in their memory and in ours.

#

America entered the war in Europe on April 6, 1917. That November, the Bolsheviks seized power in Russia. Across the country, selling liberty bonds was a top priority. Everywhere there was war talk, war news; war songs were on everyone's lips. One day late that year, while Maurice was standing out in front of the Goldblatt Bros. Dry Goods Store, a strange man bounded up to him, then hauled off and slapped him hard right across his face. Then he called him a scab because he was not in uniform. Considering the patriotic fervor at the time, such incidents were not uncommon.

Elmer and Werner Wieboldt of Wieboldt's Department Store had already been mentioned in newspapers as German; they were thought to be in sympathy with the Huns. Because he hadn't gone off to enlist, Maurice was finally drafted into the army and sent to Fort Sheridan; he was to be sent overseas. A devastating epidemic of influenza broke out in Europe at that time, then it spread throughout the United States and caused millions upon millions of deaths. Schoolchildren were instructed in means of protecting themselves and people everywhere wore face masks. Maurice not only chose not to wear one, he decided also to fast and starve himself. The result was that he, too, came down with influenza and was summarily discharged and sent home.

He arrived with his face ashen white and his weight down to 90 pounds. Most of his thick head of hair was gone, and he ran a fever of 104 degrees. Momma bedded him down on a cot away from we younger children and nursed him back to health. Henceforth, Maurice was a veteran of the Great War. Although hardly a hero, he was never to be slapped again.

Armistice, November 11, 1918! There were huge parades, and tons of confetti and shredded newspaper, showered down on the hundreds of thousands of Chicagoans who lined Michigan Avenue. Windows throughout the downtown area framed groups of office workers, deliriously screaming and waving. I had gone with a few of my friends and we perched ourselves on one of the bronze lions in the front of the Art Institute. Thus did I have a lion's share view of one of the great days in history.

Time was passing quickly and the Goldblatt brothers' stores were growing just as quickly. Joseph had been working for Maurice and Nathan for nearly three years when, at only 13 years of age, he became the buyer of fruit, toiletries, and goldfish, all in his after–school hours. My sister Rose came to work in the store, too, and was assigned to handle advertising, a sensitive post. Her job was seeing to it that she knew all the buys her brothers had made so she could make them known in the neighborhood.

Rose was as short as the rest of the family, but she was attractive, had curly hair and twinkling eyes; she was quick, clever, and highly motivated. When we were younger, she had been the plaything of her older sisters, but because she was younger she was also the one who had the unwanted job of helping Momma. She grew up a sensitive child. When a tender matter arose that might upset her, we brothers and sisters would say among ourselves, "Tell it to Rose, but be sure to scratch your left ear with your right hand when telling her." That way we would elicit her maximum sympathy. She was loved by all of us and had a way of creating her own happiness with her sympathetic and compassionate nature. Rose was good for advertising.

The year 1919 marked the start of Prohibition by means of the Eighteenth Amendment to the Constitution. The positive effects it had on some businesses weren't limited to the speakeasy. At Alex's store, we carried in stock a bevy of items necessary to the making of moonshine beer, including five-gallon copper kettles with dome lids, through which customers would drill a hole for inserting copper tubing. We also carried industrial cast-iron bottle cappers, bottles and bottle caps, malt and hops. Business was brisk. The lively pace was especially gratifying to me, as I became the buyer of all of it. With bubbling awareness, as Momma put it, I moved up from soap suds to beer suds.

The family continued to live across the street from Maurice and Nathan's store while Joe and I attended the Wells Grammar School on Ashland Avenue, two blocks from home. In class, it seemed that most of the day I just daydreamed about what I had to do at the store after school. I suppose, even then I had a career, and school was sort of a necessary evil before I could embark on it. My schoolwork had grown so bad that I was left back for four semesters before finally being allowed to graduate from eighth grade.

At the Wells School, graduates had to wear long colored ribbons for a full week prior to graduation, so as to proudly identify their status. Miss Slattery, the eighth-grade teacher, had two reasons to dislike me. One, perfectly justified, was my consistently poor record. Her other reason was purely my surmising.

I felt it was because I was Jewish. She had, for example, a way of calling every pupil by first name, except when she addressed me. She always used the name Goldblatt. In instructing the class to go buy the ribbons, she specified that they were not to be purchased at Goldblatt's. Instead, she told students to do their buying at Koop's Department Store, a few doors down from Maurice and Nathan's.

Miss Slattery and the incident stayed with me. It wasn't too many years later that Maurice and Nathan bought out Koop's. I'd probably be stretching it if I chose to believe that left her wondering about the lengths to which I would go in order to get her ribbon business.

There happened to be some real tough boys at the Wells School. They were organized into gangs, each of which represented an ethnic group of the neighborhood. Understandably, they always settled their disputes by fighting, generally during recess or after school. I managed to get into my own share of scrapes and, most of the time, badly beaten. It was double jeopardy for me; not only had I my own battles to fight, especially when called sheenee, but I had to protect my kid brother, Joseph, as well.

Somehow, I managed to know which of the gangs planned to go over to Alex's store after a fight and steal merchandise. So, bloody nose and all, I picked up my books, ran back to the store, and waited to ward them off, perhaps even to get into yet another fight. One of the gang members, named Schneider, was shot and killed by the police when caught in the act of stealing a car. Another, John Stayback, became a policeman. Then there was Manuel, a top student whose grades were always excellent on his report card. He never was a troublemaker, never had to have any fights. A few years after he graduated from both grammar and high school, I hired him to work in the store. Soon after, I had to fire him because he was not a capable worker. This experience served as a valuable lesson: neither top grades nor a peaceful disposition do a merchant nor a businessman make.

Chapter VI
Joining My Brothers in Business

I worked for Alex until summer vacation of 1919. By then, I had finished grammar school and was a dropout after six months at Carl Shurz High School. Alex had been paying me $6 for a 72-hour week. I was 16 and had put aside my knickers to wear Nathan's long pants. How like a grown man that made me feel! It was time I made a move, and Sarah had been pleading with me to come work for her and Jake. She offered me $12 a week, which I accepted. After two weeks at that new job, I again wanted to quit; instead, I wanted to work for Maurice and Nathan.

Momma would not approve. She felt it would create ill feelings among the children. I was determined. In speaking to Maurice, he told me it was up to me, but if I chose to work for him I was not to be paid. He wasn't about to hire me away from Alex or Sarah. That didn't matter much to me because I always gave my earnings to Momma and she gave me spending money. I took the job at Maurice and Nathan's even though, for several years, I did not receive a salary.

Thus, I became the buyer of pots and pans and all the housewares items down in the basement at the Goldblatt Bros. Dry Goods Store. For the next 60 years, I would be working for this family business.

Chapter VI *Joining My Brothers in Business*

Maurice and Nathan had very little schooling after having left Europe. Rose had been a good student; Joseph, only fair. I had been the poor student. Nevertheless, we all shared one point of view in the store; we saw everything as the customers saw it. In that regard, all of us were as smart as we could be toward improving ourselves, our merchandise, and our concern for our customer's needs and budget. The customer was the boss!

During my first decade with the store, Prohibition was the law of the land, and that meant we had to carry all the specialty items customers required to deal with it. Speakeasies were going strong and Al Capone came out of New York as a 20-year-old bodyguard for Big Jim Colosimo; he would climb to the top of his crime world by the time he was 26. Polish greenhorn immigrants — exactly what the Goldblatts had been called not too many years earlier — continued to arrive in our neighborhood in droves.

Nathan hired these greenhorns at a salary of $6 a week and insisted they go to night school to learn English. As employees of the store, they worked hard and were ambitious. It was their chance to get started working for all their dreams. With such drive and the ability to speak Polish with the customers, there could be no better salesclerks anywhere. Many immigrants heard that Goldblatt's was a good place to get a job. Thus, our store became a melting pot unto itself and a springboard, besides, for immigrants to learn about and experience their new country.

The Goldblatt family treated employees like members of our own family. When they had little to wear, Nathan would often outfit them with clothing. Maurice visited them at their homes when they were sick and went out of his way to congratulate them on their birthdays and other family occasions. When an employee was fired for stealing or any other reason, he or she would go to *Matka* Goldblatt across the street with the problem. Invariably, Hannah would insist that Maurice and Nathan hire them back and give them another chance. Unofficially, Momma was public relations and personnel appeals rolled into one.

The store prospered and we were able to enjoy some luxuries. Once a week on Sunday evenings during the summer, Maurice and Nathan gave the family a treat by taking Momma, Poppa, Joseph, Rose, and myself to Lincoln Park in their seven– passenger Buick touring car with canvas top. It was Nathan who did most of the driving. We brought along a basketful of food, mostly delicatessen sandwiches, spread a cloth out on the grass, and picnicked, enjoying the fresh air and being together. This was the only pleasure we managed to give ourselves throughout the hot summer.

# # #

Though by then in their late twenties, Maurice and Nathan gave themselves little time for dates. They enjoyed hard work and long hours. They knew no other way. It seemed as though each year they were knocking out another adjoining wall and enlarging the store. Soon they bought the building and expanded up to the second floor. On $500 capital, they had produced a sales volume in excess of $50,000 in their first year and the business continued to grow.

In practical terms, their objectives in doing business were simple. They sold the merchandise at very low prices and small profit in order to be able to pay the invoices that came due

Chapter VI   *Joining My Brothers in Business*

in 10 to 30 days from date of purchase. Because of the low prices of the merchandise, they created a fast rate of sales, or turnover. It followed that they enjoyed a strong cash position. As a result, vendors or suppliers liked to do business with them. After all, they paid their bills on time. In fact, they anticipated most of them and paid them before they were due, thereby earning an additional two–percent discount.

Maurice and Nathan continued to make very good buys and to sell the merchandise just a little above its actual cost. Accordingly, they were able to unload large quantities of goods before the bills came due. The result was that their store was doing its business on the vendor's capital. More and more, customers liked shopping at the Goldblatt Bros. Dry Goods Store. They knew they could buy what they wanted at good prices and that the bargains they found there were greater than those of competitive stores. Goldblatt's was the place to buy.

We all moved forward, owners and employees alike. Many of the early employees remained with the company over the years to develop into key executives. Others went into business for themselves, and in later years, still others became presidents of large corporations.

All that grew out of the greenhorn employees who learned from the very beginning to buy what the customers themselves wanted to buy. For example, when a salesman called on me wanting an order for his ribbons, I felt I knew what we needed in terms of width, color, and quantity. Nevertheless, I would consult with the Polish salesclerk. Her preference was key! Above all, she was a selling enthusiast. She was ever in pursuit of greater sales, therefore her counsel was that of the finest consultant. So it was that I used every scrap of selling information for good buying.

In those days, young girls wore ribbons frequently. Their mothers used ribbon and lace in sewing, so they were an item we carried in quantity and variety. Throughout the store, salesclerks were made to feel they placed the orders. It didn't take much time at all for such salesclerks to actually become notions buyers. In developing such methods, we did only what seemed natural and right. We produced sales from information gleaned by genuine experience with our customers, not by devising any so-called training program. That was it!

The houseware items I started out buying eventually expanded many fold into several departments, all located in the low-ceiling basement. The stockroom was in an area only six-feet high, with aisles of shelving only 24 inches apart. There was no real floor, only the damp or muddy ground. Except for some lone electric bulbs with pull chains here and there, it was mostly unlit and dark. When I was about 17, I became very aware of a pretty Polish salesclerk from my departments who frequented the stockroom looking for merchandise. So there were times I would follow her in and accidentally become wedged in between the narrow aisles with her. We both blushed and apologized and worked ourselves free. For my part, though I wasn't really trying very hard to do so.

I liked this young clerk very much and called her Mania, Polish for Mary. Later on, I did manage to give her a hug and even kissed her on the lips. That was the first time I had ever kissed a girl, except at a party once where we had played "Kiss the Pillow." Mania, I respected; she was sweet, wholesome, and innocent, and I never made any further advances toward her. I was, however, stricken with puppy love, the first time I'd encountered it.

Chapter VI   Joining My Brothers in Business

Our customers all seemed to have the same look about them, as though they'd come from the same mold. The men had large stomachs; the women, or *kobieta,* were big breasted and wore head scarfs called *babushkas.* These were good, simple, hard-working people; their concerns were family and making ends meet. In parts of our growing city, other people were concerned with civic interests and politics, with the life outside the home. Not so in our neighborhood. Some were still getting accustomed to the federal income tax, which the Supreme Court had ruled constitutional back in 1916. And of course, everyone in Chicago was interested in the growing scourge of crime. We Goldblatt brothers, however, kept our attention closely focused on business, but little did the customers know the extent to which we were prepared to go to never lose a sale.

One woman wanted a Daisy B.B. air rifle for her son as a Christmas present. Not wanting to lose the sale, I told her they were just being unpacked in the back stockroom and that by the time she would finish her shopping, I would have it for her. She agreed to wait. Then, I flew up the steps, dashed through the street, jumped on a streetcar and went all the way downtown to Butler Brothers, one of our jobbers. I ran through their offices, picked up the air rifle, and without a single wasted motion, hopped back on the streetcar and made it to the store to find the customer still patiently waiting. When she thanked me for any trouble it may have caused, all I said, still catching my breath, was, "No trouble at all. Really nothing."

That little story, in fact, portrayed the attitude on everyone's part throughout the store. This attitude gave life to our unwritten code that the customer, truly, was the boss. It was virtually a sin to lose a sale, invoking the "thou shalt not" injunction of a commandment. On the one hand, we stood far ahead of our competition in terms of the greater bargains we had to offer; on the other hand, our entire staff of employees was possessed by an unbeatable spirit to think, talk, and work, to do whatever it took, to make the almighty sale. Beating the competition went beyond the low prices at Goldblatt's. It was the people, too! No competitor could resist this double strength that was ours.

Every night after closing, a reddish compound was sprinkled on the floor to catch the dust just before it was swept up. Before doing this, the merchandise tables had to be moved out into an aisle in order to expose the whole floor. The tables, bunched together as they were, became an obstacle. In order to pass, one had almost to climb over them. This inspired some foolishness on my part. Determined that no barrier would block my path, I started to hurdle them. Eventually, I developed this stunt into a genuine skill — the skill of amateur–league high jumping. In time, from a running start, I was able to jump over tables loaded high with merchandise. What's more, I was even able to land right on top of a table from a standing start. With practice, I was getting better at this all the time. Outside the store, I couldn't pass a water hydrant without clearing it. I even hurdled over unsuspecting friends walking in front of me by bracing my hands on their shoulders and leaping over their heads. As a talent, I doubt it was marketable; but to me, knowing its simple origin at the store, it was priceless.

For Joseph and me, work was never done. We hardly ever got out at even a reasonably late hour. The store had a burglar alarm system that was the bane of our existence. Long after Maurice and Nathan left after closing, we had to stay on until the indicator on the control box showed that all the entry points were shut tight. Merchandise was just piled everywhere,

Chapter VI   Joining My Brothers in Business

including across the doors and windows. In order to check for whatever was still not shut as it should be, we had to move mountains of goods to access the trouble spot. Only when the leak was found were we able to go home. Then sometimes we were awakened when the alarm actually went off — a thief might have been in the store since before closing, and he would trip the alarm while attempting to make off with his loot during the night. And so we just went back.

We did manage to get in some play, however. Once in a while on a hot summer evening a crowd of us would get together at the local ice cream parlor. It was great fun. The dark of night seemed late in coming. It wasn't until 1918 that Congress had approved the adoption of daylight savings time, so we were still getting used to its benefits as teenagers. We'd have an ice cream soda or sundae for a dime or a banana split for 15 cents. A plain soda cost three cents or five cents, depending on size. We sat on wire-backed chairs at tables with fancy legs. We kidded around a lot to let off steam. A fellow by the name of Christian Nelson had patented his Eskimo Pie in 1922, so sometimes we'd buy one to eat in the street. The next year "Yes, We Have No Bananas" became the number-one hit, setting a record in sheet-music sales, so we'd walk down the street with its tune in our heads.

Sometimes we'd even get serious and talk about such matters as whether things had been going right for the country since Theodore Roosevelt's death in 1919. He'd been our first political hero. We heard that President Warren Harding had a radio installed at the White House, then a very novel piece of equipment. But we didn't know that Calvin Coolidge would soon succeed him upon his early death in 1923, or the Teapot Dome Scandal would erupt in 1924, or that Nathan Leopold and Richard Loeb were to be sentenced that same year to life imprisonment for the kidnap and murder of Bobby Franks.

# # #

One day, a policeman friend of Nathan came into the store to buy a shirt. Nathan hollered over for me to wait on him and even asked me to sell him the shirt at cost price, which I did. When he left, I thought I'd done exactly as told, but Nathan, furious, called me a dummy and almost hit me. He told me I should have charged the policeman even more than the shirt's actual price and that I should have told him it was the cost price.

Though I respected my brother, I could never see doing business that way. To make matters worse, except for special bargains that had price signs on the table, we hadn't yet fully become a one-price store. Until Selfridge started his one-price policy at Field's, most retailers still operated the old way, with merchandise seldom marked by the piece. Often, even when it was so marked, it was at a higher price than we'd usually sell it for. That way, the storekeeper could lower the price in conversation with the customer, making it appear that was special for him or her. Until the practice changed and all stores adopted the one-price policy, there was constant haggling. I always found that repugnant.

The Goldblatt Dry Goods Store never missed an opportunity. For instance, there was a dry goods store named Feathers on Milwaukee Avenue, which Maurice and Nathan bought out for cash with the sole purpose of running a going-out-of- business sale. Oddly enough, it would be one of the greatest sales in the store's history. Presumably, it was to include all the stock at that store. However, along with the

Chapter VI Joining My Brothers in Business

merchandise already there, Goldblatt's sent over truckload upon truckload loaded with odds and ends, goods we were stuck with. All the enthusiasm, fury, and magic of Feathers' sale proved it to be not only a huge and profitable success, but through it we also managed to clear away from Goldblatt's merchandise that was a liability as well.

Nathan was quick to buy anything and everything no matter what the item was nor how large the quantity, and he was able to obtain an even lower than low price because he bought it for cash. We were buying factory closeouts, odds and ends, irregulars, seconds and even "thirds," or out-of-season merchandise. The philosophy was that — at the right price — there was a customer for everything. And it was proven right!

For store fixtures, we improvised. We used empty crates and boxes in which merchandise had been delivered; our sales tables were converted from just about anything sturdy enough for a load of merchandise. At one time Nathan bought out a manufacturers' entire inventory, a carload full of Tingles, an item that competed with Cracker Jacks and Checkers, at a fraction of a penny cost for each box. A flake-like confection resembling corn flakes, only larger, Tingles tasted something like Cracker Jacks and were similarly packaged.

Naturally, there wasn't, by far, enough space in the store to contain so vast a quantity. We solved that by just throwing away most of the empty crates and boxes used as tables, replacing them with the cases of Tingles. Here was an opportunity that any number of sensible retailers would have turned away for lack of selling space. But for us it was the obstacle surmounted in the spirit of the store, much the same kind of thing as my jumping over all the tables. We wanted to do the impossible, and wanting to do it badly enough, we did it!

The pattern continued. Nathan made purchases in quantities so large that physically the store simply couldn't accommodate them. However, he always saw to it that the price he paid for the goods was so low that we could sell them off within a day or two, thereby never unduly crowding the store for too long. I can recall a special buy of ladies' shoes, packed loosely with each pair tied together. Most were button shoes, and the buttons had a tendency to come off from all the handling. So, we got special machines so we could replace the button ourselves right on the spot, rather than getting clogged with a quantity of straggler shoes. We even made it our business to give each customer a button hook with every pair, for free! The mob of customers was so great it could hardly be controlled.

Such purchases kept rolling in. In particular, we did a land–office business with men's shirts, the neck–band style for which collars were sold separately. Back then, shirts weren't yet made in sleeve–length sizes. So most of the time men had to wear arm bands to keep their sleeves from becoming mittens. The shirts were made in a variety of fabrics: broadcloth, madras, percale, cotton, gingham, and pure silk. They came in fancy stripes, also designs and colors. Nathan's means of procuring and pricing them was distinctly his own.

When Nathan was out negotiating and the deal was closed, he would abruptly sound off, "Cut, make, and trim!" He'd learned from experience that it took 27 yards of cloth to make a dozen shirts and what that cost. He'd also learned what it cost to trim them, depending on the number of buttons involved and whether the shirt had a breast pocket. Armed with that knowledge, he was able to bargain with the manufacturer on his own terms. His costs of course, varied with the

Chapter VI Joining My Brothers in Business

type of fabric, but for one particular sale, he averaged the costs of the individual lots and the various prices he'd paid and arrived at a single retail price for all of them

We put these shirts out for sale on a Saturday when the store was crowded with customers. We piled them high, all mixed up together, with a sign reading your choice and with the one price marked on all. Following his pricing method, Nathan was sure that the price he got covered all considerations of the separate costs of the component lots, and the customers never knew the difference. On this sale day, I climbed high on a ladder near the ceiling to open boxes of the shirts, then fling them down on the tables. All the while, I'd shout in English and then in Polish, "Come and get them. Values to $10. Now on sale; only one dollar. While they last!"

The air itself became charged with the electricity of the mad buying mood that followed. Customers were grabbing everything in sight. Then I would heighten the frenzy by throwing down a silk shirt along with the rest. When the shelves were empty, I climbed down from the ladder, picked up the shirts that had fallen on the floor, and put them back into boxes. Then I climbed up the ladder, placed the shirts back on the shelf, and started the whole thing all over again, this time shouting, "A new shipment just arrived. Because they are only slightly soiled, here they are, only one dollar each!"

It was the height of retail drama in its day. In its own way, it was a selling extravaganza. Here was the retail excitement of buying, selling, and customer satisfaction all rolled up into the most frenzied few hours that brains and muscles could produce. But the success of this sale only meant we had to do more of it. We were expendable, and no job was too grueling for our attention. Every morning at seven, which was when the store opened, we would fill, sign, put out, and line up a slew of wood cases on the sidewalk. I'd use the same shoe cases I'd prepared the soap for back in the days when I worked for Alex. Each one was made ready the night before; we would replenish the old stock or stuff them with new items. We put out unbleached sheeting, shoes, bloomers, overalls, the myriad basic everyday needs for the family. Because sunglasses weren't yet available, the visor cap, which sold for as much as nine cents and as low as three cents on sale days, was a big– selling item.

We would pin up on the awning various items for display such as corsets, blankets, raincoats, and feathers. Once, during a sub–zero spate of winter weather, the pins holding the displays up on the awning rusted. When the store closed at 10 o'clock, I went out to take the merchandise down, but the pins were stuck closed and didn't want to come unfastened. The cold was so severe, my fingers grew numb, and I barely avoided frostbite before I finally got the merchandise down.

We used every inch of space, in and outside of the store, even the ceiling. From it, we hung any number of items, then replaced them when we sold them off. Back then ladies' hose were made of mercerized cotton, silk, or wool. To display them, we strung each pair with a long strand of sewing thread and hung them from a barrel hoop suspended from the ceiling. When a customer found a pair she wanted, the sales clerk merely had to yank it loose and down it would come.

In those days, a salesgirl measured a yard of fabric by holding it out from the tip of her nose to the fingertips of her outstretched arm. If she had long arms, the store was shorted; if her arms were short, the customer was. On the counters, an improvised measuring device came into use, a series of brass tacks spaced nine inches apart. When a customer saw that a short clerk was about to wait on her and use the nose and fingers method for measuring, she would command, "Get down to brass tacks!" Thus was the expression coined.

Selling pillow feathers was a problem for many merchants back then, but we solved it in our own make–do fashion. The feathers came in two–pound muslin bags and were available in goose or duck down, a blend, or chicken feathers. The customer relied on the sales clerk to identify which. For us, feathers were a big and profitable sale, but for the customer, the purchase was laden with uncertainty. Many times she would ask *"Gdzie jest matka?"* or where is Mother Goldblatt? Then Momma would be summoned from across the street and proceed to blow into the sack. If the feathers were real down, they would float lightly around; if not, they would just sit at the bottom of the bag. In the latter case, Momma might just tell the customer the feathers weren't what they were represented to be, and she might even tell the customer not to buy them. If so, the sale would be lost and Maurice and Nathan angered, but Momma's reputation for honesty was enhanced.

Phonograph records were big business, especially those in Polish. We had a Victrola in the store that played all day long; next to it was a player piano that at the same time hammered out any one of a variety of piano rolls. This cacophony of loud, clashing tunes, with opposing rhythms, wailing sopranos, and eerie choirs rendered a startling bazaar–like quality to the store. Customers would thump, even jump and hum to the melody. Overall, it was a scene to behold with a sound that defied description, but thus we made our store customers feel as though they were home in the old country.

#

Leon and Max Lustig were two greenhorn brothers who had recently arrived from Europe. Although Leon had landed a job as a violinist, the brothers nevertheless came in asking for work. At the time, the last family still living in a flat above the store had just moved out, which was good because we needed the space for more stockroom. Then Maurice and Nathan had an idea: give the Lustig brothers a bedroom of the flat where they could open a barber shop; for this, they would pay Goldblatt's 10 percent of their sales. Once in business, the Lustigs advertised children's haircuts for five cents. The resulting lines of mothers with their children, particularly on days when there was no school, were so long that they extended all around the block.

Head lice was a common problem for schoolchildren, and mothers had to wash their children's heads with kerosene to kill the lice. To be on the safe side, some mothers decided their children should come in for a bald cut instead. That only took a minute or two and helped move the line along. Leon and Max were soon expert barbers, and in the years to come the Goldblatt's beauty salons became a large part of our business. Leon put down his violin to pick up a pair of scissors, just because Maurice and Nathan, Leon and Max, had an idea — and a vacant bedroom!

Chapter VI Joining My Brothers in Business

The First Goldblatt Bros. store, on Chicago Avenue a few blocks west of the Polska Skalp. Maurice and Nathan had opened the store in 1914, at ages 23 and 21, with $500 they had saved.

Life is a game, play to win!

During the 1927 cave-in of the Louis Store on Chicago Avenue, I helped rescue a salesclerk. Though we worried that this disaster meant the end of our growing company, it actually led to the start of a tremendous expansion, aided by the start of our long relationship with the First National Bank of Chicago.

Chapter VII
Merchandising Mania

By this time, I think we all knew that Goldblatt's could go as far as our imagination could take it. Business was growing, and I began to contemplate all that happened since I'd left Alex's store: the past, present, and future. I evaluated myself, a healthy young man of 20 with a passion for sports that, unfortunately, couldn't be matched with the available time. My life had become 110 percent work, but I imagined work as a game that I had to win, no doubt to compensate for all the street smarts and education I didn't have.

As a child, I had learned of the tribes coming out of the east, and I used to fantasize that one of my particular ancestors had come from the Far East. Why else would I have been kidded so about looking Mongolian? That couldn't be all that bad, and besides I looked like Momma and she was beautiful. Actually, the only vestige of my Oriental ancestry was almond–shaped eyes. They were, however, blue not dark brown, as my hair was. At five feet six, I was a Goliath among my brothers and sisters.

As for my dreams, I knew that if ever I were to realize them, it would be with my brains, not my looks, or by my smarts coupled with courage and an athlete's endurance. I had always been a happy person, relished meeting others, and had an ability to entertain, to make others feel as high spirited as I did. But I wanted my life to be more than just good. I would have the things I loved then and later come to know what was beyond my understanding, and have that, too. I drew comfort from my family and took pride in our working together. The store, I realized, was a conveyance to somewhere else, to something important. Someday, I assumed, I would help guide our fortunes.

At the time, Goldblatt's was bursting at the seams. We were in desperate need of additional space. Adjacent to the store was a butcher shop we wanted, but the owner had no desire to sell. Then we found we had an unwitting ally in the form of a city health department inspector by the name of Henry Appelbaum. The shop, alas, had inadequate refrigeration and its meat was often spoiled. When making his inspection one day, Appelbaum uncovered spoiled meat and poured kerosene on it so it couldn't be sold. Unable to deal with this situation, the butcher finally sold the building to Goldblatt's.

Thus, having acquired enough property, Maurice and Nathan were able to rebuild the store into a three-story building, 75 feet by 100 feet. When it reopened, they named the new store the Goldblatt Bros. Department Store.

In those days, department stores ran "dollar day" sales on which all advertised items were priced at exactly one dollar. Goldblatt's, in fact, competed with other retailers, including our own brother, Alex. In order to attract the early morning shopper, we made it a practice to feature extra-special bargains, at times below cost, on Saturday for two and a half hours only, from nine thirty to noon.

Among the departments for which I was responsible were groceries, and I had what I believed to be an earth-shak-

Chapter VII   Merchandising Mania

ing, traffic-drawing, and value-giving promotional idea. It would break all records, I thought. Little did I realize what I had taken on.

For one particular Saturday morning dollar-day sale, I would advertise a leatherette shopping bag filled with 40 grocery items, all for one dollar. We planned an ad picturing me holding a bag that listed 40 items and their regular value. It all started slowly enough, and I did my homework, too. I planned to sell 5,000 bags, which I figured called for selling three and one-third bags every minute.

I started by visiting manufacturers who supplied the leatherette used for open touring cars. I bought out all their odd pieces and remnants. Then I went to a factory and arranged to have the leatherette made into shopping bags. Next, I visited all the soap manufacturers and sold them the space on each side of the bag for their product's advertisement, thus reducing the bags' price to nothing at all for Goldblatt's. I had just begun.

I visited our various grocery jobbers, begging them to sell me 5,000 of an item below even their own cost so I could make this all happen. I'd chosen items that looked like a lot for a little money, such as a pound of cocoa or pepper, glass pepper shakers, and a two-pound sack of salt. I went to food manufacturers and convinced John B. Cannipa, the president of Red Cross spaghetti, to sell me 5,000 10-cent boxes of spaghetti for one cent. He consented with the condition that I distribute all 5,000 within the two-and-a-half-hour period. He reasoned that this way of introducing his product would cost less than were his company to deliver 5,000 samples.

Visits to other food and soap manufacturers produced similar deals, so I was soon forced to address the herculean task of receiving and storing 40 separate items in quantities of 5,000 each, then distributing the lot into 5,000 shopping bags. I would need an army to help me do it. This called for the handling of 200,000 separate pieces.

Fortunately, next door to our store was a second–floor loft I was able to use, though the building had a sagging floor and would seem to barely support the weight. I lined up the 40 items in row after row and hired school kids to work on Saturday and Sunday filling the shopping bags. One kid had the job of filling 5,000 shakers with pepper. Another had to weigh and pour the cocoa into one–pound bags, and so on. When it was all finished, I had the kids form a bucket brigade, passing the filled bags from the assembly area to the loft's far end. We had amassed a mountain in no time!

I was obsessed with what had begun as a clever merchandising stunt and had grown to be a full–fledged project of near–overwhelming proportions. It was on my mind morning, noon, and night, intensified by restrictions of time and space, inadequate help, and the rates I had to pay to purchase some of the goods. The sale day finally arrived, and the most critical part of the job lay just ahead.

Even before the store opened, a mob of customers had gathered. The crowd was so huge it spilled over into the street, blocking the streetcars. The police came to control the seething throngs. We moved the shopping bags to the second floor where the selling would take place, but to get there, the customers had to climb a narrow staircase. Maurice, Nathan, and Joe looked on in horror, fearing the banister would give way.

It seemed all of Chicago turned out. We sold 5,000 bags in two and half hours, sending as many satisfied Goldblatt's customers back into the neighborhood with four to five dollars worth of groceries for which they had paid only one dollar.

Chapter VII   Merchandising Mania

When it was over, I asked myself if I would have done it had I known its logistical consequences. I never came up with a suitable answer, but I continued to stage event after event, every one an ordeal, but I was rewarded by the supreme satisfaction of having surmounted an obstacle.

Among other departments for which I became responsible was cosmetics. Then as now, a popular way of doing this business was with a demonstrator, and we had one named Esther Cohen, who came on Saturdays. She stood on a table enthralling the ladies while giving a free makeup demonstration; her two brothers, Abe and Otto, did the same. In later years, their product, Lady Esther face cream, grew into the nationally famous line of Lady Esther cosmetics. In time, Otto was to leave the trio and form his own company, which he called Charles of the Ritz. From humble, hard-working beginnings, such people sought to create and market products, shape an image, and fulfill a dream, perhaps becoming corporate giants as well.

#

Excitement was essential to our business, and we staged a succession of attention- getting sale events without let up. Each of us would try to outdo the other. Bigger and better, more store traffic, more sales volume were our goals. We transformed the shopping experience into an adventure through which the customers, of course, would find greater bargains.

The variety of merchandise depicted the color and pace of the times and kept expanding to include important new items, such as oilcloth used on tables. This was a society without vinyl, plastic, polyester, dacron, or nylon. Gingham aprons, later to be called house dresses, were a big seller at one dollar each. For the men, there were pocket watches, as wristwatches were looked upon as feminine. Older boys who could afford them wore heavy, bulky-knit wool sweaters striped around the upper sleeve and across the chest; this, after all, was the jazz era of the 1920s. Men wore suspenders and called their underwear union suits. In the winter, boys wore the leather gauntlet gloves with fringe and cuffs they had seen in cowboy picture shows. Laborers wore blue denim overalls.

Our store became well known for price cutting, for underselling the competition, and for unusual bargains. We not only knew how to buy right, we also knew how to dramatize a value and get all the sales volume the item had to offer in the quickest amount of time. Every week, we had a circular advertisement distributed door to door throughout the neighborhood, which told of the great values to be offered in the next sales. When, on occasion, a competitor would open in the neighborhood, we would go all out, whatever the cost, to undersell him, then keep it up as long as it took to put him out of business.

The tricks of fate offered heavy blows of bitter disappointment, as well as great successes. Learning that a Woolworth store, which never sold anything for more than 10 cents or less than five cents, was to open a block from Goldblatt's, we began our countercampaign even before it opened. Woolworth filled a show window with white enamel 10-quart dishpans priced at 10 cents; a sign announced a sale to be held in two weeks, the day of its grand opening.

Like David taking on Goliath, I was immediately dispatched by train to Sheboygan, Wisconsin, to visit the Coonly Enamelware and Stamping Company; my mission was to buy

Chapter VII   Merchandising Mania

out all of their "culls," or rejects, at a specified price per pound. They led me to a huge storeroom of pots and pans piled high to the ceiling; all were damaged, chipped irregulars, but they had it all: pots, pans, covers of every size and type; white, grey, or mottled. I made my offer. Accepted! I wrote a purchase order for everything they had and said I would return in three days with cash and a truck to pick it up. I couldn't wait to tell my brothers of the great buy I made, and I set out to prepare a full–page ad in the forthcoming circular showing values of up to three dollars on sale for only nine cents each.

At the specified time I returned to Wisconsin with both cash and a truck, only to learn from the president of the company that the entire lot had been sold to a Maxwell Street merchant. He had paid more than I'd offered, and he had hauled it away the day before. I was incensed. I was outraged and said so. I described the fix they put me in, what with the circular already printed and distributed. I tried everything. I hollered. I cried. They were deaf to my pleas and threw me out, bodily. I returned to Chicago with my tail between my legs.

I didn't want to face Maurice and Nathan, but I had to. They called me a dummy and demanded that I keep faith with the customers, even if it meant supporting the sale with the regular stock, thereby incurring a great loss.

So back to Butler Bros. I went, and this time not for a Daisy B.B. air rifle. I went directly to the president and told my story with tears rolling down my cheeks; my brothers would throw me out of the store forever if I didn't replace the purchase. He was sympathetic to my plight and called the various department heads into his office. He asked them to escort me through their departments and sell anything and everything that was one or few of a kind: anything damaged or a sample, all odds and ends, plus regular items that sold for up to $15 per gross (or 12 dozen) and to charge me $10.80 per gross (or seven-and-a-half cents rather than 10 cents each). I could look into their stockrooms and under the counters and in the drawers and they were to charge me the same price for every item I found.

I was overjoyed and could hardly wait to get back to the store and brag to Maurice and Nathan of the great buy I had made. We were able to run the nine cents sale, after all, only now, in addition to pots and pans, it included tea kettles, coffeepots, wash tubs, scrub boards, pails, alarm clocks, brooms, dishpans, clotheslines, toys knives, and so much more.

The temperature hit the nineties that July day of Woolworth's grand opening. When our doors opened that morning, customers came crashing in and rushed down the stairs into the department with such a fury the police came to control them. Customers got into fights over the same item. The only way I could get through the mob was by swinging across from the ceiling pipes over the heads of the crowd. We even had to empty the show windows for fear the plate glass would break.

But the Woolworth store was practically empty of customers. I had more than redeemed myself with my brothers. It was the victory of the hunter, and I had come home with the kill. To our way of thinking, any competitor on our street was an enemy, an enemy who wanted to kill us — or at least put us out of business. So that, if we hurt him, even just a little, we were doing only what we must. Besides, we thrived on intense competition. It kept us on our toes and rendered the store always at its best.

Competition was also intense among the brothers. Each

of us were forever trying to top the other creating unusual events and techniques. With the other buyers, Joe and I had been indoctrinated by Nathan to view our individual departments as though they were the only departments in the store. Accordingly, the prevailing spirit was genuine pride of ownership — and any means to better each other. Signs for showing the price of the merchandise were always in short supply, and it was not at all uncommon to steal them off the next fellow's tables when the need arose.

There was one particular table near the front entrance that, due to the heavy traffic by it, called for merchandise that would produce the most business. Most of the time we put out fruit, cookies, or candy, unless one of us buyers could convince Nathan that his goods would produce even more sales. We all tried to come up with our own items worthy of the front table. Once I bought 20 gross of candy–filled glass toys, such as trains and telephones, imported from Japan. I paid nine dollars a gross, or six and a quarter cents apiece, then sold them for nine cents each, making more than a 30 percent profit. It was a complete sellout.

# # #

In 1924, Maurice and Nathan again confronted a dire need for more space. With only a 75–foot front, they tried to buy an additional 150 feet between their store and Koop's Department Store further down the block. Although they succeeded in buying out five of the six stores that took up this space, one little hat store held out. Located in the center of the six stores involved, this milliner overestimated his bargaining position and held out for a much higher price than Maurice and Nathan had offered. After we told him we would do without his store, Maurice and Nathan hired a dummy buyer who finally bought the milliner's shop and sold it to us as previously agreed. Now, we had it all! No sooner was all this space acquired than the excavation commenced and an addition was underway to our present store.

Until Goldblatt's started to sell them, too, cookies had been sold only in grocery stores, usually displayed in five-pound caddies on a wire stand. I had been buying large quantities direct from the bakers in 20-pound to 30-pound cartons; in so doing, I paid lower prices and thereby was able to undersell the grocery stores. I created a huge display of 15 cases near the store entrance, and believed I was doing land-office business in yet another merchandise category. But I was to learn we could do even better.

Jack Gordon was a tall, handsome man, as well as a great talker. As the representative of the Louis Weil Biscuit Company, he called on me regularly, always pleading for a 100-case order instead of the usual 50. I agreed, but only if he would come in on a Saturday and do the selling himself, as well as guarantee to take back any unsold quantity. Jack stood to win both a prize and a bonus from his company for producing the largest sales on record, and he accepted the challenge. The result was a sellout in less than half a day. We had actually broken a barrier because we were able to repeat it successfully week after week. From this we developed a cookie operation that in later years would grow into a multimillion dollar business.

We even had a wedding out of it. Jack met Rose in the advertising department and began courting her. They were soon married. There were other changes in the family, too. Though a member of the same enterprising family, my oldest brother Alex was at the opposite end on the scale of success; he

Chapter VII Merchandising Mania

went out of business in 1923 and took a job working for Maurice and Nathan. By now, Joe was spending most of his time in the operating end of the business, while I devoted all of my time to buying and merchandising. Hannah and Simon were enjoying their retirement, particularly their visits with children and grandchildren. On Friday nights in summer, we all gathered at their home for dinner. In the winter, Maurice and Nathan sent them to Miami Beach. When he was in town, Simon would visit the store often and feel he was making a contribution by picking up some string off the floor and giving it to a sales clerk to wrap packages.

Growth in business is not easily perceived on a daily basis until object lessons come along to drive a point home. I was responsible for the buying of crockery, or open-stock dishes and dinner sets. These I obtained from the Stetson china company via a weekly order following the toughest haggling imaginable. The usual dinnerware order was 10 sets. When the shipment arrived, and before paying the bill, I would generally find that one or two sets had came in broken, so I deducted the breakage from the invoice. In time, I placed an order for 100 sets. When it arrived, I noted an increased in the number of broken sets, and I decided not to pay the bill at all but to return the entire shipment. After all, in the past I received one broken set and now there were eight.

A discussion with Mr. Stetson ensued, and he instructed me that the condition of delivered dinnerware had, in fact, improved: eight out of 100 amounted to only eight percent breakage. I was persuaded to keep the large shipment and continued learning about percentages, too. Occasionally, I paid a price for my lack of schooling, but there just is no learning process as valuable as experience. At school, I'd always been poor in arithmetic, yet in business I was required to know what profit I might make from whatever I was to buy, in terms of both dollars and percent. At first, I understood this simply: if I paid 60 cents for an item and sold it for a dollar, I made 40 cents, or a profit of 40 percent. From that, I sharpened and formulated my understanding.

As a kid, I was never able to see the value of the teacher's drilling in class. Yet, eventually I had to drill and memorize until I could understand, for example, what each unit of a nine dollar gross would be. I came to know in a flash that the cost per piece of 75 cents per dozen was six and a quarter cents. I also knew that the most I could sell it for was 10 cents, thereby earning a 37.5 percent profit. Then, I reasoned, I might even hold the 37.5 percent by selling the item at nine cents, but only if I could get the cost down to $8.10 a gross. When a negotiation ended, and I was able to buy a large quantity at, say, $8.00 a gross, I would set the retail back to 10 cents instead of nine cents, as I had told the vendor. Thus I could make a profit of almost 44.5 percent.

I was motivated by the desire to make a profit and threatened by the fear of incurring a loss. I learned arithmetic that no classroom could teach me. I lived it.

###

Arithmetic wasn't all I learned during those first years of the Roaring Twenties. I made some friends and occasionally we took a break from work. Eddie Simon had replaced my sister, Rose Gordon, as the advertising manager at Goldblatt's. A dedicated employee and about our age, he became a close friend of Joe and myself. Herman Goldstein came into our circle as well.

Chapter VII   Merchandising Mania

Known to everybody as Buck, the name seemed right for the big swarthy fellow that he was; later he changed his name to Herman Buckley. With his father and brothers, Buck operated the leased lunch counter at our store.

The four of us — Eddie Simon, Hi Buckley, my brother Joe, and myself — had become close friends as we became young men. We called ourselves the Four Must Get Theirs, and we always vacationed together. Thus, one summer day we piled into a Buick with an open canvas top for a trip to South Haven, Michigan, then a popular resort for Chicagoans. The roads were unpaved back then; it was only 1923 and the trip was hard. It took about eight hours to get there. Eddie and Buck, it so happened, were already veterans at sex; Joe and I had no experience whatsoever. Our two friends were determined to have some fun watching us get laid.

On a one-week vacation, every day counts when you count on getting laid. So it became a daily routine for Eddie to flirt with his chosen object of our lust, a waitress at the resort's restaurant. In her twenties, she was a little on the plump side, but attractive with long blond hair and a pleasant disposition. All four of us kept propositioning her. Every chance we had, we'd cop a feel, and eventually she could no longer withstand the broadside campaign. Finally, on the last day, she consented, and with such overwhelming enthusiasm, she agreed to lay all four of us!

Her luncheon shift finished, we all piled into the Buick and took off down a dusty road. We parked along side a heavily wooded area. She got out and went about 50 feet into the woods to wait. Eddie was the first to go after her; the rest of us waited our turn. Buck went next. When they returned to the car, both exclaimed, "Wow, what a great lay!" Then it was my turn, and though she was obviously all warmed up, I'd developed cold feet and wanted to back out. But I also wanted to be one of the guys and wasn't about to be a sissy. I got out of the car, disappeared into the woods, and found her lying on the ground, no panties, no stockings, just a dress and sandals. Upon seeing me, she threw the dress up over her waist and was ready. I was excited. I was nervous. I was shy, ashamed, and anxious. I dallied and said, "Hi!"

She said, "What?"

In those days, men's pants had no zippers, only buttons. I looked down at the half nude girl in front of me. My fingers turned to putty as I fumbled trying to unbutton my pants. I said "Hi!" again. "Just wait a second, one second," I went on, struggling with the buttons.

She kept looking me over and said, "You're sure different from the guy I knew back there at the restaurant."

With that, my fingers somehow flicked all the buttons open, and my penis popped out at full alert! Down on my knees, I had no sooner placed it between her legs, wondering if it was in her vagina, or just between her legs, or maybe just into a soft spot in the ground, when I suddenly exploded — a rushing, unstoppable torrent. I ejaculated all over my pants. I had remained fully dressed, pants and all, during what was to be a most exciting experience of my life, my first experience at the sex act.

When I caught my breath, I said, "May I ask you a question?"

"Sure, get it over with," she replied.

"Was it in your hole?"

"Hell, no!" she shrieked. Before I had asked her, and before she replied, I thought the smile on her face had been one

Chapter VII   Merchandising Mania

of pleasure. Then, I knew it was of amusement. Well, I made her happy, anyway!

I buttoned my pants, this time running out of the woods to rejoin my friends who were laughing at the stories of their conquests. I never admitted to the guys that, in truth, I didn't know her hole from a hole in the ground. Joe took to it easily enough, knowing just what to do though it was his first experience, too. He came out of the woods with the waitress following, laughing and telling us what a wonderful time she'd had. We drove her back to the resort and kissed her goodbye. I was the only one who said thanks! Soon we were on our way back to Chicago, our vacation over. At last, Joe and I got laid. Well, at least Joe did.

Chapter VIII
From Dry Goods to Department Store

In 1925, ground was broken for the University of Chicago Medical Center, marking an appointment with destiny for Goldblatt's, for later the family would establish a major cancer research facility there. In May of the same year, Goldblatt's bought the Koop's Department Store from the owner, Julius Koop. The store had a frontage of 50 feet, operated four floors and a basement, was old–fashioned the year we bought it, and catered to an upper–class clientele. Goldblatt's customers had no time for the elaborate process of making a sale at Koop's. There, after a sale, the clerk would write a sales check, place it along with the customer's money into a container, then put the container and merchandise into a wire basket, and pull a cord that hoisted the basket up to and across the ceiling into a cashier's cage. There, the sales check was processed, the merchandise wrapped and put back into the basket, and sent down with change and a sales receipt. A transformation in the character and atmosphere of Koop's was about to take place.

Maurice and Nathan, the store's new owners, changed its name to the Louis Department Store, and put me in charge to run it as a competitor of Goldblatt's. The strategy behind all this was enlarging the Goldblatt's store on the new land they had acquired, building it all the way up to the Louis Store,

Chapter VIII *From Dry Goods to Department Store*

then running a great sale in celebration of their buying the Louis Store and connecting it with Goldblatt's. The plan would give Goldblatt Bros. a total frontage of 275 feet along on Chicago Avenue.

I was given full authority to run the operation autonomously and competitively, through to the sale events themselves. The Louis Store did its own buying, merchandising, advertising, and expense control. Maurice and Nathan rarely visited it, and I hardly set foot into Goldblatt's. Together, we gave maximum credibility to our plan of the brothers competing with each other, which in truth we were.

Goldblatt's advertised sales every week, including such major events as the President's Sale, Founder's Day, Maurice Goldblatt Day, Nathan Goldblatt Day, the Rummage Sale, Clean Sweep Sale, Anniversary Sale, Dollar Day; plus events that corresponded with all the important holidays of the year. Each brother constantly vied to make his sale greater than the other's. The first sale I ran at my Louis Store had its origin in an advertisement I made up during my school days, an idea I'd gotten from watching an ROTC class ordered to attention. The front page of the advertisement showed a mammoth-size arrow leading to the blaring word "ATTENTION." This was followed by a listing of highly recognizable items at prices well below those of Goldblatt's, along with the declaration "THE WAR IS ON! WE WILL NOT BE UNDERSOLD! WE SELL FOR LESS!" All these headlines I copied directly from Goldblatt's ad.

The customers went for it, hook, line, and sinker! The brothers were fighting, they assumed, and so they shopped both stores in order to see for themselves which offered the biggest bargains and lowest prices. But there was a surprise

Life is a game, play to win!

in store for brothers Maurice and Nathan.

July was an "off" month, and we'd never made a strong sales effort then. For this reason, I deliberately chose the month to stage my very own "Ye Old–Fashioned Bargain Carnival." For this, I pulled out all the stops. Not only was I originating a major event, but doing so obliged me to motivate a sweltering public at a time they would prefer to lay low. Were I to fail, I could already hear Maurice and Nathan saying, "Dummy, you should have known!"

I began with visits to my vendors, cajoling and pleading with them to sell me goods at cost, or a tiny bit above, for this one–day sale only. Then, I was careful to price the goods at equally low prices and saw to it that I had plenty of merchandise stacked high on the tables. I made signs carrying the name of the sale and placed them throughout the store, hung pennants from the ceilings, and strung balloons everywhere. On the windows, I posted pictures of animals to give the store a carnival feeling. Inside, I placed authentic–looking street posts up and down the aisles reading "Bargain Lane," "Cut Price Street," "Thrift Avenue." All of this was intended to create a mood that would pre–sell the bargain message, which the merchandise itself would bear out.

Trained to see all of this as the customer would see it, I examined my every move, every sign, every merchandise location, and detail. I would not leave a bit to chance nor an inch of space unaccounted for. Color was everywhere. I even had the 30,000 circulars printed in carnival colors to match the balloons and pennants. On the awnings, too, was item after item, all priced for success! The salesclerks were primed, and above all enthused and ready to make retail history.

Came the morning of the sale, it was a 94 degree day.

Chapter VIII   From Dry Goods to Department Store

The crowds gathered at the entrance spilled out into the street. Maurice and Nathan couldn't resist and tried to get into the store, only to find they had to wait with all the others for some customers to leave before the doors were opened to admit a like number. Representatives of stores from other areas, even State Street, came to see what was happening. Word of the enormous success of the event became even more widely known, and bargain carnival was to be copied by retailers across the country.

Goldblatt's, naturally, did poorly during the Louis Store sale, and I couldn't refrain from teasing my brothers. "Well, you have your Maurice Goldblatt Days and Nathan Goldblatt Days. Now, I have my own bargain carnival sale!" I gloated.

In those days, the weeks and months of the two years I ran the Louis Store, I was still only in my early twenties. I took no time for play or dating. My mind was always racing like a turbine, constantly generating new ideas for new sale events and gimmicks to produce more and more sales. I would look at almost anything and be able to envision some promotional possibility.

In this light, one day I saw a child's balloon and a scheme popped into my mind, I ran into my makeshift office and started to figure its angles and costs. I multiplied, one day, two days, prizes, advertising, display, excitement — always excitement. Hence, the birth of the Ten Cent Balloon Sale!

My idea was to place a small coupon for a particular piece of merchandise inside a drug capsule and put each capsule in a balloon. We would inflate thousands of them and display them everywhere, along with a vast array of items out of every department on every floor of the store. Plus one balloon would contain a coupon for a $10 gold piece. All the signs and advertising informed the customer that the balloons cost 10 cents and coupons were worth at least 10 cents, but the lucky coupons might win them great merchandise values. If they weren't completely satisfied, we would even refund their 10 cents. The excitement struck the neighborhood like a brand-new holiday, and they converged upon the store in droves.

They'd buy a balloon, burst it and, find the coupon reading, "Go to the third floor and receive a wash tub." The idea was to get the traffic to all the departments on all the floors. It just couldn't lose. Any dissatisfied customer had to go to the refund cashier located on an upper floor. The cashier, in turn, was required to prepare a refund slip, which took time and caused a long line. Not wanting to wait, many customers gave up and went to do the rest of their shopping in the store. Although there was a limit of one balloon per customer, some went and bought still another balloon after they got their refund. The result was that the customers were having fun and getting value, too. The store had a successful sale, and I added still another pearl to my growing collection of lessons in human nature.

And then, the building's profit generator screeched to a crashing halt. It was the ninth of May in the year 1927. The Louis Store had a bay window in the vestibule, with an entrance on either side and a show window bordering each entrance.

It was noon on a warm Monday morning. The trimmer was inside one of windows; a sale was in progress, and the store was busy with customers. Workmen were just leaving the excavation being dug between Goldblatt's and the Louis Store, and I had just left the store for lunch. I stopped to see how the window was being trimmed, and all of a sudden, right before my eyes, the plate glass cracked straight through from top to bottom. At first, I

Chapter VIII From Dry Goods to Department Store

thought the trimmer had caused an accident, but just then the window next to it cracked, too. Then another, and still another. Frantic, I ran to the side of the building, looked up at the roof, and to my horror, saw bricks dislodging and hurtling down. This couldn't be happening, I cried. Near panic, I ran over to Goldblatt's and shouted, "Maurice, Nathan, come quick! The Louis Store is falling down!"

Within minutes, the police and fire departments arrived. Crowds gathered across the street. Suddenly, there were police barricades all around and no one was allowed to enter. Anyone still inside the store was doomed, so they believed. I, too, was held back, but broke loose. I hurdled the wood horses and before anyone could stop me began running through the store, shouting at the top of my voice, "Fire! Quick, get out! The building is falling down! Murder! Hold–up! Gangsters! Everybody out!" I kept it up everywhere I ran. On the fourth floor, I saw Sherman, a stockboy, getting into the elevator. As I shouted to him, "Get out, Sherman! Get out," the elevator plunged down with him inside.

I ran as fast as I could down the stairs, not knowing that a salesclerk from the yard goods department, Mae McGuinness, was in the ladies' room at the time. When I reached the second floor, I heard a sickening rumble. I could feel the building tremble as though in an earthquake. Some of the lights went out. I had to jump over the last three steps; they had already shattered. When I landed, I stopped to help a salesclerk who had fainted, and I carried her down to the first floor, shouting all the time for everyone to get out of the store.

With the girl in my arms, I was about to leave the store when I saw the cashier at the front gathering up the money out of her register. I shouted to her to drop it and run. I got to the street and started to trudge onto the streetcar tracks, still holding the girl. Behind me, I heard the crash of the big electric sign, the Louis Store sign, my Louis Store. The street was teeming with police, firemen, ambulances, Red Cross trucks, and onlookers. The police chief, a man named Collins, began to question me as to how many employees were in the store at the time, what their names were, and whether any customers were still inside. I told him that, as far as I knew, there were no customers there, and that we had 35 employees working at the time. I thought they'd all gotten out, except for Sherman.

Finally, the whole building collapsed into a pile of rubble, right into the excavation. The fourth floor went one direction, the third in an opposite direction. It took what seemed like the longest time for the thick clouds of dust to settle. Then, slowly, like a dim, red, nightmare, the whole ghastly specter came into view, midst the deafening screams of the crowd that had gathered.

Immediately a wrecking crew began to dig through the twisted steel and merchandise where the elevator had gone down carrying Sherman. By then, we'd presumed him to be lost, but thank God, he was spared. The elevator that trapped him had also saved him! Everyone cheered when he was pulled out. It was a neighborhood rejoicing for its own! It was also a neighborhood that had witnessed the destruction of one of its distinctive assets. Next, Mae McGuinness, trapped in the third–floor washroom, was pulled from the heap and rushed to the hospital. She only suffered two broken ribs.

The Louis Store kept mannequins in a basement storeroom. During the cave in, some had been splattered with red paint. When they were carried out, they presented a spectacle

Chapter VIII   From Dry Goods to Department Store

of death and mutilation that evoked the sympathy instinct of the screaming crowd. The Salvation Army was there with coffee and doughnuts. We were all grateful that there was no fire. Momma and Poppa had long since come down from their apartment across the street. Along with Maurice and Nathan, Joe, and myself, we stood in a group sobbing when Walter Heymann, vice president of the First National Bank, walked over to console us.

It was easily determined that the shoring of the Louis Store had been weakened during the excavation. Intended to support the 40-year old building, the shoring gave way, causing the store to collapse. Goldblatt's was not insured for this kind of disaster. Maurice and Nathan worried that they'd been wiped out. The brothers' banking history was as dramatic as everything else they had done. Back in 1924, they'd been banking with the Northwestern Bank on Milwaukee Avenue. At the time, Wieboldt's, a big account at the bank as well as a fierce and angry competitor of ours, threatened to take its business elsewhere if the bank continued doing business with Goldblatt's. So, Maurice went to see Eagle Brown, chairman and chief executive officer of the First National Bank, who not only doubled Goldblatt's credit rating but offered a lower interest rate besides. Now it was 1927 and the bank, in the person of Walter Heymann, was there. But he wasn't there just to witness our tears or to see the brothers' years of plans and dreams turn to dust in a few hours. He stepped between Maurice and Nathan and placed his hands on their shoulders, which by then were stooped as though in acquiescence to a tragedy beyond even their ingenuity to resist. "Maurice, Nathan, my friends," Heymann said, "it's not lost."

Nathan replied, "It's our hearts we've lost. It's not an

arm or a leg. Our lives are laying in a hole. There, see for yourself. When that's covered over, our store is gone."

"No, no, not at all," Heymann replied, "On the contrary. I am able to see what you both don't see. Maurice, Nathan, let me tell you what I see. I see a store, a bigger store, a five-floor store and basement, right there where you see a grave. I see the two of you with the help of the bank rebuilding and rising like a phoenix from the ashes. We'll rebuild a Goldblatt's of tomorrow, leaving the past behind. I mean to see that you have all the money you need.

"Then," he continued, "true, the building perished, but the dream is alive. Your hearts are strong. The fight and the spirit of you brothers are all the assets the bank needs. We ask nothing more to guarantee the investment. We ask for no collateral. I have the Goldblatt brothers. You have the First National Bank behind you — and Walter Heymann."

Now Maurice and Nathan cried as they hadn't cried before. They gripped Heymann's hands until he grimaced. Then they remembered there was work to be done. Late that afternoon, when it was determined that no bodies were missing, Maurice, Nathan, Joe, and I surveyed the heaps of twisted steel, plaster, fixtures, and merchandise to plan the salvage operation. Apart from merchandise, there were cash registers, safes with the money still inside, fixtures, and store records.

Shortly, Maurice and Nathan rented an empty store a block away, to which we sent all the salvageable merchandise; some weeks later we held a successful rummage sale. Before that, however, we four of the salvage crew had been so battered by ill weather we all came down with bad colds. When we were able to replace ourselves, we went to the Turkish Baths on Division Street for the cure and some well-deserved rest.

Chapter VIII   From Dry Goods to Department Store

The following morning, we took our positions and resumed the operation. But then, toward evening, we had another disaster to endure. A severe rainstorm hit with winds so strong they broke the show windows of the Goldblatt's store. Coming on the heels of the cave–in, this made the brothers, employees, and even customers wonder if, despite Heymann's offer, the final blow was actually on its way. Our little world, at least, seemed coming to an end. But no, the storm's timing was just a terrible coincidence.

Newspapers carried the story with headlines that screamed "LOUIS STORE COLLAPSES." The story following said, "It is believed many were killed." Newsboys throughout the city shouted, "EXTRA! EXTRA! READ ALL ABOUT IT. THE LOUIS STORE CAVE–IN!" In an editorial, the *Chicago Daily News* offered a rather heartfelt view of the story, even suggesting to the Carnegie Hero Fund Commission that it award Louis Goldblatt the Carnegie Medal for heroism. Later, representatives of the commission came and visited me to get the story firsthand, but alas, my status as hero was short–lived.

Three days after the terrible accident, the news of the Louis Store moved inside the newspaper. The front pages now carried the story of Charles Lindbergh, who was to fly across the Atlantic Ocean on May 12 of that year. All the country waited with him for better flying weather; finally, he was able to take off and land in Paris on May 21. The story of the store and my assumed heroism seemed pale by comparison; the *Daily News* campaign lost its momentum. But for those of us who had been there, the story was never to die.

As the years went by, the Louis Store incident settled into my memory; it was never to blur, nor could I forget any of its harrowing details. Since then, a nightmare has recurred countless times. In it, I recall faces and names as though the collapse happened yesterday. While these recollections still quicken my heartbeat and bring on a cold sweat, I have the compensating awareness that my cries, my legs, and my arms served in the divine intervention. It was ordained that no one was to perish and no one did. The angels were watching over me again.

# # #

The nation had passed the first quarter of the century, and 1927 was indeed a newsworthy year. There were strikes, memorable events, and scandals, too. There were some fledgling conceptions afoot that would grow to enrich the world, and a villainy that would grow to oppress the world was under development as well. Television came into being, but it wouldn't reach the public for another 20 years. Talkies were introduced to moviegoers, and Mickey Mouse was born. Americans were able to have telephone conversations with Europe as commercial transatlantic service was inaugurated between New York and London.

In sports, the nation was captivated by the fight in which Jack Dempsey knocked out Jack Sharkey; later that year, he lost the heavyweight championship to Gene Tunney. Babe Ruth hit his sixtieth home run of a season, setting a record that was to last for 34 years. Sacco and Vanzetti, convicted of being the alien anarchists, were executed. Thomas Edison celebrated his eightieth birthday, and Albert Einstein had a year of prolific publication.

In Chicago, the word was that Mayor William Hale Thompson, reputed pal of Al Capone, was ripping off city

Chapter VIII   From Dry Goods to Department Store

schools, defrauding charities, and providing police protection for the mob. His private yacht sank in Belmont Harbor, overcrowded with celebrants of his election to a third term.

# # #

The grand opening of the new Goldblatt Bros. Department Store was set to take place March 10, 1928, just 10 months after the collapse of the Louis Store. This additional 175-foot frontage, a five-floor building and basement, was annexed to the 75 feet of the original three-floor store, plus 25 feet of the one-floor annex. Goldblatt's now had a total of a full 275 feet on Chicago Avenue, or a 169,000- square-foot store.

On opening day, a giant canopy made of green foliage stretched the full 275 feet. We'd hired a loud band and located it on a platform out front. People came from far and wide, jamming the street and bringing traffic to a standstill. We erected barricades to prevent the mobs from crushing into the windows.

When the doors were opened, the multitude broke through like a torrent breaching a dam. In no time at all, every floor was filled. The entrances were closed before any more of the crowd could be admitted. Babies in carriages were left by their mothers out on the sidewalk in the care of a special security force.

Merchandise was stacked high in every available square foot or hung from the ceilings. Hundreds of cash registers were located at 10-foot intervals; wrapping desks were loaded with supplies. Never had we seen such spirit. Employees and customers shared our elation. We brothers were ecstatic; our eyes were moist with joy and our hearts pounded like trip hammers. Maurice, Nathan, Joe, Alex, and myself ran throughout the store all day, making change, fixing registers, wrapping, greeting, handling complaints — and receiving best wishes, even blessings.

Momma and Poppa were drunk with the kind of pride that heaven reserves only for parents. There they were, and this was infinitely more than a store. It was a saga, that had its origins in the tiny boot shop in Stachov, the Polska Skalp, the money they had saved and added to their son's investment. This was the culmination of the raising of their eight children. For glowing Momma, this was the neighborhood and all of her beloved friends. For Poppa, this was God's reward; it was the steamship *Peace* and *Halifax*, the kielbasa down in the old basement, and South Water Street Market — and it was his family. They shook hands with the customers using both hands, even with the tumultuous crowd. Momma kissed many of them. It was a triumphant day for us all.

As the cost of advertising for Goldblatt's had always run at a high percent of sales, Maurice and Nathan bought their own plant, the National Printing Company, of producing our advertising circulars. For the grand-opening sale, we hand delivered 300,000 circulars, and advertised, naturally, in the foreign language newspapers, too: Polish, Bohemian, German, and Jewish. We also ran ads in the *Herald American* and the *Daily News*. On every ad read the slogan, "AMERICA'S FASTEST-GROWING DEPARTMENT STORE. WE GUARANTEE CHICAGO'S LOWEST PRICES. WE SELL FOR LESS!"

This extraordinary, highly personal customer response continued throughout the day and into the late evening. There were incessant compliments for the brothers; many customers remarked about having known Hannah and Simon in the days of the grocery store. Many went on to pledge the loyalty of themselves and their family to Goldblatt's — forever! We delivered purchases free of charge. On this day, the shipping room was inundated. Without stop, Joe Merric, delivery head, routed mountains of packages onto the fleet of trucks that Goldblatt owned. He tried so hard, renting additional trucks and hiring more help, that many deliveries arrived home before the customers.

Over the hundreds of items bought for the grand–opening days, the prices and values were startling, even for Goldblatt's. Two worlds of retailing were watching us. One was that of customers, who couldn't believe the prices they were seeing. They couldn't be misprints as there were too many of them; these prices were real! The other was the world of retailers. Now that we were a full–line department store stocking almost every category of merchandise, they were taking stock of this upstart in an out–of–the–way location in Chicago.

The grand–opening ads declared "WE WILL NOT BE UNDERSOLD," and we didn't intend to be. We offered women's all–leather shoes at $1.55 and house slippers at 19 cents; for boys, there were all–leather shoes for $1.17; men's famous Endicott Johnson leather shoes were $1.49. Bananas were 17 cents a dozen; donuts, 19 cents. Hand–dipped, chocolate maraschino cherries, individually wrapped, went for 23 cents per pound; O'Henry candy bars, one and a half cents. The deals went on. No item of clothing was sold for over a dollar; a 35–piece porcelain dinner set went for the same price, a large assortment of pots and pans for half that. A rebuilt sewing machine was $12.50, and a five–piece dining room suite, $39.50. Bedsheets were 59 cents each and zinc washboards, 39 cents. The saturation advertising we showered on the ethnic and

Life is a game, play to win!

mainstream public set off a bargain–hunting furor; word–of–mouth acclaim carried news of the sale from one end of Chicago to the other. The store had to stay open way past the advertised nine o'clock closing time; the customers simply would not leave. Everyone's hard work and dreams culminated into one history–making day.

We had grown to a full–line department store, including even furniture. On the buying trip to New York in preparation for this sale, we'd reached new heights in negotiating deals. I begged for free goods, for half–price items; we even demanded manufacturers' cost! When approached by Nathan and one of our buyers, our vendors, fearful of antagonizing him and wanting to remain in Goldblatt's good graces, would say, "All right, damn it! I'm losing money, but I'll accept. This one time only though." Back on the street, Nathan and the buyer would rejoice and hug each other for the show they put on and the great buy they had made.

On regular buying trips, when the buyers returned after a day out in the market, they would visit Nathan in his hotel suite, boasting about their buys that day. Nathan would be quick to show his pleasure and motivate them to go out the next day to make even better buys.

At the end of one buying day, Nathan took us all to a large restaurant down in the Bowery, where we ate and drank in celebration of the bonanza buys we made. We'd been organized with objectives, and having achieved them, we shared our self– satisfaction. Nathan was a dynamo. Well–liked and respected by his buyers and vendors as well, Nathan was looked upon as shrewd, cunning, and an excellent horse trader. A vendor, for example, would ask $10 a dozen for an item and might be willing to take it down to nine. Our buyer was insist-

Chapter VIII   From Dry Goods to Department Store

ing on six, although he would gladly pay nine, if need be. Then the buyer would raise his offer to seven — and call upon Nathan for help. Nathan would come up, inspect the merchandise, hear both sides of the argument, and proceed to reprimand the buyer unmercifully for his seven dollar offer. Then, Nathan would tell the vendor to split the difference and order the buyer to write the purchase order for eight dollars, at once. After a week of buying, ruses with vendors, chats in Nathan's suite, and group dinners, the buyers all headed back to Chicago. Though they took some time for prankish fun on the train, they'd also rehash their experiences, review the money they'd spent, and discuss the prices at which they would offer merchandise to customers.

After the grand-opening day sale, it was time to move on again. We took our signals from this experience, exploiting the potential the sale made so clear to us. Certain categories of merchandise had neither been tried nor tested in a department-store environment, so merchandising a new line of goods was a challenge. First one had to recognize, then seize, an opportunity. Starting up a new department was a daring undertaking, and we set off disadvantaged by the lack of adequate store space as well as experience. But we saw the opportunities and we took up the challenges. To provide us with more money to expand, we took the company public in 1928. Its first board of directors consisted of us four brothers, plus banker Robert Straus and Charles Cushing, a businessman.

#

Chicago was growing rapidly at the time; jobs were plentiful and salaries good. Block after block of bungalows were filling in former farmland at the city's edges. Families could move from cramped tenements to their own little brick houses with backyards. This presented an opportunity for Goldblatt's that no department–store retailer had tried before. A garden shop.

I went out to the Welch Nursery in Shenandoah, Iowa, where the proprietor instructed me in the nature and care of his extensive line of horticulture products: the myriad of names, when and how to plant them, relative climate, and on and on, another education in itself. For example, the *Catalpa bungi*, a tree native to Asia and North America known also as the umbrella tree, was in almost every front yard back in Chicago. Nearly as popular was the tall, graceful, Lombardy poplar, originally imported from Europe.

I bought a truckload of each, and another of *Spiraea Van Houttei*, or bridal wreath, plus one of Armour River privet hedge, and half a truckload of Barberry Thunbergia, or Japanese thorny hedge. The grand total came to 20 truckloads, an incredible variety of flowering bushes and bulbs: gladioli, peony, caladium, plus fruit trees, weeping willows, birch, elm, and oak trees. Assortment was key; we took no halfway measures. The delivery schedule was spaced out across the shrubbery season. The shopkeeper's son had become a nurseryman, too.

I'd coordinated the arrival time of the first truckloads to coincide with the morning of the day the department was to open, and I'd placed additional orders with local vendors for grass seed, fertilizer, and trellises. Content labeling was still an idea of the future, but I poured the three different kinds of grass seed into three separate barrels, each carrying a sign with its price and ingredients, such as "mixture of Kentucky Blue Grass, white clover, timothy and inert matter," the last of which the customers in those naive days often took to be something espe-

Chapter VIII   From Dry Goods to Department Store

cially worthwhile. Though I'd paid only a fraction of a penny more for one seed than another, I priced the three at 19 cents, 29 cents, and 39 cents per pound. Hence, I got another lesson in human nature: the bestseller was the seed priced 39 cents. There were things for which customers wanted to pay more, and grass seed apparently was one of them.

The Vigoro Company refused to sell us its nationally advertised product, a bone–meal fertilizer. Its retail price was upheld by all stores, and they anticipated, justifiably so, that Goldblatt's would sell it for less. So I went out and found a retailer in Milwaukee, Wisconsin, who sold me a carload of the fertilizer at five percent above his cost. No obstacle was going to stand in my way; the Vigoro Company's policy was no more a hurdle than all those tables I used to jump over. Everything was set. A barrage of advertising would bring the customers flocking in for privet hedges, fertilizer, rose bushes, gladioli bulbs, and our leader item, the popular, Vigoro, all priced at practically their cost.

Opening day was a challenge in logistics. I was rolling dice and selling mostly perishables to boot. The department, located in a small, crowded corner of the basement, could hardly contain even a representative array of the many truckloads of bulbs and bushes now pulling into the alley behind the store. The only course I had was the one I took. Since we offered free delivery of the customer's orders, we simply unloaded their purchases from the vendors' trucks right on to the Goldblatt's delivery trucks. A back–alley operation, one might say. As a matter of fact, the customer orders went out so quickly that, with the COD's, which most were, the driver had to wait for the customer to get home in order to collect the charge. It was a one–day sellout, and I found myself on the phone that afternoon pleading for immediate reorders. Thus Goldblatt's became the first department store to originate a shrubbery department; not only that, we guaranteed that every shrub would grow! In later years, this department came to be known as horticulture and grew to become a very big business.

#

During the latter part of 1928, I was sent to New York for a month. My job was to change our resident buying office from Ben F. Levis to Jack Hartblay and to scout the markets for our buyers before their trips to New York. It was a lonely period for me. For nearly 25 years, I'd hardly ever been alone, and I didn't like it. Although during the days I was always out at the vendors, in the evenings I just roamed around alone. I never accepted any gifts from vendors, neither theater tickets nor even lunches and certainly not the prostitutes sent up at their request. Politely, I told them I was tied up with appointments, though that was hardly the case. Though this policy led to loneliness, it never obligated me to a vendor, and thus I was always free to negotiate the best buy I could make.

I took in the sights on Broadway, went window shopping, had a beef sandwich on Jewish rye at the Brass Rail, and saw an occasional movie. None of them lessened my utter loneliness in the great city, but my singular purpose there was business. I would have company enough when I got home.

Chapter IX
One Store Becomes Four

In 1928, my brother–in–law, Jack Gordon, had opened a dry goods store at 47th Street and Ashland Avenue, kitty–corner across from the large, four–floor Lederer Department Store. A short time later, Maurice and Nathan bought the Lederer store, arranged for Jack to go out of business, and named him store manager of the new Goldblatt's. So here was another grand opening, held while Maurice and Nathan were negotiating the purchase of still additional stores.

Goldblatt's was expanding, and in 1929 we acquired two more stores, one at 91st Street and Commercial Avenue on Chicago's far southeast side and another on the north side at Lincoln and Belmont avenues. We also acquired a warehouse on the south side near the Union Stock Yards; all merchandise was sent there and distributed to the four stores. Administrative functions were also housed there, namely, the buying and management personnel, the advertising department, accounts payable and receivable.

This marked the beginning of a centralized chain operation. Prior to this, a salesman representing a vendor had to call on each store individually; now, with the warehouse's central role, salesmen had only to make one stop for a four–store order.

Just 13 years earlier, with his famous *Chicago* poem published in 1916, Carl Sandburg had claimed the city was "hog butcher for the world." Built in 1865, the Union Stock Yards had attracted many other buildings nearby, but the pace of slaughter there was slowing down and we could get good space inexpensively. Further, it was located near the railroad yards. So there we were, in the world-famous center of butchery. The stench throughout the warehouse and offices was almost unbearable. Nearly 33,000 men, women, and children still worked in the stockyards, slaughtering equal numbers of hogs and cows. But the "city of the big shoulders" was where Goldblatt's had inalterably staked its claim, and if the stench was the price for the privilege, so be it.

 A consequence of success is becoming well-known, thus many nationally marketed brands followed the Vigoro Company's refusal to sell to Goldblatt's. They feared we would destroy their markets by cutting prices, and they dared not risk any damage to their own advertising. They also feared that other retailers who upheld their prices would discontinue selling their products.

 But as far as we were concerned, if brands were what the customer wanted, brands were what the customer would get. We would just manage to obtain the merchandise from other sources. We would buy it from jobbers, bootleggers, and even from other retailers at five, 10, or 15 percent above their cost. When we needed to accumulate large quantities, we even bought from competing stores and paid full retail price. Then we advertised the goods at a price below cost. Goldblatt's did play havoc with the vendors of nationally branded merchandise, but this was all before the price-controlling fair trade laws. When we had begun in business 20 years earlier, goods were seldom even priced, and retailers could sell items at whatever price they chose, frequently

Chapter IX   One Store Becomes Four

bargaining with the customer. Then Harry Selfridge adopted the one-price policy for Field's, and stores around the country did the same, including Goldblatt's. In the early years of this century, a new phenomenon had hit retailing, the national brand. Companies like Procter and Gamble were advertising their goods nationally, and the role of merchant was about to undergo the second major change to affect it this century.

The vendors of these nationally advertised goods vowed never to sell to Goldblatt's, even if we would promise to maintain their prices. Similarly, stores that competed with us vowed to discontinue the vendors' lines if they did sell to Goldblatt's, whether or not we'd uphold the prices. The lines were drawn, and we were fighting on two fronts.

Wieboldt's was our closest competitor. A traditional, full-line department store, they carried all the leading brands and never cut prices. Naturally, we'd been giving them a rough time. Then, they attacked. First, it was a skirmish. Wieboldt's advertised, of all things, goldfish at four cents following our ad for them at five cents. We came back at three cents. This continued until the price plummeted to one penny, then two for a penny, even to the Wieboldt price of three for a penny. That's when we quit. But not really, because we intensified our stance on selected housewares, which, of course, provoked retaliation on their part. And so it went.

I called a meeting of the buyers, outlining a strategy to hit where it would hurt them the most. Fighting in terms of national brands would prove too costly for us, but not for them; the vendors themselves were subsidizing the Wieboldt's effort by reimbursing them the difference between normal markup and their price. To compete we would have had to procure most of our goods from retailers, and that was much too costly.

So we launched a major assault on another front.

Wieboldt's had been doing an outstanding job with Fruit of the Loom bedsheets, which was their line exclusively in Chicago. So I sent salesclerks out with lots of cash to head for Wieboldt's and buy all the Fruit of the Loom bedsheets they could. It took two months to accumulate enough for the barrage of advertising that I planned at cut prices. Wieboldt's not only lost face in the eyes of the public, but the big business in these goods that they had developed over many years just slipped from their grip.

The Fruit of the Loom people, also headquartered in Chicago, came to plead with me to stop. I invited them to eliminate Wieboldt's and sell the line to Goldblatt's exclusively, in which case we would promise to maintain their price as well as guarantee to double the business they had been doing with Wieboldt's. They agreed and we kept our word. Furthermore, we more than doubled the business the first year. Subsequently, Goldblatt's cut Wieboldt's prices, but they no longer fought back. The goldfish came back to haunt them in the size of a whale!

Nevertheless, nationally known top brands in cosmetics, toiletries, drugs, and cigarettes were not available to Goldblatt's from the manufacturers and were only to be gotten through diverse sources. Yet, in the American competitive system, nothing is more assured than the consumers' demand for greater value. So long as we gave it, our market would continue to clamor for our products at our prices, and our growth was inevitable. So long as we were denied avenues of supply, there would be pressure from small entrepreneurs, apart from our own, responding both to consumer demand and to their own ambition to rise and prosper.

Such a young man was Louis Zahn. A visionary even in

Chapter IX   One Store Becomes Four

his early twenties, he would pull up to Goldblatt's in his van loaded with branded drugs and toiletries and offer them to me at two to four percent above his cost. Eventually, his Zahn Drug Company was to grow to become the largest drug jobber in the country, and Lou Zahn himself would become my close personal friend and golfing partner.

When Goldblatt's advertised a leading cosmetic line obtained from Louis Zahn, such as Coty or items like Guerlain's Shalimar, other retailers demanded that the vendor put a stop to it. However, because those vendors did no business with us, they were powerless to prevent us from selling their goods at our prices. When Jean De Prey, general sales manager of Coty, came to me pleading that we stop, I consented, but with a condition. In the future, Coty would sell to us directly. He agreed and we maintained the retail price. Later we became close friends, and later still Jean married the hat designer Lily Dache. Eventually many vendors of similarly nationally advertised famous brands succumbed to the Goldblatt's onslaught. They, too, agreed to sell to us direct in return for our upholding their prices. This was, however, for cosmetics, drugs, and toiletries. We did not make these agreements in apparel departments.

As the company developed, so did its image. Goldblatt's had become the place to buy practical, everyday needs, not a store where one could expect to buy fashion selectively. There were many reasons for this. Our crowded advertising screamed with bargains. Fashion, per se, was hardly an apt counterpart of brooms, bloomers, boiled ham, nor the Copenhagen snuff, for example, that we sold in greater quantity than any other retailer in the country. Goldblatt's even sold more donuts by the dozen than any other store. Our ads resounded with spectaculars: enough hotdogs to circle the globe several times, the country's largest retailer of bulk cookies. Our candy and cookie sales were so immense, we placed orders by truckloads, carloads, even by the ton. It was common for us to buy a carload of Rockwood milk chocolate in 10–pound slabs, break it up with ice picks, and sell it out within two weeks as "broken" milk chocolate.

Customers could often find a barrel of steaming hot, freshly roasted, salted Spanish peanuts inside the entrance, which they were invited to sample. This led to a bit of fun one day. Mary, our candy department manager, had a clerk by the name of Max Katz who waited on customers at the peanut barrel. One busy day, spotting an impatient customer in the candy department and wanting to see that she was taken care of, I shouted over to Mary, "Where is Max Katz?" to which Mary shouted in reply, "I got Max by the nuts," at which point, everyone, customers and employees alike, broke out in laughter throughout the main floor. I was kidded about it for years after.

In other stores, clerks waited on customers from behind counters. Goldblatt's displayed its merchandise out in the open, stacked or dumped on tables. This enabled customers to see and handle it, encouraging impulse sales. We called this self–selection; it grew up to become the self–service at the discount stores. Goldblatt's was about the only store in the country that tied a pair of shoes together with its own laces and dumped them on a table, inviting the customer to find the right style and size, rather than selling them from a box which required a clerk and space–taking chairs.

Our displays were inspired, high–impact visuals, created with volume sales in mind. Once I took spools of black and white sewing thread with which I built a five–foot replica of the Wrigley Building. I raised this high on a platform and stacked

Chapter IX One Store Becomes Four

boxes filled with a dozen spools each from the floor to its base. Soon we were selling spools of thread by the dozens. I pasted together hundreds of sugar-coated almonds to form a large heap and signed it "The Snowball Mountain of Sugar Coated Almonds . . . only 26¢ lb. . . . While They Last!" We sold 500 pounds in one day. The customer required only a dramatic suggestion to respond.

Nothing came easily. We worked hard, and with our hands and hearts for our sales in order to create forceful messages of availability, of value and confidence. It was the same creativity we used with vendors to make our great buys. Selling we regarded as an impassioned bid for more than could be gotten from complacency. Enthusiasm energized us. Success, a sellout, was its own reward. With some refinements, this grew up to be what corporate retailers call visual merchandising, but no manual of operations could ever substitute for our good-natured determination to create attraction for extraordinary sales. The floor display was the only communication with the customer that we knew, and our customers loved it. Display was my forte, and "talking" with the customer that way was my hobby.

It was the same all over the store, whether men's socks, washboards, or curtains. Goldblatt's was living in the eye of the storm, and no less than in the early days, the customer was our boss and inspiration. She (because our customers were mainly women) told us how to buy and how to sell; she told us we had to master the art of finding the goods she wanted and devise strategies to get them into our store. In return, she would protect us from the vendors and retailers who had vowed to deny us our place in the market.

Life is a game, play to win!

#

By the late 1920s, Goldblatt's had 35 buyers, 18 of whom carried the title merchandise manager, as was the custom for anyone who bought for more than one department. If buying were truly an art, not all of them, including myself, practiced it every day in every way. Of necessity, whether for lack of time or experience, artless buying happened because we had to keep moving. We depended less on art, therefore, than on our own initiative, good luck, and what have you in order to carry out our assignments.

I wound up buying yard goods in addition to my other duties when Maurice relinquished his soft-line departments to Nathan. I learned all I could, which wasn't very much, before going to New York on a buying trip. Once there, I scouted around, visiting the jobbers on Worth and Broome streets, to learn what they had to offer. I was ready to buy, knowing full well how ill prepared I was for the task.

My primary interest was in one- to 10-yard remnants in percale and broadcloth, both of which were generally sold mixed in many colors and patterns. I chose the jobber whom I felt had the lowest prices and largest selection, and learned his name was Mr. Wolf. He quoted me a price of 15 cents per yard if I bought a large quantity.

In replying, I said, "My brother, Maurice, just made me the buyer of yard goods and I don't know anything about the department. I'm going to have to leave it to you. You tell me what to buy." Then I continued, "I was told to buy 5,000 yards of percale and broadcloth that we will advertise on sale for 15 cents per yard. Maurice told me not to pay more than 10 or 11 cents. I want to show my brothers that I'm a good buyer, and

Chapter IX   One Store Becomes Four

you'll have to help me this one time."

After a while, Mr. Wolf dropped his price to 13 cents; I raised my offer to 11. Finally, he split the difference and offered the lot at 12 cents. I agreed to write the order for 5,000 yards, but added, "Look here, Mr. Wolf, I leave it to you to pick the patterns for me, but please don't include any remnants that are less than two and half yards. My customers sew their own dresses and need at least two and a half yards. If you take good care of me and don't cheat me, I'll come back and give you a lot of business. If, on the other hand, when goods come in and I find poor patterns and remnants of less the two and a half yards, you'll never do business with me again. Remember, you are my buyer and you are writing the order. I leave it to your honor."

Mr. Wolf had done his work well, and when the shipment arrived, I divided the lot into three groups of 16, 19, and 22 cents per yard. It sold all within a week -- at a good profit.

When the Great Depression hit, Goldblatt's buffered it for our customers. There were catastrophic declines in industrial production, bankruptcies, and massive unemployment everywhere, but Goldblatt's kept pounding out its sale events. We continued to pay less for what we bought and strove to give our customers bigger bargains than ever. They were not the people who had bought stock on 70 percent margin, not the suicides, nor recipients of the lowest-interest government issue yields in 10 years. Our customers were those hardest hit by the layoffs and plant closings. For a dollar, we offered customers a 10-pound bag consisting of four pounds of pigs' feet, one pound of lean, sugar-cured sliced bacon, one pound of tender small steaks, one pound of lamb stew, one pound of frankfurters, and two pounds of sauerkraut. Also for a dollar, we sold two collar–attached shirts, five yards of fabric, a girls' dress, or 16 bars of Palmolive soap. The deals went on and on, making our promotional department store even more the mainstay of the family. Goldblatt's price cutting had become the Goldblatt's way of life.

The Nathan Goldblatt Sale of May 1933 was no doubt the biggest and most successful retailing event of the year in Chicago. To celebrate its success, Maurice and Nathan threw a huge party for the company's employees. There was another reason for the party as well. A few years earlier, both the brothers had been married in a double ceremony. Now, Nathan and his wife Frances (whom he'd nicknamed Frenchy) were also celebrating the birth of their son, Lionel.

The party was planned by Eddie Simon and held at Mann's Rainbow Garden Hippodrome on the corner of Lawrence Avenue and Clark Street. The event was to be unbelievably elaborate, and the preparations were lengthy. The *Herald American* even ran a special edition for the event, replacing its front page with a headline and story about the event for distribution to employees, their spouses, and other invited guests. Three thousand people attended this bash, politicians, bankers, entertainers, newspaper executives, vendors, close friends of the Goldblatt brothers, and relatives. Chartered busses transported the employees from all four stores and the warehouse. Abe N. Pritzker, who had joined our board and whose sons now own the Hyatt Hotel chain as well as a lot of other businesses, was toastmaster of the evening. One could hardly imagine that a depression was raging outside of Mann's Rainbow Garden Hippodrome that night.

Not only was Goldblatt's well–known throughout Chicago as a company that sold its merchandise quickly, at a

Chapter IX One Store Becomes Four

very low price and small profit, but vaudeville itself picked up the theme. At one theater, a performer came on stage doing a somersault saying, "that was a Goldblatt's turnover!" In another skit, the performer squeezed a lemon dry and offered a prize of $100 to anyone in the audience who could get one more drop from it. Then a shill would appear in the audience, normally a meek-looking little fellow, who would come up on stage and squeeze a pitcher full of juice from the dry lemon. Asked how he was able to accomplish the impossible, he replied, "It wasn't hard to do. I'm a Goldblatt's buyer!"

We were also the subject of local jokes. Henry Applebaum, the former meat inspector who had married a Goldblatt's bookkeeper named Dotty Martin, was rising fast and looked upon as a future officer of the company. So were Eddie Simon and Herman Buckley. When serving in France during the First World War, Henry had developed a friendship with a fellow Chicagoan named Matt Schulien, who opened a saloon on Halsted Street after the war. A burly man with thick, fat hands, Matt, nevertheless was adept in sleight-of-hand and card tricks, and he entertained his patrons with his magic.

One evening, shortly after the end of the war, Henry asked Maurice, Nathan, Joe, and myself to join him at Matt's saloon for a beer and a sandwich. Although radios still weren't to be found everywhere, Matt's place had a large one that blasted away most of the time. We were listening to it and eating our sandwiches when suddenly a news flash came on saying there was a four-eleven fire raging at the Goldblatt's on Chicago Avenue. The store was burning to the ground. We dropped everything and rushed there, expecting a disaster. Nothing of the kind! There was no fire and there hadn't been any. It was nothing more than a Matt Schulien prank.

Another time, we were all at Schulien's again, this time with a Mr. Abrams, a chemist who worked for a Goldblatt's subsidiary. Matt reached into the large, prominently displayed, goldfish tank and, raving what delicacies goldfish were, pulled one out and ate it. He then attempted to induce the brothers to try it, but without success. Abrams was game, though. Matt reached in again, snared a fish and handed it over to Abrams. He bit down and hastily spit it out, complaining that it was bitter and awful tasting, and then proceeded to vomit. This, of course, was another Matt Schulien prank. Actually, he'd just cut up come carrots in the shape of fish and put them in the tank. When he reached in, he came up with a piece of carrot, "wiggled" then subdued it inside his fat hand, and promptly devoured the fake fish. Abrams, however, was given the real thing.

One wonders where such nonsense gets its start. About the same time, college students across the country got into goldfish, or rather, goldfish got into college students who competed for who could swallow the most. But it was Matt Schulien's saloon that first broke the sanity barrier, and the actions of a poor, unwitting chemist by the name of Abrams managed to prove nothing.

When I think of Abrams, many memories cross my mind. In 1934, prohibition was repealed, and during this period, the Goldblatt company added many subsidiaries. One was Ann Marlow Candy Kitchens, which manufactured items for us and other retailers, including Marshall Field & Company. We had already acquired the printing plant, plus manufacturers of sausages and hot dogs, venetian blinds, and comforters, a coffee–roasting plant, a maker and canner of preserves, and a bakery. We'd taken a large space in our warehouse and installed huge copper vats to serve the vastly increased demand for alco-

Chapter IX   One Store Becomes Four

holic drinks, cordials, and whisky. These we marketed throughout the country. Mr. Abrams was employed as the chemist at another subsidiary, one that bottled drugs and toiletries. Goldblatt's maintained a fresh-fish department within the food operation, and naturally it was known for having lower prices than its competitors. One day, other retailers of fish in Chicago banded together and decided to boycott any fisheries that would sell to Goldblatt's. When Maurice and Nathan found out about this, they bought out the Morris Fishery, and in fact, began to sell to their competitors at lower prices than were available elsewhere. We'd turned the tables. Goldblatt's no longer depended on the fisheries, but the other retailers were dependent on Goldblatt's as their supplier. We also became headquarters for police, fire, and streetcar motormen's and conductor's uniforms.

In the late 1920s, my brother Joel (which he'd taken to calling himself as an adult), our two close friends Eddie Simon and Hy Buckley — the Four Must Get Theirs — had rented a duplex apartment at 20 East Cedar Street and decorated it as only four bachelors would. We entertained in similar fashion.

Lou Pelton was a salesman for Fleishman's Yeast, a bachelor playboy, and a close friend of all four of us. While we were entertaining some girls at the apartment one evening, Lou came by with a lawyer friend by the name of Eugene Bernstein. He, it turned out, was an accomplished hypnotist with a talent, besides, for card tricks. None of the people there had ever met him before, so we were enthralled by his "magic." Later in the evening, he hypnotized the girls and they obeyed his various commands. Fortunately, he hadn't asked them to do anything too embarrassing.

I was captivated by it all, especially as I had never

believed in hypnotism in the first place. Now, I was seeing it with my own eyes, at close range, and in my own apartment. When I asked Eugene how he did it, he replied, "It's because I have magic power. A gift from God."

I didn't sleep for nights thinking about it, trying to unravel the mystery of one human being having such power over another. I began to read up on hypnosis and learned that it dated back to the work of Franz Anton Mesmer who lived from 1734 to 1815. His unusual theories and techniques sparked an interest in the possibilities of using animal magnetism or "mesmerism" for psychotherapy. It is said that he cured people of their ills by having them sit around a tub of water with cords tied from their bodies to the tub while he spoke his therapy in a monotone.

After a while, I began to practice hypnosis successfully, applying it initially to friends. After reading the text of C. Hull's *Hypnosis and Suggestibility*, I discovered that I was able to perform feats that Hull's work indicated couldn't be done. In realizing that hypnotism could be used therapeutically, I was not inclined to demonstrate it as entertainment. I never exploited a subject by making him bark like a dog or inducing other self–demeaning behavior. Nonetheless, through posthypnotic suggestion, I was able to cure headache, fingernail biting, sleepwalking, overweight through hypnotic–induced dieting, and a host of other mentally controlled disorders. I was even able to induce a subject to recall memories out of childhood.

Leaving hypnosis to the therapists, I went on to study mind reading, telepathy, extrasensory perception, and with it, human anatomy. In more casual moments, I added sleight–of–hand, card tricks, and fortune telling. It was all just a hobby, for after working hours; most of it I learned from read-

Chapter IX   One Store Becomes Four

ing. I had, during the 1930s, embarked upon an extensive course of self-education. Mainly, I read the biographies of notable businessmen and the histories of important corporations. As I had moved out into the world, I became aware of my limited education and this reading was intended to compensate for that. It had several other effects as well, one of which was improving my ability to communicate my goals and intentions to our buyers. I came to believe strongly in motivation and teamwork and in generating a will to achieve. In this, I was to see an increasing number of differences between myself and my brothers. Although I had learned much from Maurice and Nathan, I found myself frequently disagreeing with them in matters of store policy. Eventually, I felt I was learning more from them in terms of what not to do. My reading, I believe, contributed to the growing differences between us. I was becoming an American businessman; they remained the ambitious immigrant merchants.

In the meantime, my buying trips to New York for Goldblatt's continued, and during one such trip, Momma was there as well. I never ceased to learn when I was with her. This time it was a lesson in the philosophy of charity, and it probably came at a time when some humility served me well. We were in a taxi together, stopped for a red light in Times Square, when a crippled beggar selling pencils came over to us. I promptly turned him away, and the cab went on. "Louis, why did you let him go that way?" she asked.

"Momma, there are, I suppose, at least a hundred fake beggars in just any small area in New York."

Momma admonished me, saying, "My darling son, if there were only one beggar out of a hundred who was not a fake, it would be a *mitzva,* a blessing, to give to all of the hundred so that the one who was truly in need would be taken care of. It's God's will to be charitable, and it makes the giver a happier, healthier person."

I never passed a beggar again without giving something, nor would I ever forget the logic of Momma's numbers. They were more profound than all the numbers I taught myself and didn't learn at school. Another lesson about real life, and it came from my first teacher.

As I hadn't yet quite reached 30 years of age, I craved a hectic pace and I found it. First and foremost, I had a job that demanded 125 percent of me, that is, 100 percent creative and 25 percent routine. I was pursuing the chase, or the bachelor's life, within the circus–like society of the Four Must Get Theirs. I had Joel to watch out for, too, a responsibility, considering his susceptibilities. I read my business books whenever I could, and I had my hobbies, too, particularly hypnosis and all the peripheral interests to which it led.

I had my hobbies inside the company, too. My fascination with the shrubbery department never waned, and going back to the days when we carried only goldfish, I was always attracted to the pet department's potential. From fish, I went on to buy canaries from Max Stern, who brought them in from the Hartz Mountains in Germany (he had recently acquired a small birdfeed company of the same name and went on to turn it into what it later became). Stern had recently come to America and was himself a bird fancier, caught up in marketing his hobby. Canaries, I learned, are themselves finches, which in the wild are usually gray or green. The tame birds, valued for their lovely song, have been bred in Europe since the 16th century to produce the characteristic canary yellow.

I added parakeets, macaws, cockatoos, parrots, finches,

Chapter IX   One Store Becomes Four

and mynas, plus other canary breeds like Yorkshires and mules to our stock. I also brought in small monkeys like ring-tails, the South American spider monkey, and the soft, woolly haired marmoset from Central and South America. Goldblatt's sold over a thousand monkeys during the course of a year, causing people to say that Goldblatt's did more monkey business than anybody. We also sold baby alligators, garter snakes, hamsters, Japanese waltzing mice, turtles, rabbits, baby chicks, and ducks. And we carried these in a department that included all the accessories too: foods, cages, incubators, toys, and what have you.

It was only natural that some customers would change their minds about owning monkeys or other unusual and not-so-unusual pets; others may simply have tired of them. Intending to do the right thing by their pets and perhaps for the community, many turned them over to the Lincoln Park Zoo. Thus it was that management there asked us to stop selling monkeys; they just couldn't handle any more! Little baby chicks along with incubators were an absolute sensation, too, but for a different reason. Our customers were raising chickens in their front yards as a prime source of poultry and eggs, not as pets. For them, this was food, and that also applied to the demand for ducklings.

We also did rather well with the canaries, too. As only the males are singers and the sex of the young birds cannot be determined, we were able to buy the birds at a low enough price to advertise them as a leader for only one dollar in order to bring traffic to the department.

So, it should come as no surprise that eventually I staged a Pet Parade Sale. And we advertised that, along with the animals, a bird doctor was to be in the department.

Customers were invited to bring in their sick birds for free treatment. In they came: birds with broken legs, matted feathers, some close to death.

To treat them, the doctor would lay them on their backs on a table, with their heads extending over the edge. This rendered the bird totally immobile and provided me with an idea for an addition to my repertoire. I, too, would be able to place a bird on its back in the palm of someone's hand where it would lie motionless. Then, I would clap my hands and it would come "awake" and fly away. The bird doctor's trick was etched in my memory that day, to be recalled on a later day in another, wildly different circumstance.

The pet department grew to become big business and brought other attractions. A high-kicking jackass, part of an act in town, was brought to the store, and all hell broke loose. The animal went on a rampage, kicking not only its well- padded owner, but everything else in sight. It even caused a monkey to break loose and bite the owner of the donkey on the ear.

Foolishness aside, there was serious business to attend to as well. There were still nationally advertised brands whose manufacturers didn't want to sell to Goldblatt's. In the pet department, we sold Ken-L-Ration and Rival dog food as traffic items, but selling the latter presented a problem. Its company insisted I stop bootlegging it in and cutting its price. So I met with Meyer Katz of Rival and offered him a deal, which he accepted. Rival was to sell direct to Goldblatt's; we, in turn, would pledge to maintain the price, but we added a proviso. They would also sell us full carloads of the same quality dog food, and we would sell it under the Goldblatt's private label Barker brand. We bought this, at a lower cost than the Rival brand, which enabled us to undersell all the other national

Chapter IX   One Store Becomes Four

brands. Thus in one stroke, I had added both the national brand and a quality private label that would be worth almost immeasurable sales and traffic to the department and to the store. Goldblatt's had almost unwittingly devised another merchandising method, one that in following years was to be adopted my most chain stores around the country.

Life is a game, play to win!

Chapter X
Growing Through the Depression

The country's economic doldrums continued, and because of it we responded all the more to whatever excitement we could find. Attractions drew our attention and admiration. The Empire State Building, dedicated in 1931, thrust our imagination to the heavens and away from the malaise that so gripped the nation. The Baha'i House of Worship opened that same year in Wilmette on the Lake Michigan shore; spiritually and architecturally its splendor rang far and wide. On the other side of the thirties, Al Capone was convicted, if only on the charge of income tax evasion, and Nevada legalized gambling.

To us, these times meant only one thing, promoting and fostering even better values. We had to give the customer an ongoing, self-generating, habit-forming method by which she would save money on all her purchases and then use those savings for even more store visits, buying more and more bargains. Thus we came up with the Goldblatt's Trading Stamp Plan, which meant that for every 10-cent purchase, the customer would receive a trading stamp. Once she accumulated a book of the stamps, which represented $150 in purchases, she would receive three dollars worth of merchandise. Not incidental was the location of the stamp booth;

Chapter X Growing Through the Depression

it could be reached only by walking through the store.

Some of our promotions were meticulously planned, touch–and–go–operations, like the turkey business at Thanksgiving time. This was a matter of high–profile identity, and Goldblatt's, price leader that it was, seized it to assert our indisputable position of leadership. We prepared a full–page ad for our turkeys and held the price open until just before the newspaper went to press. This enabled us to check and double check every competitors' price, then we priced our own the lowest in all Chicago. We also advertised a complete, hot, cooked turkey dinner to be delivered just in time for the family. And of course we had these delivered by well–marked motorcycles and trucks so they could be seen going on their appointed routes throughout the city.

No one could hold a candle to Goldblatt's during holiday time, and once we actually held it ourselves, candling eggs we bought direct from the farmers. We discarded the unwanted ones and sold the others for Easter at the lowest price of six cents a dozen.

We sold candy corn at Halloween, chocolate–covered cherries for George Washington's Birthday, and one Mother's Day, Nathan gave away thousands of potted geraniums. These were delivered along with a tender greeting card from the firm that cared, of course, by saving the customer money.

With its promotional and price–cutting policies, Goldblatt's was a constant thorn in the side of the competition. With our growth, we were able to increase our advertising expenditure in the metropolitan newspapers, waging a competitive fury felt all the way to State Street in the Loop.

Marshall Field's, on the north end of that street, also owned the Davis Store just five blocks south. The Davis Store made it a policy to do battle with Goldblatt's; their ads showed a bulldog with the caption "The Watch Dog of Chicago," and they claimed, "We will meet anyone's prices. Our prices are the lowest in Chicago!"

So the next day, we'd run an ad, with the same items at still–lower prices. "Proof Positive!" the copy ran. "No one in all Chicago can beat Goldblatt's lowest prices!" Soon, the Davis Store gave up and ended the war.

We knew our place in the market and guarded it closely. We catered to the low–income, blue–collar, working–class family and were able to save them money by maintaining large sales volume per square foot and low expenses. We had no carpeting on the floors, no expensive fixtures, or fancy treatments. Cartons and paper cluttered our stores. The Selling floors were a hodgepodge of grocery tables, wearing apparel, and household needs, interspersed with hawker demonstrators of, perhaps, knife sharpeners or furniture polish. Goldblatt's was a beehive of excitement and fun; it was not intended to be fancy or even comfortable.

Our selections were incomplete but loaded with bargains; we picked up closeouts and irregulars with no special concern for what they were. So long as the item would sell out quickly, we were able thereby to pay the bill quickly with what we took in for selling it. This is the way we stayed in business. By paying our bills within 10 days, we were usually entitled to vendor discounts. These two techniques — fast turnover and maximum vendor discounts — are what enabled Goldblatt's to grow so quickly and to thrive.

Our greatest asset was our employees, most of whom were from the old country and upon arrival couldn't read, write, or speak English. Together they could make other Chicago

Chapter X   Growing Through the Depression

retailers tremble. Only on rare exceptions would Maurice or Nathan hire a buyer or executive from outside of the company. For a while, it seemed that there was hardly a person in Chicago who hadn't worked for Goldblatt's at some point in his or her life, either after school or as a weekend extra. The employees called all of us by our first names, and everyone felt free to voice their own opinions, debating Maurice, Nathan, and anyone else, if need be. Their dedication and devotion as family was the fuel of Goldblatt's growth.

During the six years following the stock market crash, the country struggled to repair a wasted economy. In 1932, Charles A. Lindbergh turned $50,000 over as ransom to an unidentified man in a New York cemetery, hoping to regain his kidnapped son, who was later found murdered. Franklin Delano Roosevelt, elected president in 1932, declared a bank moratorium the next year. Chicago civil service employees were paid in script, and schoolteachers who had not been paid for 10 months stormed the Chicago banks demanding back pay that totalled $30 million. Very few retailers honored the script, which was all the cash that most policemen, firemen, and transit workers had.

Goldblatt's ran an ad announcing that we would honor the civil service workers' script the same as money. This proved a master stroke in good will for us, not only for civil servants but the general public as well. We also carried a full line of police, fire, and transit worker's uniforms and sold them at only eight percent profit. These people vowed never to trade anywhere else.

Goldblatt's had become nothing short of a phenomenon. Here was a retailer that had scratched its very existence out of concrete with its fingernails. But the store had also made such

Life is a game, play to win!

a bond of mutual loyalty with its customers that it would come to national attention at a time when debt, insolvency, and foreclosure were the order of the day.

###

By the close of 1933, Goldblatt's had become a chain of six department stores with a sales volume of $22 million annually. Our profit margin and expense cost were 33 and 25 percent respectively, yielding an after–tax profit of $1,275,100. Joel and I were now earning $100 a week. But our family was not unscathed by the depression. Sarah and Jake lost all their money when the banks failed, so they closed their department store and went out of business.

In spite of the times, there was opportunity, too. In retail, giving value was king! National brands had instant identity. Their quality went unchallenged, and they were commanding prices set most of the time in their executive suites. What a chance for retailers if only they could provide equal or better quality at substantial savings. In order to do so, we sold our own merchandise as counterpart to the brand names through packaging and describing it in certain ways. We had to create new brands that mirrored the existing proven ones, then name and label them as our own. This done, we knew we would capture for ourselves a piece of the market these famous name brands had already developed, and at great expense to them if not to us. Adding to this was our own creative advertising. We had a host of additional traffic and sales. Ah, the marvels of private–label merchandising!

These were the years for it, so Nathan went to Cuba and arranged for the Questa Rey Cigar Company to make

Chapter X Growing Through the Depression

their Havana cigars under the Goldblatt's Bond brand. When they arrived, he sent a box or so to each of the cigar wholesalers with whom we did business, along with a sample pack of three cigars. He enclosed an invoice for the box of cigars and a letter inviting them to try the samples. If they enjoyed the cigars, he asked them to pay the bill for the box. If they didn't like them, they could return the box at Goldblatt's expense. None of the boxes were returned, and the reorders started to come in. Goldblatt's Bond Havana cigars were not long in becoming popular.

Determined to create a razor blade equal or better in quality than Gillette, I visited manufacturers and finally located one who could do this. I had the blades packaged somewhat similarly to the famous brand, advertised them via billboards and newspapers, and sold them at half the price — with a money-back guarantee. From there we copied, as it were, other items and sold them under the Goldblatt's Bond label with growing success. Thus we sold "Bayer" aspirin, "Listerine" mouthwash, "Colgate" toothpaste, "Delmonte" canned foods, and on and on.

Sears enjoyed big business with its five-gallon can of Coast-to-Coast motor oil. I introduced our own brand and called it Gold Coast. I brought on Gold Coast hosiery, bedsheets, auto batteries, knitting yarn, duplicates of many brands heretofore considered invulnerable. I even created a takeoff on Lifebuoy soap, down to its aroma, odd shape, size, and color. I named it Body Guard and sold it profitably at half the price.

During the bank moratorium, manufacturers were in desperate need of ready cash. To keep from going under, they had to keep their factories going. They were willing to sacrifice inventory at any price to get the cash that would keep them alive.

Life is a game, play to win!

Goldblatt's recognized this, so we sent our buyers to market with their pockets stuffed with money to buy goods at their own prices for cash on the spot.

We sent out anywhere from a dozen to two dozen buyers at a time and took full page ads in the trade paper *Women's Wear Daily* announcing that a staff of buyers would be arriving with millions in ready cash in their pockets to purchase goods from anyone willing to trade. We were able to visit and comb every market on the East Coast within a week. Hence, we had unbelievable buys available in all departments. The buys were so compellingly good, our buyers bought much larger quantities than there was room for. As a result, in order to clear space, the values offered were even beyond the norm of Goldblatt's usual bargains, even for depression time. Sales and profits zoomed, while the competition suffered decreases in both sales and profits.

These were the days when a dollar was actually a dollar, and many items sold for pennies, nickels, and dimes. We sold window shades three for $1; the beauty parlor offered a ladies' shampoo, finger wave, haircut, manicure, and eyebrow arch, all for $1; Wisconsin potatoes in one hundred-pound bags sold for $1, delivered for free; Libby's Red Alaska Salmon in a one-pound can was 14 cents; sugar-cured ham could be had for 9 cents per pound; a large box of Kellogg's corn flakes was 6 cents.

Bombast and frivolity characterized that year of 1993. The nation's recovery effort was finally underway, new records were set in sports, and new conquests were made in aviation and transportation. The authorities were in hot pursuit of crime. At mid decade, America and the world were pushing toward the turbulent contest between good and evil

Chapter X   Growing Through the Depression

that lay ahead.

The country took wide-eyed notice of a nude fan dancer named Sally Rand, a top attraction at Chicago's Centennial Exposition in 1933. We Four Must Get Theirs cashed in some favors and invited her up to see a "sister" nude painted inside our closet door. During her visit with us Ms. Rand wore white gloves and hardly anything else.

The Chicago Bears beat the New York Giants at Wrigley Field in the first world championship football game; the winning players got $210 each. The first all- star baseball game was played at Comiskey Park that year.

President Franklin Roosevelt signed a measure legalizing wine and beer containing 3.2 percent alcohol. In order to prevent hoarding as the nation went off the gold standard, he ordered Americans to surrender private stores of gold to the Federal Reserve banks. The New Deal recovery programs were launched, and Roosevelt narrowly escaped assassination in Miami when a bullet intended for him fatally wounded Chicago's Mayor Anton Cermak. The Works Progress Administration (WPA), later declared unconstitutional, provided jobs for more than four million people.

American aviator Wiley Post completed the first solo flight around the world in his plane, the *Winnie May*; Chicago celebrated the completion of a waterway from the Great Lakes to the Gulf of Mexico a day after the first tow arrived from New Orleans. Shirley Temple's film career was launched with the release of *Stand Up and Cheer*. Bank robbers Bonnie Parker and Clyde Barrow were killed as they drove into a hail of police bullets in Louisiana, and "pretty boy" Floyd was shot by federal agents at an Ohio farm. An entrepreneur by the name of J.F. Cantrell installed four electric washing machines for rent by the hour in his Washateria in Fort Worth, Texas. Bruno Richard Hauptmann was indicted for murder in the death of the infant son of Charles A. Lindbergh. The ominous persecution of the Jews began in Nazi Germany, and a dark cloud was to form across the world.

These were the years the Four Must Get Theirs took their 10-day Miami Beach vacations together, staying at the Roney Plaza. In visiting the nightclubs in the evening, we would invite some of the chorus girls to our beach cabana the next day. There, amidst all the fun we always had, I would perform hypnosis, careful still not to cause any real embarrassment to anyone.

On these occasions my routine would attract movie stars and V.I.P.s from the nearby cabanas. Among the funsters one day was a fellow named Jack Emeil, who happened to own race horses as well as the Turf Restaurant in New York. He became so fascinated that he begged me to teach him hypnosis, and we developed a friendship that led to his inviting us to watch him roll the dice at the gambling clubs. We saw him win or lose as much as $30,000 dollars in an evening. A short man with shiny black, slicked-down hair, Jack also had eyes that had a way of bulging out of his head at the very moment the dice stopped rolling. When he won, he would toss $100 bills as though they were ones to each of the chorus girls.

Early one morning, he invited me to watch him clock his horses, and he pointed out a particular one, saying, "That horse is a winner. He's going to win high stake races; only for now I'm holding him down because I want him to lose a half dozen races to get the odds up." Although to my knowledge he never tipped his friends on any of the horses he thought would win, he did whisper the "sure things" to me.

Chapter X   Growing Through the Depression

I never gambled and couldn't care less for the races. Furthermore, I had serious doubts whether it was possible to delay and store like the energy in a battery a horse's ability to win, then release it at the owner's will in a sudden burst of thrust. Knowing that hypnosis was my own kind of magic, I wondered if Jack was able to . . . No, no that would be too much! The more I refused to bet on his tips, the more he tried to induce me. Once, he even bet $100 and told me the bet was for me. Sure enough the horse won! He entered a horse, Count Turf, in the Kentucky Derby and pleaded with me to bet heavily. Again, I declined and again Count Turf was the winner.

Many years later, after I had married Bobbie and we were in New York together on a buying trip, we were invited to Monmouth Park by Charles Bloom, the drapery manufacturer. Charles hardly ever missed a day at the track and on this particular day was running a streak of bad luck. That's when Bobbie and I ran into Jack Emeil, whom I hadn't seen for years. He insisted we bet on his seventh race entry and went so far as to guarantee his horse to win. He was so sure he asked Bobbie and me to place the winner's wreath on the horse after the race. Charles didn't bet on the horse, saying, "It's a nag with a poor record."

This time I acquiesced to Jack's insistence. I placed a bet. The horse won by a long shot and Bobbie and I won $600. Poor Charles could only kick himself for not having bet on the nag with the poor record. Those episodes with Jack Emeil stayed with me far longer than other details of those trips. It seemed Jack had something there, maybe an art of his own with a control that baffled my imagination. I gave it a lot of thought, but decided I could never get a horse to concentrate anyway!

In 1934, Babe Ruth made his farewell appearance as a regular player with the New York Yankees, and John Dillinger, age 31, was shot and killed by the F.B.I. outside the Biograph Theater on Lincoln Avenue in Chicago. The year may have put an end to their eras, but not to Goldblatt's.

Our circular advertising was going full force, distributed door-to-door mainly by the bums and drunkards, who would take odd jobs for booze money and flop- house lodging. One day an underworld character by the name of Leonard Boltz called on Nathan at his office. Boltz was about five foot ten, 180 pounds, blond complected, and soft spoken. He had made several visits before, trying to unionize the distributor of our circulars and demanding initiation dues. At the time we were distributing an average of 300,000, 12-page circulars every week, printing them at our own plant. The distributors, most of whom were marginally employable men, were being paid little enough to begin with, had no interest in paying union dues, and refused to join. Though Boltz had failed in his attempts to unionize them, he demanded that Nathan deduct the dues from their pay and make them join, to which he added the threat or else!

Nathan and Boltz got into a heated argument. Nathan reached into his desk drawer and pulled out a gun, laid it on the desk, and warned Boltz never to come around again "or else!" Soon, when another group of gangsters headed up by a mobster named John Rooney attempted to unionize distributors, Nathan, figuring the best way to fight fire is with fire, contacted Boltz and hired him as the Goldblatt's security officer. Soon, Boltz and the Goldblatt brothers became friends.

Leonard had a summer home in Eagle River, Wisconsin, and he invited Maurice, Nathan, Joel, and myself to drive up for the weekend one Fourth of July in the early 1930s. He intended to show us how he lived there: hunting deer, fishing muskee, and being a woodsman. For sheer entertainment, he would set off sticks of dynamite. We all knew he was a daring and fearless guy and were captivated with his stories about the underworld.

He told Joel and me he wanted to have some fun with Maurice and Nathan, so he told them the area was still inhabited by Indians, and that when they got drunk they'd go on a scalping rampage in the dark of night. However, he reassured them, they need not worry because the Indians hardly did that any more.

Late that evening, he invited the four of us for a walk through the woods. Earlier, he'd arranged for some of his friends dressed as Indians, with painted faces and feathers, to "attack" the four of us as we walked. Leonard had even hidden catsup to smear on his face when the time was right, and he brought along a rifle "just in case" of an attack by wild animals or Indians.

At precisely the prearranged moment, out came his friends screaming and "shooting!" Leonard made sure he got all bloodied up, and shouted for everyone to run for their lives back to the house. When they got there, Maurice and Nathan were trembling and as white as sheets. At the time and ever after, they never regarded this a laughing matter. They were furious with all three of us, but I couldn't help laughing at the thought that, if it weren't a gag, a Chicago headline might have read, "Price Cutters Scalped at Eagle River!"

#

I had learned to consider the Sears Roebuck catalog my retailing "bible," and based on the number of pages or space devoted to an item or a category, I decided which hard–line items were important to Sears business. Then I instructed our buyers to get those items Goldblatt's hadn't carried before.

After these trips, the buyers would come back telling me it couldn't be done. The price they would have to pay was higher than Sears paid. Moreover, it was higher still than the Sears retail price. Because of the large quantities of goods they bought, Sears could command very good prices. Goldblatt's couldn't buy as cheaply because our quantities weren't as large. I refused to accept their argument and began to take my program forward by instructing a buyer to buy bicycles even though we would be paying more for them than Sears was selling them for. The plan was for us to advertise them below our cost, but also lower than Sears price.

I explained that in so doing, Goldblatt's would sell enough to place carload reorders from the manufacturers at a reduced cost. We could continue to undersell Sears, and then make a small profit, too. As a result, Goldblatt's became the largest retailer of bicycles in Chicago, except for Sears and Ward's.

I then saw my way clear to duplicate this strategy many times over to get us into a variety of other hard–line items. We added an auto accessory department to the company and contacted Firestone, Goodyear, Fisk, and other makers of nationally branded auto tires. They all refused to sell to us price cutters. So in desperation, I purchased quantities of tires from retail dealers and gas stations at from five to 25 percent above their cost. In that manner, I accumulated a carload full of tires representing all the national brands and ran a full–page ad to sell them, highlighting "Goldblatt's Sells For Less. We Guarantee Chicago's Lowest Prices." There it was, "all the top brands in

*Chapter X   **Growing Through the Depression***

all the sizes to fit every make car — at half price." The sale represented a huge loss, but . . .

No sooner had the ad appeared than the tire manufacturers contacted me imploring me to stop. All the local dealers were beside themselves, and when I refused to comply, I received a call from Harvey Firestone, Sr., inviting me to visit him at his office in Akron, Ohio. Once there, I went into a long meeting with Mr. Firestone and made it clear the only way I would stop was when Firestone sold to Goldblatt's directly. To that he replied, "Look, Mr. Goldblatt, I have one hundred dealers in Chicago, and if I sold directly to you these dealers would be upset and might even discontinue selling Firestone tires."

"Mr. Firestone, you ought to worry about your competitor Sears Roebuck, instead. You need Goldblatt's to give Sears a licking. Besides, I will guarantee to give you as much or more business than all your hundred dealers combined, and I'll uphold your retail prices. Furthermore, how do you suppose I purchased all these tires? I bought them from your dealers at cut prices!"

After lengthy negotiations, he consented to sell to Goldblatt's directly. That was the beginning of our auto accessory department, and the first time in the history of Firestone that they sold their tires to a department store.

In my heart I rejoiced at the creative leverage that was ours, here, there, and everywhere, just waiting for the doing. I came away from the Firestone deal with a sense of exhilaration, exalting enough to lift me from negative emotions whenever I thought of it. I saw lemons made into lemonade at every turn, from the rise of a wisp of a business to the collapse of the Louis Store to our thriving through the Great Depression. We'd done battle with Wieboldt's, the Davis Store, and now the giants, Sears and Wards, and the powerful hard lines for which they had a clear field all to themselves. This was driven home to me by an encounter with the great tire industry and Harvey Firestone himself. The present was ours! We buy the future with the present! Nothing could stop us, or so it appeared.

To celebrate, we ran a double truck ad, or a two-page spread, with a powerful illustration of the two companies in a hand clasp; the Firestone Corporation and the Goldblatt Brothers, united in a major city and major market.

I followed this up with private-label auto needs and a complete line of accessories. We continued it with a series of hard line items, using the Sears catalog criteria to bring on virtually a parade of Sewmaster sewing machines, Freezmaster refrigerators, Cookmaster stoves, and still more. We were competing with the leaders, now. In fact, at the time Goldblatt's was the only department store in Chicago to compete with Sears and Wards in appliances, hardware, and auto accessories.

Yet, there was a fallacy in this. With the competitiveness we had come to master with our aggressiveness, our strongest competitor was Goldblatt's itself! Our objective, like a banner held high, was Buy! Advertise! Sell! and always for less than ever before. But the race was getting out of control, and we were losing our perspective. Our buyers never comparison shopped to gauge whether we might raise a Goldblatt price so as to make more on an item and still undersell the competition. Instead, they shopped as hunters, targeting items they might sell for less and less, in ever-larger quantities. It was a false God. Our objectives were going awry. Our profits were small by habit, and bad habits are difficult to change.

Chapter X   Growing Through the Depression

There were other drawbacks to our one-dimensional buying, buying by price only. I had to learn all of them, one by one, hard lessons all. We were still growing quickly, and with that growth should have come the responsibility of adding knowledge and scope to performance. I recall negotiating a mattress buy from Ira Pink of the Englander Mattress Company for what was to be the biggest sale in our history. The advertising plan, of course, called for items from every department at the lowest prices of the year. Considering all the business I had given him over the years, and that all our other vendors were cooperating, I had reason to expect the usual "this-time-only" kind of help from Pink. I expected him to sell me full-size mattresses to retail at $3.98.

Ira finally acceded to an order at a cost of three dollars each, but with the understanding that he would be forced to lower quality. When the shipment arrived and I saw the deplorable quality of the merchandise, I immediately called him to register my complaint. "What did you expect for only three dollars?" he replied. "I had to use cotton stuffing, straw, and saw dust. You're lucky I didn't stuff it with manure!"

For the times that they were and the company that we were, to thus be calculating quality as overriding price hit me, first with a jolt, than as a cardinal lesson in merchandising. The three dollar cost didn't buy a mattress, it bought a poor substitute for a mattress. The incident took me back to my childhood days with Alex. It was a reminder that, whatever the price, the customer must be pleased and made to want to come back. I would never need another lesson of that kind.

There were other lessons, too. The buying personnel, of which I was one, were responsible for sales, advertising costs, expenses, and profits. Eddie Simon in advertising was responsible for creating traffic at the stores. I became infuriated when he advertised as leaders items from my departments at below cost. I complained to Nathan that end–of–the–year profits were my responsibility, and that I lost control when Eddie would misuse my items on his own. Nathan always supported Eddie in such matters. Store traffic was paramount, he said. I came to realize that, over a full year, Eddie's infringement on my profit was minuscule. His consideration was the store as a whole, generating traffic was a valid contribution to the profits of the company as a whole; nevertheless, it was also my place to protect my turf and voice my feelings.

I think of the adage about how England is best defined by her contradictions: it's a democracy imbued with royalty; it's a European nation but a separate island, whether they live in cottages or castles, that the English are English. At Goldblatt's, we pulled together for collective value–giving and excitement. We bought as a team and sold as a team; within that framework, each department was autonomous. Each buyer was expected to produce a profit, which was the determinant of his year–end raise or promotion. Naturally, there were the prorated charges of utilities and rent, but each buyer's destiny was his own. We succeeded or failed as individuals and, thus, were taught to run our departments as our own stores. Such was the double standard indoctrination of the Goldblatt's buyer, a contradiction of team and individual that we lived with and profited by.

Some members of our buying staff not only felt like family, they were family, a thought that brings back very pleasant memories of Esther Terry, our aunt and Momma's half sister. She worked at Goldblatt's as an excellent housedress buyer, but she was equally capable as a cook. Her *kreplach*, the triangle-shaped dough stuffed with meat that was delicious in

Chapter X   GROWING THROUGH THE DEPRESSION

soup and rather close in appearance to Italian ravioli, was as good as Momma's. I called it my piggy in a blanket. Aunt Esther's son Bill Targ was our book buyer for a short time and later left to become an editor at the World Publishing Company as well as a noted author.

My desire to fully understand merchandising went far beyond the Sears Roebuck catalogue. One thing we always took a dim view of was concessions, or leased departments. Though most stores leased out some departments, such as shoes, millinery, the lunch counter, and better jewelry, we felt we could operate them better ourselves and avoid any possibility of cheating or overcharging the customers. As innovative merchants, it was not our way to lean on others, to oversee at arm's length the activities of outside operators inside a Goldblatt's store.

My curiosity into other methods of merchandising and operating often acted like grains of sand in pearls, ideas leading to practice, practice to expansion, expansion to encouraging others with talent, all giving rise to new enterprise. Typical was the focus I first applied to Woolworth. It carried all the top brands of cosmetics and toiletries that were sold in the department stores, except that Woolworth's selection was in five- and 10-cent sizes. Woolworth was also better than department stores at selling such classifications as school supplies, hardware, electrical accessories, toys, notions and jewelry, even though their selection was confined to the five- and 10-cent price range.

So one day I went to Woolworth and bought about $300 worth of individual items and laid them out on the floor in my office. I learned of the catalog service that listed all these items, the vendors that supplied them, as well as their costs. I subscribed to this service and further learned which items were carried by both Woolworth and Kresge.

I proceeded to stock the items I'd gathered and set up a booth of tables in the basements of the stores, pricing 10-cent items at nine cents and the five-cent ones at two for nine cents. As all the items were small and the units many. The booth tables required glass bins and shams, so I hired a Woolworth glass cutter by the name of Allan Neimark to do this work. If Woolworth presented advertised items on front tables, so would we. Soon, one such booth became many, and the limited area to which they had been confined grew, so half of our stores" basements became known as the Goldblatt's 5¢ to $1 Basement. As this business grew, I separated the classifications into complete departments — hardware, electrical, stationery — and Allan Neimark, glass cutter, became Allan Neimark, buyer.

Goldblatt's New York buying office was always a beehive of activity, with everyone scrutinizing the samples in the huge, noisy bull-pen — feeling fabrics, squinting at stitching, checking for strength of construction. Girls' dresses, men's pants, jewelry, roller skates, handbags, flatware. Jabber, jabber, jabber went the hum of the dialogue of examination. Some were quiet and pensive, other duos and small groups were laughing, still others disappointed or disapproving. Colors, grades, sizes; guarantees, delivery, terms, packaging, returns, credits, exchange privileges.

In the late morning, the buyers headed out to their appointments with the vendors at the showrooms and offices. They visited old dependable firms with huge plants and new

Chapter X *Growing Through the Depression*

firms and start-ups with, perhaps, only a few machines in old dilapidated, low-rent, walk-up lofts. Both felt the sweat of anxiety about the Goldblatt's order and the fast cash it was known for. Slow, quiet discussions. Quick, loud arguments. Negotiation. Truth and deception. First-time buys, trial runs, ultimatums, reorders. Friendships, too. There was drama and pathos, tragedy, too, when our handbag buyer, Henry Schwartz, fell or jumped to his death from the 18th floor of the Pennsylvania Hotel.

Perhaps, we might be off to one of the product-center cities like Gloversville in upstate New York, the glove capitol of the country. Almost every family in town was somehow involved in their manufacture, and a buyer needed only walk the street there and go into any home to buy. The buyers went to Providence, Rhode Island, for jewelry; to Passaic, New Jersey, for laces and handkerchiefs; to Red Lion, New York, for cigars; and to Philadelphia for police uniforms.

I made it my business always to visit Macy's and insisted the buyers do likewise. I walked the entire store, making note of everything I saw that Goldblatt's should copy. Displays, merchandising, private-label items, everything. I never visited any city that I didn't shop the local department store to find at least one outstanding merchandising or operating idea. I felt I had conquered the pitfall of vanity by training myself to pass quickly by anything I saw that Goldblatt's might have been doing better. My mission, always, was to correct our weaknesses with self-criticism, not waste time with self-flattery. Who was better, and why?

In January 1934, Momma and Sarah took off from Miami Beach and flew to Cuba, making them the first members of the family to fly. Knowing that Poppa would be fearful and disapprove, they waited until after they'd arrived to phone him to say they were in Cuba, adding that they were looking for gigolos to show them the sights. At first he was livid, then he collected himself and pleaded that they be careful and come home soon. It took Momma and Sarah to prove that flying was safe; thereafter, we brothers gave up the train and traveled to New York by plane.

That was also a sad year, for Poppa died of a heart attack at the age of 69. The Goldblatt's stores were closed for a day of mourning. On the way back from the cemetery, Joel and I remarked to Momma how astonished we were at the huge crowd that attended. She replied, "In a lifetime, a person either makes friends or enemies. Poppa was a good and righteous man, loving if stingy. His many friends were at the funeral to protect him from the devils," she said, a remark that has stayed with me ever since. Whenever I attend a funeral, I observe how many others are there, how many others care to protect the deceased from the devil. Momma was strong, a stoic; she kept her head high and refused to cry in the presence of her children. We all took her lead, and when I stopped to think about it, all of Chicago had come to know the name Goldblatt only because of Shimon Youna.

#

In the company, no sooner was one sale event over than it was challenged by another, also identified by superlatives. Our promotional pace was forever on the climb — bigger and better sale events. While it would appear that we'd nearly hit a peak — hence, that nothing bigger or better was possible — this was not the case. Each succeeding event actually was larger, considering the addition and expansion of depart-

Chapter X   Growing Through the Depression

ments, the acquisition of new stores with added sales volume, and the general improvement in our technique from one year to the next.

Early one morning in the spring of 1934, I called a meeting of all the merchandise managers, buyers, and assistant buyers, store managers, and all members of management. This meeting, I told them, was to be kept a secret from Nathan. I had decided to stage yet another sale event to surpass all previous sales by far; a Nathan Goldblatt Sale, true, but this one, the star of all the others, was to be called the Star Sale of the Year.

It was to be a single–day event, held the Saturday prior to the Decoration Day (now called Memorial Day) holiday. Our goal was to produce one million dollars in sales, more than double the sales of any one day ever, including any day in the Christmas season.

I made an impassioned appeal to each of the buyers personally, challenging their talents and personal goals. I sought to uncover the hidden, untried capability, if not genius, that lies in every man. I could hear my own voice ringing in a room that was hushed. I articulated the goals they must demand of themselves, rather than what I was demanding of them. I generated a vision of superachievement, and it must have taken because when I concluded, the buyers went wild with enthusiasm.

They were chumping at the bit, anxious to get out of the meeting and into the market to make the most earthshaking buys of their careers. Furthermore, there was the motivation of Nathan's name. He was well loved, and Goldblatt employees would do anything to make his sale a success. The vendors responded as well, some offering 50 percent off regular price. Others who couldn't cut prices for fear their own customers would learn of it gave cash allowances to be deducted from the

Life is a game, play to win!

buyer's purchases.

Weeks before the event took place, store managers began taking advance orders; these sales were rung up on cash registers hidden in stockrooms and held to be credited on the mammoth Saturday. It went so far that, without management approval, some department managers asked their customers to wait for the big day and come back. Hearing rumors of this, I chose to look the other way rather than dampen the spirit.

On the actual day of the sale, none of the precautions we'd taken seemed adequate to control the crowds that descended upon Goldblatt's — the police with their barricades, the fire department, our own special security force. When the opening bell sounded, there was suddenly a whirlwind of feet, hands, faces, cash, packages, crying babies, packed stairwells and elevators, darting stock boys, ankle– deep paper litter, lines outside the washrooms. Faces we'd seen in the morning were still to be seen late into the day. Tables that started chock–full of merchandise were suddenly emptied as though devoured by locusts. Goldblatt's had hand– distributed a million, 32–page circulars, four pages in color, and they brought in the customers.

The stores did ring up more than $1 million, but more importantly, a precedent was established that would represent next year's challenge. The theatrical banquet that followed, held again in Mann's Rainbow Garden Hippodrome, lauded the achievers. Top performers were given a leather–bound volume, personalized with their own pictures engraved on the first page.

All the evidence clearly supported our claim to be "America's fastest growing department stores." By the close of 1935, there were eight Goldblatt's stores with combined sales of $33,000,000 and a profit of $1,100,000. The company paid a dividend of 37_ cents per share in cash, a total of $843,000.

Chapter X   Growing Through the Depression

The board of directors was comprised of Maurice, Nathan, Joel and myself, our brother–in–law Jack Gordon, and Nicholas J. Pritzker (a lawyer, father of original board member A.N., and grandfather of the current generation of Pritzkers).

The Social Security System, proposed in 1934, went into effect that year. A social safety net was established in this country. In Germany, the Nazis deprived all Jews of their citizenship; ghettos were reestablished and the swastika became the country's national emblem.

Life is a game, play to win!

Nathan, Maurice, Joel, and myself celebrate the 25th anniversary of the Goldblatt Bros. Department Stores in 1939. By then, we had expanded to 10 stores and were recognized around the country as a new kind of retailer. The chain store hadn't yet become the standard for merchandising most household goods. Goldblatt's was not only one of the early discount stores, it was also one of the first to establish branch stores.

Chapter X   Growing Through the Depression

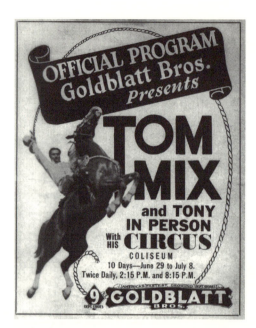

One of our extraordinary promotions during the 1930s was to bring legendary movie star Tom Mix and his western show/circus to Chicago. In following years, trying to beat the success of that promotion became an increasingly difficult challenge.

Goldblatt's had become a national phenomenon by the time we opened our store on State Street in 1936. Conflicts among my brothers and myself over what kind of company we had become–cost-cutting discounter or value-driven but mainline department store–first surfaced with the opening of this store, on what was then the nation's leading street of retailers.

Life is a game, play to win!

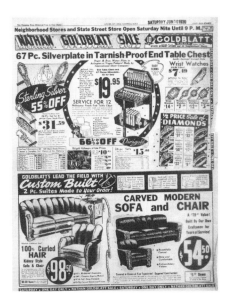

A 1938 newspaper ad and two circulars done in 1938 and 1939 indicate the wide variety of goods carried by goldblatt's stores. Note that at one point even our State Sreet store was open until 9 on Saturday night.

Chapter X   Growing Through the Depression

Portrait of me at age 30, taken during the Century of Progress Exhibition in Chicago by the photographer Maurice Seymour.

Life is a game, play to win!

Chapter XI
Goldblatt's Gets to State Street

In 1933, I moved to the Drake Hotel on Lake Shore Drive in Chicago's Gold Coast, and soon after that Nathan bought a harborside mansion in Wilmette, one of the wealthy North Shore suburbs.

We immigrant boys had made it into Chicago's exclusive residential neighborhoods, and in 1936, Goldblatt's acquired a store on State Street, at the time, the country's busiest shopping center.

Overlooking Lake Michigan, Nathan's extraordinary house was originally built by noted architect Benjamin Marshall, as his home and studio. Nathan bedecked it with even more innovative surprises than Marshall had; its one–of–a–kind artifacts and grandiose features included special effects, both horticultural and zoological spectaculars. Its total effect teetered between the shockingly flamboyant and the breathtakingly beautiful.

An Egyptian room housed an authentic mummy case, complete with a mummy. At party time, the fully set dining table would come up through the floor; that portion of the floor itself converted to a canopy over the table. A part of the huge living room replicated the stage of the Chicago Theater, complete with backdrops and lighting effects. A kidney–shaped

Chapter XI Goldblatt's Gets to State Street

swimming pool was surrounded by a vast, enclosed tropical garden replete with exotic birds. This area had a glass ceiling 25 feet high that opened electrically, exposing the jungle around the pool to the open sky. When watering was required, a special sprinkler system created the effect of rain. Banana trees, tropical plants, and foliage were so thick one had to part the vines as though going through a forest. Marshall, who had designed the Drake Hotel and several other Gold Coast buildings, reportedly had entertained the Prince of Wales, Charles Lindbergh, and Herbert Hoover there.

Shortly after moving in with Frances and their four children, Nathan proceeded to expand the place, adding wings of exotic rooms. He adopted the letter N as a monogram, and he brandished as Napoleon himself would have, setting it into specially woven rugs in the new dining room, on all the dinnerware and flatware as well. He built a Chinese bedroom in which he included a hundred–year– old Chinese bed. He added a gambling casino, complete with crap tables, roulette, bird–cage dice, and other gambling devices; he asked guests to burn their autograph into a long teakwood table. In still another room, known as the Zebra Room, the bar, stools, and walls were covered with zebra skin.

On his trips to Europe, Nathan would arrange to disassemble and send back complete rooms, which were reassembled as part of the mansion. There were antiques, fine paintings, and even solid gold flatware that had belonged to Czar Nicholas of Russia, every piece of which was set with rubies and other precious stones. There was a Japanese rickshaw converted to a telephone booth, even a life– size ivory eagle with outstretched wings. This fantasy palace exceeded the bounds of any ordinary mansion. It was an art and historical repository, a museum where Nathan entertained movie stars, politicians, dignitaries, and vendors.

Meanwhile, the Four Must Get Theirs occupied a lavish suite on the eighth floor of the Drake Hotel, also designed by Marshall and overlooking the Oak Street Beach. During Prohibition and afterward, we were well–known at the night–clubs. We entertained an endless parade of show girls and collected many memories.

Our suite at the Drake became a place where stage and screen stars from New York and Hollywood would visit when they were in town. Joel and I cut dashing figures in our white cashmere coats and white fedoras; I was photographed wearing mine by Maurice Seymour, a celebrity photographer in Chicago. With his Valentino–like appeal, Joel met and fell in love with Helen Morgan, the well–known nightclub entertainer actress. Unlike Eddie Simon, who later made a disastrous marriage to another actress, Joel resisted the temptation to move out beyond the world in which we had done so well.

One of our memories, however, was horrifying. On a New Year's Eve while we were still living at 20 East Cedar Street, we had the chorus girls of the Chez Paree, Chicago's most famous nightclub at the time, over to our place. Suddenly, "Machine Gun" Jack McGurn, one of Chicago's most notorious gangsters at the time, broke in with his three bodyguards looking for McGurn's moll, who had gone and hidden herself in a closet. It was thought at the time that McGurn was the one who did the killing at the St. Valentine's Day Massacre. To say we were scared stiff would be an understatement.

We immediately brought out the girl, explaining that she wasn't the girlfriend of any of us, and invited McGurn and his men to have a New Year's drink. They stayed a short while, then left, taking her with them. When the door closed behind them, we sighed with relief and felt we had a new lease on life.

In 1936, everyone gathered around their radios to hear that Bruno Hauptmann had been executed for the Lindbergh baby's murder, and the black American athlete, Jesse Owens, shattered Hitler's attempt to demonstrate Aryan superiority at the Berlin Olympics.

The year also meant a great leap forward for Goldblatt's. In rapid fire succession, we opened a large department store in Hammond, Indiana, another in Gary, and still another on 26th Street in Chicago. The biggest acquisition of them all was buying our former competitor, the Davis Store on State Street, from Marshall Field & Company. Now, truly, we stood with the heavy hitters, the giant department stores.

To offer even greater values, our buyers would sometimes demand half-price merchandise for a special sales event, and in obtaining them we would advertise and sell them at correspondingly low prices. We didn't, in other words, inflate the prices at the retail level because of the lower costs. We truly gave the values that we strove for. Growing chain that we were, we had a similarly growing number of competitors; to some of them, Goldblatt's represented a mortal threat. Our buyers grew increasingly sharp and powerful, with the additional buying power of the sales volume generated by our new store acquisitions. Besides, they had the freedom to make opportunistic buys when they ran into a situation of surplus inventories, close outs, bankruptcy buy-outs, and the like, all of which compounded the hazards of competing with us.

Then we had another labor crisis. Our circular distributors continued to represent a temptation to gangster union organizers; the hiring of Leonard Boltz hadn't put this threat to rest, not by a long shot. We had a crew of– a crew of derelicts on the payroll who by then were distributing a million or more circulars a week. They were mainly bums and winos, and as far as we knew their situation with Goldblatt's was much the way they wanted it.

But it wasn't what the union wanted, and one day our old foe John Rooney popped back up, heading a gangster-ridden local. He and his men approached the circular distributors in the alley behind the Chicago Avenue store, which served as the base of the circular distribution operation. The gangsters demanded each distributor fork over $2.00 from his pay each week for union dues. The men refused.

Goldblatt's had grown out of the dynamics of Chicago, rising as hard-working, hard-thinking immigrants; even *Fortune* magazine gave us credit for that. It had been a fight to get started, a fight to hold on, a fight against competition that wanted to see us perish, a fight against those vendors who said we weren't fit to buy their goods, and now a fight on State Street itself for the core of the Chicago market. Yes, we were fighters primed in the combat of the American dream. We weren't about to give in to those gangsters, this scum of the city. And if we had to do it without the aid of the authorities, we'd just have to go it alone!

Nathan backed the distributors and promised to protect them from the union organizers. After much fighting, and even threats of bodily harm, Rooney and his gang drove by, shooting up our show windows. It was a warning to stop resisting, or else! A war was on. As though we didn't have enough to watch over already, Nathan, Joel, and myself armed ourselves. We were ready, come what may.

One morning Rooney and gang drove by the State Street store in their touring car, shooting up the windows. They also killed an armed guard standing out front, a young man who was the brother of Joel's secretary. Nathan vowed that he would get the killer Rooney and bring him to justice. Getting no cooperation from the police department, he took the matter into his own hands. He asked Leonard Boltz along with some of his men plus police friends to hunt for Rooney, who was now hiding out.

Leonard, former underworld character that he was, knew exactly where to hunt for Rooney. He led his men to a remote cottage in the woods of Wisconsin where Rooney and his gang were holed up. They surrounded the house and, using a bull horn, ordered them to come out with their hands up. Rooney and the gang were finally brought to trial, a rarity as important gangsters were seldom indicted. They were all given jail sentences, but it was Rooney who drew the longest term. He swore that the first thing he would do when he got out was to kill Nathan Goldblatt.

Released from jail a few years later, Rooney was gunned down and killed after walking no more than half a block from the jail gate. The murder was never solved. Throughout our entire business career, we brothers stood our ground against intimidation and gangsterism.

Another event in the year 1936 was that the Four Must Get Theirs went on vacation to Europe, our first trip there. We visited Austria, France, Switzerland, Italy, and England. The highlight of the trip was traveling on the French luxury liner, *Normandie*, which we sailed on with our friend Harry Richman. At the time, he was in his prime as a nightclub entertainer, most famous for his song "Puttin' on the Ritz." The chef enjoyed cooking to order, so rather than ordering from the lavish menu, we asked him to prepare anything and everything one could possibly dream of. The kitchen would also serve large portions of Russian caviar, bringing it to one's stateroom at any hour of the day or night. What a tragedy when that $60 million superliner burned and sank at her berth in New York three years later!

We were in London during the coronation of King George VI and saw royalty in unimaginable splendor on parade. Pomp and circumstance on every corner. Here, I suppose I finally found an event that beat anything Goldblatt's could ever dream of staging. We also visited Harry Richman at his lavish Paris apartment where he always surrounded himself with lots of women, several usually in the nude. He'd throw hundred dollar bills around as though they were 10 cent pieces.

# # #

I loved retail showmanship, the will and the wherewithal to excite the public, to make them "feel" something in order to make them do something. With our move to State Street, I was motivated to make these even more spectacular. The Bargain Carnival Sale, which I'd first staged at the Louis Store in 1926, had over the years turned into a model retail promotion that was copied across the country. Our version in 1937 included a circus parade, which took more than an hour to pass by viewers lined four and five deep along Chicago Avenue. Live wild animals paced in cages mounted atop colorfully decked out trucks provided by our vendors. A statuesque, macho–looking, lion–tamer dramatically cracked his whip while thrusting his chair at an imagined king of the beasts. Oh, what a thrill to watch the faces on those spellbound kids.

Inside the stores, we continued the carnival theme with

vivid, ferocious-looking animal heads we'd rented from taxidermists and mounted on the columns. We piped in real circus calliope music and strung balloons, pennants, and signs throughout the store, including in the windows. Free balloons were given with purchases, and we encouraged customers to carry them out into the streets throughout the neighborhood.

Thus another Bargain Carnival Sale was behind us, another success, but as with all such events, it left a vacuum after it was over, and left us asking how we could possibly top it again the next year. At least with the English coronations, they're "kings" apart. Retailers move in 12-month cycles. We could have relaxed, thinking next year would take care of itself, but we knew nothing ever really takes care of itself!

So, Eddie Simon and I embarked on a trip to Cheyenne, Wyoming, where for one solid week we lived with the incomparable, the one and only, the movie star, Tom Mix. We shared his large, luxurious bus, which was decorated with guns and saddles and all sorts of western gear. We watched him pitch his tents and prepare for and execute every phase of his one-day circus performances, day after day, in town after town. At the end of the week, we signed a contract with Tom Mix. We had his entire circus and the rodeo, too, coming to Chicago and the Colosseum!

It would be the first time Tom Mix had ever traveled east of the Mississippi River. In addition to the attractions of his circus, we added a tight rope walker and a lion taming act.

We ran the circus for 10 days, two shows a day and it proved to be a bonanza. We sold tickets for 10 cents each with the purchase of $1.00 or more. For additional revenue, we set up concessions, selling popcorn and hot dogs, Tom Mix autographed photos, toys, and souvenirs. With heavy advertising in all the metropolitan newspapers, the ethnic and community papers, and more than a million 40–page color circulars hand distributed throughout the city, there probably wasn't a Chicagoan who didn't know Tom Mix had come to Goldblatt's 1938 Bargain Carnival Sale.

Crowds streamed into our stores and into the Colosseum as well. At the conclusion of each circus show, an announcer told the happy audience that for 25 cents more, they could remain to watch Tom Mix star in the rodeo show. Naturally, everybody did. The enthusiasm for this sale reinforced the lesson I'd learned from the early days of the Louis Store: not to leave anything to chance, that there are no shortcuts, and the idea is to get an idea! Tom Mix was the idea for this one, and it worked. The circus broke even, which, not incidentally, was a triumph in itself. The Bargain Carnival Sale hit a new sales high. And in answer to the question about what we should do the next year, we decided that this particular event had been unsurpassable. When, a few years later, the Second World War started, the Bargain Carnival Sale was reduced to a mere title.

Though our sales were inimitable, stores like Sears, Ward's, and Wieboldt's, who'd been advertising exclusively in the metropolitan newspapers, began emulating our use of advertising circulars. Then Nathan got another idea. Now that we were situated on State Street along with the retailing greats, why couldn't Goldblatt's sell higher–priced fashion just like they did, but cut the prices and take away their business? I was skeptical about such a radical change in our approach. Goldblatt's wasn't recognized as a fashion store; we catered to lower–income, blue–collar families, and our identity was merchandising lower–priced, everyday basic items; $10 was the top price for any dress we carried.

Chapter XI   Goldblatt's Gets to State Street

Nevertheless, Nathan went to New York and bought 100 dresses from a manufacturer that sold to Marshall Field. The dresses were identical in styles and fabrics to those Field's was selling for $100. Our cost was $60 each on an eight percent trade-discount bill, and when they arrived, we advertised them for the State Street Store only. Boldly highlighted Was copy stating that these dresses were selling regularly for $100 at other department stores. We had them on sale at only $69. The sale was a flop! We sold three dresses at that price and very few more in the weeks that followed. In order to clear them, we had to take markdown after markdown, finally selling them out at $10 each.

I tried to tell Nathan that it had taken Field's a hundred years to develop the business it enjoyed in fashion apparel and that Goldblatt's could not expect to capture that market overnight. If we truly wanted to get into this, I felt, we would first have to trade up, stepping our highest priced dresses up from $10 to $12. Then, when we'd learned to sell $12 dresses, we could step up to $15 dresses. It would take many years, I argued, before we could actually get into the fashion business. Such a business has to be built by image and reputation, and we had built a different one for Goldblatt's. Though a decade later, we did begin to change our image, it was a change we accomplished only after much thought and coordinated throughout all the stores in response to a changed marketplace.

#

I suppose my interest in magic coupled with a flair for promotion sparked a lot of ideas I thought applicable to the store. One in particular came to me while studying a roll of tissue mounted on a bathroom wall. Christmastime was approaching and I thought I had an idea for an unusual promotion. I called in our carpenters and decorators and asked them to create giant rolls similar to those inside the toilet tissue. My notion was to paint them to look like life-size wooden soldiers with their arms outstretched downward as though marching. We would wrap them around each of the columns on the toy-selling floor, and have them motorized to gyrate so that each of the soldiers became animated, creating an illusion of a magic world of toy soldiers. They were a sight to behold. They dominated the toy floor, their magic reached out to touch the hearts of everyone. I advertised this as a special children's Christmas attraction at the Goldblatt's Toyland at State Street, and it drew an endless stream of children and parents.

There had been a midget village exhibit at the 1933 Chicago Centennial Exposition. It was an elaborate affair, though very real with little houses in which the midgets and their families actually lived. Their houses, in fact, had no roofs, so children could look right into the rooms from above, and through the windows, as well, seeing the little people in their homes and how they live, the small furniture and everything else downsized. It was an exhibition that, with today's sensitivities, would never have been built, but this was long before the Americans with Disabilities Act, and midgets back then could really only make a living as midgets, putting themselves on display. Recalling Midget Village, I hired a fellow from the Ringling Bros. Circus at a fee of $5,000 to develop such an exhibit for Goldblatt's, beginning a whole year in advance.

This young man's job was to assemble a group of midgets, known at the Rose Midget Troupe, so that our designers could create a 25,000 square-foot replica of the village as it

Chapter XI   Goldblatt's Gets to State Street

appeared at the Chicago world's fair. This meant that almost one half of our State Street store's entire 55,000 square-foot Christmas toyland was to be devoted to this attraction. This, too, was advertised as a free attraction, along with a visit with Santa Claus, for our Christmas celebration. The resulting crowds were so large, they lined up throughout the floor and down the staircase. Additionally, the Rose Midget Troupe village attracted lengthy newspaper publicity stories.

A commonplace approach to promotion would not work for our State Street store; the stakes were just too high! Particularly when we made a bid for fashion attention, both our efforts and the customer's response had to be dramatic in order to challenge the image shoppers had of Goldblatt's, to let them know they could buy fashion there as well as housedresses. So we devised some innovative ways to get the customer's attention.

Most retailers on the street were members of the State Street Council, a chamber of commerce-like organization concerned with common promotion and standards. The council did not permit live displays, meaning real people, in the show windows, but I figured out a way to put female mannequins in sitting and standing positions to achieve a fashion impression in each of the State Street windows while staying within these guidelines. We dressed the mannequins in the fashions we were promoting, then we positioned them right close to an opaque fabric background. Behind this curtain we had real-life models dressed in the same fashions. They put their arms and legs through holes in the curtain so they appeared to be those of the mannequins. Every so often, the live models would move their legs or wave an arm, catching the attention of passersby. They'd be forced to stop and take a second glance, to wait and then ask themselves, "Is it a mannequin or is she really alive?"

Life is a game, play to win!

The curious collected at the windows, and the sight of this crowd brought more crowds. Complete strangers began conversing with each other: "There, you see, she moved again!" One said she didn't see it; another said she did. Still another said she saw a leg move that never moved at all. Many came back later with their friends. The display was a sensation; shoppers and office workers had to see for themselves the mystery of the Goldblatt's windows. All the while, they got to see that the latest fashions were on view there, too.

There were many such creative attractions. One year for Easter, we had a real parade of mannequins dressed in the latest fashion gliding along on a moving track the full length of five windows. To do this, we'd removed the partitions between the windows and laid the track. At the end of its run, the mannequins were redressed behind a backdrop, invisible to the crowds on the street. Then the mannequins would reappear, passing again through the length of the five windows in completely different outfits. An all-day parade of new Easter fashions. Again, conversations sprang up between strangers, who couldn't help but ask, "I wonder if that dress comes in my size." Most importantly, customers stayed watching as though the display truly was a parade. It got them to wait in anticipation for Goldblatt's next new fashions, and for every woman enthralled with our windows, there had to be one less at our competitors!

We also came up with some clever promotions of hard lines at the State Street store. One was for a felt-base linoleum floor covering, a practical and essential item, if not necessarily a fashionable one. It came in six-foot wide, 500- pound rolls that couldn't easily be placed in the window. Instead, we cut two yards off a roll and mounted it so it appeared to be a full and heavy roll. Then, we removed a piece two feet in length,

Chapter XI Goldblatt's Gets to State Street

cut it at about a 25-degree angle, and affixed it on the outside of the show window, which we marked to look shattered and cracked. The total visual impression was that the heavy roll had broken the glass and protruded through to the outside. As if that wasn't enough, we covered the sidewalk with the linoleum, in a path that led into the store and continued straight through to the rug department, where a sensational linoleum rug sale was in progress!

Though by this time I was in my mid 30s, but when it came to merchandising, I was still the kid who vaulted over the display tables in our Chicago Avenue store. I would not be a me too merchant! My mind was steadily leaping forward, planning for seasons far ahead, struggling to surpass what we'd done before, or what any other store had done before. On State Street, there was a hunger for drama and excitement that would invite public attention; it was a need unlike those at our stores in outlying neighborhoods. So I decided to create a Christmas toy window that would outdo them all!

In a large corner window, we placed a red brick chimney and built an animated Santa to pop in and out of it. We simulated snow on the floor and displayed a huge selection of toys strewn about the window, then we spotted several life-size animated dwarfs here and there. One was set on a moving track that traversed the entire window, our Easter parade all over again. When the dwarf reached the end of the track, its course curved out of view behind a partition. There the animated dwarf was replaced with a live dwarf, done up in identical clothes and makeup. Each time the track circled the window, we'd alternate between the live fellow and the maché facsimile. One, then the other. The result was captivating!

The live one would wink, and there would be an uproar

from the crowd. He'd move his hands or his head, and the crowds were baffled. "Look, he's alive!" someone would say "No, it's a dummy!" a disbeliever would counter. The next time around, no one could quite remember what they'd seen the last time, so they'd wait to see it yet again. The ensuing cycle and just a wink or two from the real dwarf threw the crowd into renewed commotion. Their puzzlement went on all day. Many onlookers wanted desperately to solve the mystery; others wanted to bet the dwarf was alive and real. Children stood with their mouths agape; mothers turned their infants heads to see the miracle of Santa's elf that came to life.

At the time, *Look* magazine was running a series of mystery stories that their detective Mr. Cobb, naturally, always managed to solve. So he came to tackle the mystery of the Goldblatt's window. The magazine went on to do a feature that included illustrations and photographs of the window and our behind-the-scene transfer that, naturally, solved the mystery, but *Look* and all the local newspapers agreed that the Goldblatt's toy window that year was the best in all Chicago.

#

In 1936, Joel and I purchased a 91-foot yacht, which we named the *Hannah G*, after Momma and paid for with money saved in our joint account. We would have bought it sooner had it not been for a loss we suffered in a show business venture. We bought out the New York musical stageplay *Shuffle Along* and brought it to Chicago to play at the Shubert Theater. It was an all-black review with a cast of 100 starring Ethel Waters, and we thought it would be a hit. As it turned out, we shuffled along right out of show business. The show was a flop in Chicago and closed in a week!

So that summer we learned we weren't impresarios, and we also learned that our talents as retailers exceeded our talents as yachtsmen. One warm, starlit Saturday evening after store closing Joel, Eddie, Buck, and myself, plus Joel's best girl, the singer Helen Morgan, set sail for Green Bay, Wisconsin. Unfortunately, with her narrow beam and a five-foot draw, the *Hannah G*, wasn't built for rough waters. Though the evening seemed calm under a full moon, at midnight a storm suddenly broke loose and we found ourselves caught in 15-foot waves with deep swells. The boat, its crew, and our guests were tossed about like corks. In the galley, the stove and refrigerator broke loose and pitched from one side of the boat to the other; in our own lounge, the piano broke loose, as did many other objects, which crashed about everywhere. To keep her from tumbling, we tied poor Helen to a column, while all night long monstrous waves nearly swallowed our entire craft. Though we were only 200 feet off Milwaukee, but we dared not bring her about to try to make for shore, for fear that a towering wave would hit us broadside, roll us over, and sink us.

Fortunately, the motors didn't zonk out; they were our salvation, enabling us to battle the waves by staying in one place. The storm kept up until early morning, and then we made a run for it, turning between the swells and heading for the harbor. It was a ghastly experience for all of us, but we finally reached safety.

The following summer I had another waterborne brush with death. We were visiting our good friends the Pritzker family at their home in Eagle River, Wisconsin. Abe Pritzker's sons, Jay, Bob, and Ted, along with their friend Jerry Wexler and Jay's girlfriend Cindy, to whom he is now married, were playing around the swimming pool. Knowing I couldn't swim, they decided to have some fun by throwing me into the pool and then rescuing me. They did and I was, but not without some frightening moments. They were teenagers at the time, and I was 35 years of age, but games were a way of life for them. I remember how their father Abe Pritzker would play games about buying and selling real estate with them.

It's interesting, what connections one makes in life. That adolescent Jerrold Wexler, who died in 1992 at age 68 (after becoming famous as actress Daryl Hannah's stepfather), eventually bought the Drake Hotel, where I had lived for so many years. With his partner Edward Ross, he owned or helped develop a host of glittering downtown properties, particularly along North Michigan Avenue, and when it went into Chapter 11 bankruptcy after I had left the company, he also bought the Goldblatt Department Stores.

Two years after our disastrous trip on the *Hannah G*, Joel and I sold it and bought at auction a new boat, actually a 284–ton sea–going yacht named the *Carolita*. She was 134 feet long, had twin propellers, a steel hull, a 10–foot draw, 18–foot beam, and carried four Chris–Craft lifeboats. The *Carolita* was well equipped, with a large galley, a dressing room, and a number of marble staterooms, plus furniture and a piano we provided. It was the last word in improvements. We could even skeet–shoot off the top of its three decks.

Before we bought her, the *Carolita* had made several voyages across the ocean, and she had quite a history of owners, which included some infamous characters as well as famous ones. Guglielmo Marconi, the physicist and inventor of the wireless telegraph, was among the latter. But the boat's pre-

Chapter XI   Goldblatt's Gets to State Street

vious owner was among the latter: a man known as Donald Coster. Once president of the pharmaceutical firm McKesson and Robbins, he became better known as a swindler and embezzler of his company's money who committed suicide after he was exposed.

The *Carolita* was anchored about 250 yards off Navy Pier, a convenience when we chose to live on board. Neighboring yachts included one owned by Leon Mandel, of the Mandel Bros. department stores, and another belonging to Gene McDonnell of the Zenith Corporation. We entertained a lot on board, and once a year we would invite six male guests to cruise with us to fish for bass in Canada; one year we took Nathan, another year, Maurice. Except for the crew of 18, none of us on board shaved for the entire two-week trip. We ate lavish meals prepared by a French chef who offered a fancy menu so guests could request their own preferences in advance.

After returning from one of those fishing trips with us, Harry Kohler, publisher of the *Chicago Herald Examiner*, gave a party for all its guests plus several columnists from his newspaper. Among them was the poet Louis Sarat, who had written articles declaring mental telepathy nonexistent. When told that I did, in fact, practice mental telepathy, he challenged me to read his mind. I accepted.

I asked Sarat to concentrate on someone he had known, but who was now dead, and I told him I would identify the person, say his name, and describe how the person died. As I spoke with Sarat, I was careful to observe his facial expressions, the twitch of his eye, and the quivering of his lips. By sheer trial and error, I was able to tell him he was thinking of his father. Then I determined his father's name by a similar process of letter elimination: "Oh, there's a k in his name? . . .

You say, no, there isn't! . . . Then there's an s, . . . and so forth, thereby eventually becoming aware of some letters the name did and didn't include. Eventually, I was able to piece together the name Julius. The "train accident" in which the senior Mr. Sarat died was a matter of even simpler deduction.

All my answers were indeed true! So there must be something called mental telepathy. The fact is, I didn't believe in it then and used trickery to arrive at the facts. But I had left Louis Sarat astounded. The following week in his column he retracted his views on the subject.

Christmas, with its myriad opportunities in toys attractions, held great fascination for me. One year I got a jump on it. In January, right after the Christmas season, I sent the toy buyer, Stanley Lipinski, to New York for huge quantities of items that manufacturers were anxious to dispose of. I asked him to buy toys that at Christmastime had sold for 50 cents and more and to pay no more than $21 per gross for them (14 or 15 cents each). I stressed that they must be shipped at once and that the bills would be paid with 10 days.

Stan was able to make huge purchases of all sorts of toys and games, both imported and domestic; toys that sold for as much as $5 each, for which he was able to pay as little as $9 and as high as $21 per gross. We accumulated these toys and, all during the year, wrapped them in Christmas paper: red for boys and green for girls.

As Christmas approached, I asked Ray Bianchi, our display manager, to design and build a 20–foot long kind of a Rube Goldberg contraption. The parent would insert a quarter in a slot at one end, which activated a whole chain of reactions, one setting off the other: grinding gears would move swinging parts this way and that, pounding and clanging all the time. In addition, bells rang, sparks poured out, and big puffs of white smoke billowed forth. At the end of this incredible apparatus, a surprise gift package — as though manufactured midst all the noise and animation — came sliding down a chute, red for the boys and green for the girls. Also, waiting there at the end of this tantalizing operation was Santa himself sitting on a throne, and right across from a photographer ready to snap the child on Santa's knee for another quarter!

The customers waited in long lines with their quarters ready. Their response to this fantastical contraption, as well as to the exceptional toy value itself and the element of surprise, was so successful, we repeated it in one form or another for many years to come.

While we did this in Chicago, Momma was spending the winter in Miami Beach. One year, when she was in her early 70s, Joel and I sent her a heart-shaped valentine card that was four-feet high by three-feet wide with a large ribbon proclaiming her our love, our sweetheart, and our favorite valentine. We also sent her a diamond ring. Nathan, vacationing there at the time, had a party for her and invited her friends. Momma was overjoyed and showed off the gifts from her loving sons. We were delighted to be able to at least partially repay the love she had so generously raised us with.

But life was not so cheerful back in Poland. In 1939, the Nazis had bombed Warsaw. We may have been enjoying yachts and diamonds in America, but we knew in Europe the talk of war was ominous, particularly after a military and political alliance known as the Rome–Berlin Axis was announced by fascist governments in Italy and Germany. At home, the U.S. Supreme Court outlawed sitdown strikes, and Franklin Roosevelt became the first president to appear on television when his speech opening the New York World's Fair was carried by N.B.C. Lou Gehrig, calling himself the luckiest man on the face of the earth, gave a farewell speech to his fans at Yankee Stadium. Congress passed the Selective Service Act, providing for the first peacetime draft in U.S. history. In 1940, Roosevelt was elected for a third term, and among the first things he did was put into effect price controls to prevent runaway prices and hoarding, making that a very bad year for business.

Despite that, we still found time to play. Among the famous guests at our suite in the Drake Hotel was the popular song and dance man Al Jolson. At the time, he was brooding that his wife, dancer Ruby Keeler, had left him, so we fixed him up with a lady of the night. But he didn't know that we'd wired the bedroom with a silent-nurse transmitter and connected it to a speaker in the living room. The occasion inspired him to parody his popular minstrel tune, so it went something like, "Mammy! Mammy! The sun shines east; the sun shines west; but you–oo–oo do it best." And so on. Later, we told him how we'd enjoyed his new song and, after he regained his composure, responded, "Since you know everything about me and there aren't any secrets, I might as well strip and run around in the nude!"

Like many retailers at the time, Goldblatt's loaded up on all kinds of merchandise in anticipation of war. I had directed the buyers to buy most everything in sight, not to adhere to any purchasing budgets. As a result, the company became heavily overbought and was forced to borrow from the bank. Walter Heymann, still our banker a dozen years after the Louis Store collapse, objected to our heavy inventory, and feared we'd have a problem if no war was declared.

Chapter XI Goldblatt's Gets to State Street

But in 1941, Goldblatt's managed to improve both sales and profits over the previous year. Our director Nicholas J. Pritzker died, and he was replaced on the board by his son Abe, whose law firm represented the company. (Known as A.N.) Abe Pritzker had been instrumental in closing deals for added stores, and Maurice and Nathan had earlier recognized his talents. In fact, they once suggested he quit his law practice to join Goldblatt's at a $90,000 annual salary. Abe said he'd come on only if they gave him a 10-year contract, $100,000 a year, and a one-third ownership in the company. The brothers responded, "We can hire President Roosevelt for less!" And there was no deal.

Advances in technology kept creating new consumer goods, among them ladies" nylon hosiery, which came into the market in 1940. It fast replaced silk hose, and was the hottest selling item to hit the stores in many years. Retailers could buy it on allotment only, but because Goldblatt's bought direct from the hosiery mills, which few other department stores were able to do, our allotments were generous. Customers formed long lines, even though we were selling it with a limit of one pair per customer.

During the Fourth of July holiday in 1941 my friend Buck, brother Joel, and myself invited our girlfriends aboard our yacht for a sail across Lake Michigan. Looking forward to a night of romance, we left in high spirits and were equally joyful upon our return the next day. But our self-indulgent jaunt came to an abrupt end. Upon arriving in Chicago, we anchored near Navy Pier. A messenger in a Chris-Craft was waiting for us there with word that our dear, wonderful mother had died. The news sent me into shock. Her radiant angel face was no more; her sparkling blue eyes had been closed. The tea and sympathy she'd always given so freely was to be there no longer. I thought of her strong, stubby fingers, of her charity and generosity, of how she simply was the embodiment of love. All her children took her death very hard, but especially me. For a long time, I cried and trembled, unable to control my emotions. Again and again, I became hysterical and vomited.

Momma, I later learned, had been at Nathan's home, teaching Abe Pritzker's mother how to rhumba, when she simply dropped. She was 74, had a weak heart, and had been warned by her doctor — and by her children — to cut down on her two to three packs of cigarettes a day. But she insisted on living it up, saying that one doesn't live forever and she intended to enjoy life while she could. I was despondent for weeks afterward, and felt I had nothing to live for, so I cried and cried, and eventually I cried it all out.

During the balance of that year, the talk of war grew even more. Jews were being slaughtered in Germany, and the Nazis occupied several other countries. Robert McCormick, publisher of the *Chicago Tribune*, advocated isolationism in his editorials and urged the nation's leadership not to meddle in a European war. In a speech in Des Moines, Charles Lindbergh charged that the British, the Jews, and the Roosevelt Administration were trying to push the United States into World War II. Joseph Stalin became premier of the Soviet Union, and President Roosevelt ordered the freezing of German and Italian assets in the United States. The German battleship *Bismarck* was finally sunk by the British navy, resulting in about 2,300 deaths and the destruction of a menace on the seas. In December of that year, the Japanese attacked Pearl Harbor, and the United States and Japan were at war. A few days later we were at war with Germany and Italy.

    With Momma's death, the strongest bond among the brothers together was no longer there. So her children, the Goldblatt brothers, began drifting apart. Business was not going well, and there were many disputes among us. Many employees had been drafted, causing a serious shortage of help. Merchandise was more and more difficult to come by. Joel and I donated the *Carolita* to the Navy, after removing the equipment and furnishings we wanted to keep, and we began preparing to enter military service ourselves.

Life is a game, play to win!

Chapter XII
Lt. Louis, at War with the U.S. Army

Buck, Joel, and I wanted to leave the company and join the army, and in the spring of 1942, Joel became the first to do so, enlisting in the Quartermaster Corps with the rank of captain. Buck and I tried to enlist in any branch of the service that would accept us, but we were turned down as overage. I then asked Frank Folsom, a Goldblatt vice president who at this time was stationed in Washington with the navy, to see what he could do. (Folsom, who had come to us from Montgomery Ward's, later was appointed interim president of R.C.A. while its founder, Gen. Robert Sarnoff, served overseas.) Soon after that, Buck and I got telegrams ordering us to report for army duty within 10 days. We jumped for joy. We were leaving the hectic pace at Goldblatt's for what seemed a more relaxed life in the armed forces during a major war.

Buck and I, now second lieutenants in the U.S. Army, went to Princeton, New Jersey, to report for duty and basic training. After only five days of basics and drilling, we were lined up and called to attention. The officer in command ordered all the men who knew how to make up a bunk bed to take three steps forward. I thought, if that's what it takes to excel, I'll volunteer. I certainly knew how to make up a bunk bed, tight as a drum, in fact. You could bounce a coin off my

Chapter XII Lt. Louis, at War with the U.S. Army

bunk bed! No sooner had I stepped forward than I was ordered to make up all the bunk beds in the barracks. "This will teach you to keep your fuckin' mouth shut in the army!" the officer barked.

In 1943, Joel was transferred to Washington, D.C.; Buck and I, who were to remain together throughout our term in service, were sent first to Fort Meade, Maryland, to train in jungle warfare, then later, to Fort Riley, Kansas, as first lieutenants. Our assignment was to activate the 21st Special Service Company, a group of 128 newly inducted men, one of which was the then unknown Burt Lancaster. From Fort Riley we were sent to Camp Seibert, Alabama, for bivouac training in gas warfare, then finally to Newport, Rhode Island, before being shipped out to Europe. Eventually Buck and I were put in charge of a unit charged with procuring provisions for front-line troops. Somehow, the army found a way to make good use of our talents — and in an assignment that gave us considerable leeway to enjoy ourselves.

While still in the states, we had kept in touch with Joel by phone and, when opportunities arose, visited him. When Buck and I went overseas, we began an intense campaign of letter writing. Most often, we had so little to do we spent the bulk of our time writing, and as our letters were strictly censored, we confined their content to nonsense. Consequently, the writing became fun and dwelled on information of social happenings, health, business, mutual regard, and just plain ribbing. Before going overseas we had developed a code through which we could reveal our whereabouts as well as some experiences that were normally censored. The three of us received many letters from the family and employees, too, making us aware of what was going on in the company and in retailing in general. As I saved them all, I had a marvelous trove of memorabilia with which to write this book.

Thus, we learned of merchandising and other retailing problems in the country, especially those of Goldblatt's. During the war, many merchandise classifications were not to be had at any price, and what could be gotten was bought with ration coupons. Customers were able to purchase limited quantities of meat and shoes, some leather and rubber items, gasoline, and many other products; still, many butcher shops closed for want of meat. Taken off the market as unavailable even with ration coupons were items needed to fight the war, like auto tires, motors, major and small appliances, and almost anything made of metal. Other classifications, though nominally available, were scarce and difficult to get: lumber, building material, paper (particularly toilet tissue and newsprint), items made of wood, and the critical necessity nylon hosiery — most of this newly invented fabric went into the making of parachutes.

Merchandise allotments were based on the amount of business manufacturers had done with retailers during the pre-war years. The manufacturers of branded goods had done little business with Goldblatt's, the price cutters, so the company encountered more difficulty buying goods than did its competition. Our buyers went begging for merchandise, but they were turned down.

Goldblatt's was doubly hurt. As newsprint was scarce, the company had to discontinue its advertising circulars, then the *Chicago Tribune* raised the price of the daily edition from two to three cents, and the *Herald American* and *Daily News* from three to four cents. Not only did the store have little merchandise to sell, it also could barely afford to advertise what merchandise it did have.

Chapter XII Lt. Louis, at War with the U.S. Army

#

In May of 1943, the 21st Special Service Company was fully activated at Camp Seibert, headed by four first lieutenants, of which Buck and I were two, plus a commanding officer called Capt. Mobly. The captain, a full-time regular army man, easy going and lazy, permitted Buck and me to virtually run the company. Throughout our assignment, we organized a group of capable and talented men to serve the front-line troops.

And did we maintain standards! When a goldbrick (lazy soldier), incompetent, or apple polisher overstayed a five-day sick leave, we had the authority to requisition his replacement; in so doing, we could chose a man of talent and character to replace him. We would investigate pools of men awaiting assignment and request transfers of talented individuals into the company.

We selected men for a broad range of needs: from truck drivers to librarians, cooks to newspaper writers and movie projection operators, plus bookkeepers. We also attracted athletes and performers from singers and dancers to magicians, even fire eaters, and more.

On several occasions throughout our term in service, we were called down for not adhering to the blue book, the army's *Manual of Rules and Laws*. For example, while the 21st Special Service Company was to consist of four platoons of 28 men each (or 116 men), we had at times as many as 145 in total. But, no sooner did some high-ranking officer issue an order to reprimand us or cut our size than we would be moved on to some other area under other new commanding officers, so we could ignore the order. When faced with the blue book, we would comply, though usually in somewhat less than by-the-book fashion.

Because our backgrounds were in merchandising, we were, by strict definition, to operate as a PX (post exchange) unit, meaning under army rulings. However, we chose to make our own rules, and we usually got away with it for the duration of the war. We even created our own newspaper, the *Stars and Gripes*!

During my term of service, I had several duties and titles, one of which was transportation officer. When our unit was stationed at Fort Riley in Kansas, I received orders to transfer the 140-man company to Camp Seibert in Alabama. The train on which we were loaded was so overcrowded, the accommodations and sleeping facilities so poor, that when we finally pulled to a stop at Camp Seibert one Sunday morning at 5:30 A.M., I decided to let the men stay bunked down for a while. A sergeant, however, presented me with orders to disembark at once.

Not being much of a soldier and unaccustomed to following orders that lacked common sense, I refused to rouse the men from their sleep. When they did finally disembark at 7:00 A.M., tired and hungry, we were marched to our quarters in the bivouac area and put under quarantine. Then, I was handed orders by a major requesting a written report, in duplicate, as to why I refused to obey an order to remove my men from the train, a copy of which was to go to Camp Seibert's commanding officer.

I brought my lengthy report to the major's office and no sooner had I handed it to him than he barked, "Stand at attention until I put you at ease. When you address an officer, you salute! What kind of an officer are you, L. Goldblatt! Where

Chapter XII Lt. Louis, at War with the U.S. Army

did you get your basic training!" He continued to berate me, threatening to make it tough for me. Finally, he put me at ease and began reading.

With his hand trembling, his face turned white and his brow started to wrinkle. When he finished reading, he told me to return to quarters. The quarantine would be lifted at once, he said, and he would not send a copy of my report to the C.O. He would, in fact, appreciate it if I forgot the entire matter.

What he had read was my account of the condition of the men as well as some comments I'd written on the train about what I saw after our arrival. When the train pulled in at 5:30 that Sunday morning, the sergeant's detail of soldiers awaiting us were listless, dirty, and ill disciplined. Some had broken rank and started walking to church. I described the sergeant who handed me the orders as shabbily dressed with dirty shoes, unkempt hair, and slovenly in general. When a noncommissioned officer had addressed Lt. Goldblatt to present the orders, he had not only failed to salute, he had said, "Hey, you guys, get off the train!" The report also brought out that the grounds of the base were littered with paper and cigarette butts, an indication of inadequate discipline, and it went on to criticize the camp and its personnel.

Thereafter, Lt. Goldblatt and his company were given free reign and treated with kid gloves.

The 21st Special Service Company had two distinct halves: the service platoons, which consisted of six separate sections with individual complements of personnel, talent, and ability; and the exchange platoon, a special group that operated a mobile PX. Buck and I could not have been more ideally suited to fulfilling the particular duties assigned to us: showmanship and efficient distribution of goods were our forte and that's what the army had us doing.

Even before our arrival with the company, presentations by the entertainment and music section of the service platoons had received enthusiastic acclaim throughout Kansas. Among its members were many remarkable talents. For one, there was Sgt. Thomas Conroy, producer and director of many Broadway shows, who had also appeared in many dramatic hits. His last previous gigs, before joining the army, were roles in *Arsenic and Old Lace* and *Johnny 2x4*. Not yet a star, but still incredibly talented, was Sgt. Burt Lancaster, an acrobat, vaudevillian, and actor with many years of experience in circuses, vaudeville, and musical comedy.

Some of our productions starred Cpl. Arnold Belnick, one of the foremost violinists in the country. He'd appeared in concert at New York's Town Hall and Carnegie Hall and played with the New York Philharmonic Orchestra. Cpl. Boris Barere was a gifted son of a gifted father, already following closely in the footsteps of Simon Barere, one of the world's finest concert pianists. Boris himself had performed in Latvia, Sweden, and Denmark, and as a solo pianist with the Chicago Symphony Orchestra. Appearing together, Belnick and Barere had become a symbol of the most beautiful music played wherever they appeared.

S/Sgt. Irving Feirstein, music supervisor at the James Monroe High School in New York City, was a fine violinist and another member of our unit. As conductor of high school orchestras and bands, he had been chosen to lead the All–City High School Band made up of specially chosen players from throughout New York City. Cpl. Lawrence Dahms, a fine popular pianist, was a composer in residence and producer as well. Another

Chapter XII Lt. Louis, at War with the U.S. Army

pianist was Joseph Quintile, who had appeared with Harry James and Bob Crosby.

In Cpl. Gilbert Baerwaldt, we had a big–time drummer, and with Cpl. Carmen Londino, a string bassist who had played with Les Brown and Vaughn Monroe. Sgt. Frank DeSimone was an easy singer of popular songs; Pvt. John Sakas, a professional ballroom dancer, Pvt. Arthur Zeyen, a former radio crooner and stage vocalist; and Cpl. Murray Schreier, a famous tenor.

Despite all this individual talent, our entertainment section encouraged group work as well as solo appearances. Our production numbers drew upon the personnel of the entire unit, yielding a number of hilarious skits, a dancing chorus, a band, a glee club of 80 voices, duets and quartets. Our composers and lyricists wrote a number or original songs that reflected the life, emotions, and longings of the American soldier. We had piano duets with Cpl. Barere and Pfc. Carpenter, a violin duets with Cpl. Belnick and S/Sgt. Feirstein; a five–piece dance band, 20–voice glee club, a male quartet, a can–can chorus of eight dancers, a jitterbug chorus of six. We had talent and we had fun.

Though our entertainment section received the most publicity, our service unit consisted of specialists in numerous other endeavors. The motion picture section had nine movie projectors equipped for sound and a staff of 16 trained as pro-jectionists. They put on the outdoor movies so popular with troops everywhere. The public address section included four sets of equipment and men especially trained in its operation. In addition to its use by our entertainment section, it was available for large public gatherings, shows, athletic games, and radio programs. The library section has a mobile library of 8,000 volumes staffed by four trained librarians.

The physical training section had eight specialists and a large variety of sporting and game equipment used by soldiers in their free hours. The newspaper section was a mimeograph machine, men with practical experience running it, and a newspaper.

The exchange platoon, the other half of our unit's activities, wasn't quite so much fun but surely as essential. It operated a mobile exchange with a staff of accountants, managers, salesmen, clerks, stock clerks, and sundry others. Just like Goldblatt's, the unit's responsibility was to supply soldiers with every comfort, form of recreation and entertainment, and all spiritual and mental sustenance omitted in their regular routine.

# # #

Naturally, word traveled quickly that being part of the 21st Special Service outfit was fun; capable men from other branches of the army made their talent available to us by requesting transfers. When the company was shipped overseas, it was assigned to the forward echelon of the Fifth Army under Gen. Mark Clark. We took upon ourselves performance of the duties and functions we felt were most needed by the men in the front lines. The work was mostly freelance; we did what the army couldn't figure out how to do any other way. Buck and I and our entire company, plus 5,000 enlisted men, were shipped across the Atlantic as part of a convoy flanked on either side by warships and blanketed above by fighter planes. Our debarkation point was itself protected by a huge barrage of balloons suspended by cables. Their role was to be an obstacle preventing possible Nazi air assault.

During our short stay in Casablanca we met with our

Chapter XII   Lt. Louis, at War with the U.S. Army

friend, the entertainer Al Jolson, who had come there with a USO troupe. We took him on a tour of the Casbah, the ancient native quarter with a large Arab population. There we saw walls of the dwellings lined with cement slabs, which were used as beds by the government–controlled prostitutes. The three of us had more than we could handle warding off their advances with the canes we carried.

We visited with Al every day of his stay in Casablanca. When he returned to the States, we gave him two pair of hard–to–get–nylon hose to barter for a roll in the hay with any girl of his choice. We never heard what he got for the hose. When he arrived home he visited Joel and tried to see if he could get Buck and me transferred to a noncombat zone, an effort that met without success. Soon after his departure, the 21st Special Service Company received its orders to move on to Bizerte, also on the North Africa Coast. Burt Lancaster managed to get a transfer out of the company and remained in Casablanca, a move that angered Capt. Mobly because, in order to do so, he had to go over the captain's head.

The company boarded a train made up of cattle cars, with two sliding door openings, one on either side. The car was large enough for only 20 standing men, so we had to take turns sleeping because there wasn't space enough for all of us to lie down at one time. It was a journey of 1,000 miles and it took 10 days and nights. As a preventive measure, I had ordered them not to drink any water other than that provided by the army in their canteens, nor to eat any fruit or melons offered them by the Arabs. I further ordered the men not to sell any bedsheets, cigarettes, shoes, or anything, for that matter.

Enforcing this order was futile! The men were able to get one dollar for a pack of cigarettes that cost them only eight cents at the PX; they could get $50 for an army-supplied bedsheet, even $100 for a worn pair of shoes. When the train stopped, which happened every few miles, the Arabs would gather at both openings of the boxcars and barter with the soldiers to buy whatever they had to offer.

When the men bragged about how they had robbed the Arabs and the great deals they made, I gave them a talk from an old, experienced merchant. They weren't as smart as they thought, I told them, because obviously the Arabs found these items to be worth far more than they'd paid for them. In fact, I said, it was the wily Arabs who had robbed the dumb American soldiers. The real trick to merchandising, I said, would be to sell the Arabs their own type of item at a profit, not the American items!

When the train stopped the next time, I demonstrated my point. I went first to one side of the boxcar and purchased a melon for 20 cents in francs from one of the many Arabs there. Then I went over to the opening on the other side of the car and sold the very same melon to another Arab. He was in a frenzy, begging to buy and waving his money to get most anything from the dumb Americans, so I gave him the melon for 40 cents in francs!

My point made, I no longer had to admonish the men for disobeying orders. They just stopped selling!

Once, while we were stationed in Bizerte, Buck and I took our jeep, along with a dozen men and a truck, and drove 500 miles to Algiers where many supply ships were docked. For two days we lived in our vehicles, fearing the Arab teenagers would steal anything they could lay their hands on. Another threat came in the form of the many mad and emaciated dogs who roamed the area; rocks with which to shoo them

Chapter XII   Lt. Louis, at War with the U.S. Army

away were our only weapon.

For two days, the 14 of us stole all sorts of equipment, whatever we could get away with without getting caught. We had a two-and-a-half ton truck loaded with pillows, cases of fruit salad, potatoes, bats and balls, movie projector and cameras, whatever, then drove off during the night back to our base in Bizerte with the loot.

Then one morning, when all the men of the 21st Special Service Company were feeling enriched by all our booty and pleased with ourselves for the shows we'd put on for enlisted men in the area, Buck and I got some bad news. We were to appear in the office of the colonel who was CO for the entire Bizerte area. He was displeased with the manner in which our company was operating, he said. We weren't functioning according to the blue book of rules. Thus, Buck and I would be separated and the company split in two.

He gave us a choice. One of us would be shipped off to Sicily with half the men and from there on to Salerno; the other one, along with the other half of the company, would remain in Bizerte assigned to quartermaster functions.

Inconsolably upset with these orders, we pleaded, but to no avail. Finally, we tossed a coin in the colonel's presence to determine which of us was to go to Italy. Buck won and prepared to move out with half the company at once. This left me and my 70 men assigned to a 21-year-old captain who was in charge of a supply warehouse.

At the warehouse, I found the stockkeeping deplorable, the records all bungled, and the inventory unbalanced. Whenever any branch of the army wanted supplies, they first had to see my 21-year-old superior officer and get a requisition. Then, my men and I filled their orders. Being methodical by nature, and having long experience handling inventory, I proceeded to install a perpetual, basic–stock control system, and then began to line up the supplies neatly in rows.

The captain did not approve of what I was doing. So he ordered me to put things back as they were and to discontinue the system I had installed. There I was, a first lieutenant refusing to obey a captain's orders. He said he would have me court martialed and reported the incident to my commanding officer. A major by rank and a schoolteacher in private life before the war, CO Bates called both the captain and myself to his office. Upon hearing my side of the story, he ordered the captain to take orders from me and thereafter be under the command of Lt. Louis Goldblatt.

In the meantime, I was very lonesome, separated from my friend Buck for the first time since we had joined the army. I craved action and wanted combat duty. I exchanged many letters with Joel at the time. Before Buck had left for Italy, we'd devised a code that couldn't be censored so that we could learn what the other was doing and where he was stationed. At long last, I received my first letter from him in which he "told" me he was in Salerno. More than ever, I wanted to find a way of joining him.

First, I contacted several commanding officers in different parts of the army, seeking permission for my half of the company to be transferred to Italy. They all turned me down. In desperation, I decided to stow away on an LST, a landing ship designed to bring transport tanks to shore. The men and I then managed to steal more trucks and equipment and waited for the right time in which to steal ourselves aboard. I didn't dare trying to obtain any food such as C or K rations, because that would give our plan away. I was, however, able to get

Chapter XII Lt. Louis, at War with the U.S. Army

enough Hershey tropical chocolate bars, a very hard, concentrated bar that provided several-days nourishment, from the PX for all the men.

Just two days before we were to leave, Burt Lancaster found me, asking to be taken back into the 21st. He was unshaven, looked haggard, and wore dirty fatigues. I told him that Capt. Mobly, now in Italy with Lt. Buckley and half the company, was angry about his having transferred himself out of the unit. Then I told him of our plan to steal aboard an LST and meet up with the captain in Italy. I was, however, willing to chance taking him along, but only under the condition that he be broken as staff sergeant, become a buck private, and no longer be a member of the company's "Stars and Gripes" show. He was to be a truck driver. He told me that when he had stayed behind at Casablanca, he was placed on KP duty. No more acrobatics for him; he was peeling potatoes and scrubbing floors. He said he'd abide by my conditions so long as he might rejoin the company. I took him back.

Came the morning of our planned departure, I ordered all the men into a convoy of two and one-half ton trucks along with the equipment and drove to the docks where LSTs were being loaded. The air was heavy with anticipation. With our trucks lined up around the corner, I waited out of sight for the MP sergeant, who let only those pass with proper papers for transport to Italy, to leave his post. Then, in double time, I ordered the men and trucks aboard!

After loading onto the LST, I ordered the men to stay and even to sleep in the trucks throughout the entire voyage. After several hours at sea, I was asked for my transport papers and credentials. Not being able to produce them, I was ordered to report to the commanding officer in Salerno and was quarantined. As soon as we docked, I was able to contact Buck and, through his commanding officer, a Col. Ray Novotny, we were shortly released. Once more, the entire company was intact and operating under its own rules. We functioned as a volunteers plus, entertainment unit in Gen. Mark Clark's forward echelons.

From Salerno, we moved up to Naples, then on to Caserta, a few miles north of Naples, where Buck and I, along with officers of some other army units, were billeted in the Caserta Palace. At the time, it was a palace in name only. The roof of the tall, spacious home was bombed out, the elevators were out of order, and we had to climb 200 stairs to get to our room, which also had no roof and was cold besides.

Since our main function was to organize and stage shows of USO entertainers, we both got to meet many important stage and screen stars in the process. We were also quite busy in the planning and staging of the talent in our company. One of the famous people we met there was the famous comedian, Joe E. Brown, who had arrived there with some other entertainers. Buck and I played the card game Hearts with him constantly.

There was never a dull moment!

# # #

When Mount Vesuvius, an active volcano situated on the Bay of Naples, erupted in March of 1944; I wrote Joel describing what we had witnessed: "It started one evening about six o'clock. At eight o'clock, Buck and I saw its bright red tip. . . . [It] looked like a huge cone, almost like a bottle with a bright red cork. . . . The next morning, we could see three huge red stripes down its sides, . . . streaming red hot lava. Mind you, Joel, rivers of lava a quarter mile wide, 90 feet deep, and miles long! . . . Later that

Chapter XII Lt. Louis, at War with the U.S. Army

morning, Buck and I, in the spirit of adventure, decided to ascend the mountain in our jeep to see just how close we might get to the top without getting ourselves killed. Ever upwards we drove until we reached the Observation Tower . . . [which] was at about 900 feet and we climbed to about 1,200 feet, where we could not go any further. The path was blocked by a river of flowing lava. . . . We got out of the jeep and looked around in complete amazement . . . and just gaped at the smoldering river of ashes practically at our feet; so close, we dropped pieces of paper into it and watched them ignite in flames. Just imagine! Here and there the ground around us was still splotched with snow. . . . Standing, just marveling at the wonder of it all, a red hot rock the size of a baseball came down striking earth right between us! It was then we realized what danger the place held for us and we darted for the jeep . . . when, lo and behold, right before our eyes, the wind shifted and we were directly in the path of a black cloud of hot ash! . . . we didn't want to see any more and got into the jeep and sped away. . . . We actually watched this hell on earth as it engulfed and knocked down houses like match boxes and buried a city! . . . Some days later, it began to calm down and now with its top blown off, had come to look like half a mountain. Weeks later when we passed through, we saw these Italian families with their belongings, their carts and burros, trudging back to what might have been left of their homes. . . . Then, we drove down to the wasted city below and came to the end of the 30-foot high lava flow that had buried it — a mass of smoldering ashes that had stopped in its course at the wall of a building. We climbed on the parts that had already cooled. I picked up one hot rock that was still smoking between two sticks of wood and brought it along in the jeep. It stayed hot for many hours. . . . Later, we had a pilot fly us over the crater in his Piper Cub. What a sight! What a hole! Now, we know what hell must look like!"

After the volcano, the 21st Special Service Company moved up the boot of Italy to Santa Maria and Buck and I moved into what was actually an empty barn next to where our men were quartered. We cleaned out the spider webs, made it spic and span, furnished it with two bunk beds, placed a wooden crate in the center to be used as a table, drove in nails as coat hangers, and built shelves for all the "goody" foods sent us from Chicago. We also had a two–burner hot plate fueled by sterno. With our housekeeping in order, we began entertaining the stage and screen stars who came for USO shows. One rainy, muddy day we drove to Naples to pick up Marlene Dietrich, then brought her to our quarters to attend a party we had put together that included Danny Thomas, Irving Berlin, plus six other lesser–known show people. Buck cooked the dinner and we spread a bedsheet over the wooden crate to use as a dining table.

Our guests were served food and drink that was, indeed, scarce, let alone heard of, in Italy at the time. We had been saving most of what we received from friends, relatives, and employees for just such occasions — spaghetti, Mrs. Grass's concentrated noodle soup, sundry canned foods, candy, salami, and brandy disguised in Coca Cola bottles. At that, only a quarter of what was sent ever arrived.

In a letter to Joel about the party, I described Marlene Dietrich as not "such a much" and told him how we impressed her with a pair of nylon hose. We even arranged a pail of sand for her to pee in when the need arose during the shows. We enjoyed Irving Berlin, too; he was practicing new army songs on Buck and me, and I gave him a can of Goldblatt's Bond salmon that I'd received from Chicago. The letter continued:

"that can of salmon was so rare, so wanted, I was offered a hundred dollars for it by army personnel. Irving Berlin was so delighted that he invited us to dinner at the home of an Italian family where we ate carno soco . . . and with it another rarity, chicken, which we had for the first time since we left the States. He actually saved the can of salmon and, get this, he presented it to the pope when he visited him!

"Can you imagine! Goldblatt Bond salmon . . . dinner for His Holiness at the Vatican! . . . The pope was absolutely elated with such a gift, and I was told that when he looked at the label he remarked to Irving Berlin that he remembered passing the Goldblatt Bros. store when he visited Chicago during the Eucharistic Congress, which I learned was before he was the pope in 1926. That's not all, Joel! Irving Berlin told the pope that Lt. Goldblatt is here in Italy, to which His Holiness responded that he would like to meet him."

And so, in early 1944 it was arranged by the Fifth Army hierarchy for Col. Chaplain Ryan to accompany Buck and myself to the Vatican for an audience with Pope Pius XII. It was ten minutes before noon. There were several cardinals in the anterooms awaiting their turn to be escorted into the papal study when, to our astonishment, we were ushered in before them. A tall, lean man in a long white robe and skull cap, he welcomed us in halting English. He spoke of his visit to Chicago and how much he appreciated the can of salmon given to him by Irving Berlin.

He then gave us an autographed color photograph of himself and a rosary, both of which were stolen some time later. Fortunately, Buck and I had purchased some rosaries at the Vatican catacombs which we brought along with us and asked his holiness if he would be kind enough to bless them as they would be so dear to our friends in Chicago after the war. He replied that not only would he do so but that he would bless everything on our person, and proceeded to do so.

It was now noon, time for him to appear on the balcony to bless the throng gathered in Saint Peter's Square. We walked through the corridor with him and his aides. On the way, we passed by the colorfully dressed Swiss Guards, who knelt before the short procession of which Buck and I were somewhat uncomfortably a part.

The pope was hardly the only luminary Buck and I met in Italy. We later welcomed the renowned violinist Jascha Heifetz to our area as a USO entertainer. His performance caused a sensation among the enlisted men, especially when he played "Mares Eat Oats (and does eat oats, and little lambs eat ivy, a pig'll eat ivy too; wouldn't you)." I gave him one of our treasures at the time, a kosher salami I'd received from Chicago. Heifetz visited us every day at our barn, repeatedly expressing his gratitude for this gift. When he took sick with a bad cold, we visited him often to cheer him up with funny stories. We enjoyed our interlude with him and were pleased to have been perhaps his only audience who paid for the privilege with a kosher salami from Chicago.

# # #

Of course, there were the hardships to our lives in the army, but so there were for the other men in the service. Buck and I seldom wrote home about them, but recalling them now, nothing ever happened in half measures. Once, we happened to be near a mountain when it exploded with a force that destroyed a city and almost eliminated the two of us.

Chapter XII   Lt. Louis, at War with the U.S. Army

Amidst our fun, the war went on, and Gen. Mark Clark's Fifth Army was advancing, city by city, up the Italian boot. Our company was among the first personnel in these regained cities, as our function was to set up rest centers for the front-line troops and entertain them with the "Stars and Gripes" show.

Buck and I, free to come and go as we chose, did much traveling by jeep. We were always warmly welcomed into chief of staff headquarters, where I was frequently asked to entertain with magic tricks and mass hypnotism.

Showoff that I was, I'd also mastered hurdling the hood of a jeep on a running jump without using my hands. Then one day I missed, and for a while I had to hobble around on crutches. Once I got permission to put what had been a wrecked train back in operation, and then I began to organize train trips to Pompeii to entertain front-line troops during their rest periods. One time I entertained them by hypnotizing actor John Garfield, who was there with the USO.

At another time, again as transportation officer, I was required to lead a convoy of trucks, several with trailers attached, to another area. In that I had a poor sense of direction and very often lost my way going from base to town, the army couldn't have done worse for this particular assignment. As a consequence, I led the convoy up a narrow dusty road, and it wasn't until after several miles that I discovered I was taking us in the wrong direction. If only the discovery itself had been the solution, but as the road was too narrow for the convoy to turn around, we were forced to continue. Continue we did for many more miles before finally reaching a town with an area wide enough for the required "U" turn.

It was a long time before I lived that down, what with all

the other officers and men, especially my friend, Lt. Buckley, ribbing and laughing at me. I was not, however, unaccustomed to this sort of embarrassment since I had taken wrong turns many times before — and, I might add, a few since!

One of our pastimes was playing poker with higher–ranking officers. One moonless night during a blackout, while walking to our jeep after a game in a sealed tent lit only by candlelight, we were groping our way in the darkness when I fell, kerplunk, right into an open, abandoned latrine. It was horrifying! Although I got out of it, I never got over it! For Buck, the thought of it was a source of hilarious laughter throughout our army careers. Not so for me!

One day when we were quartered in our tent on the outskirts of the small Italian town of Presenzono, a Col. Porter, under the direct personal command of Gen. Mark Clark, came and presented me with an invitation to the general's 47th birthday party, which was to be held April 1, 1944. With my hypnosis and magic tricks, I was to entertain Gen. Clark and all the allied generals who would be there, plus some high–ranking army nurses.

My anxiety was intense. There I was, a mere first lieutenant, with the daunting prospect of hypnotizing a general! I grew obsessed with a consuming fear I might fail, and were I to do so in the presence of such a collection of army brass, I would, assuredly, be branded a faker far and wide. Apart from the consequence of monumental embarrassment, there was the real possibility I would be transferred out of my unit and separated from Buck. Now, the showoff in me wanted to hide behind a rock.

Even though I knew an invitation from a general was tantamount to a command performance, or an order, I pleaded

Chapter XII   Lt. Louis, at War with the U.S. Army

with Col. Porter to please excuse me, telling him I was not a professional hypnotist and might fail and spoil the party. "After all," I said, "I was only a merchant in civilian life, not a performer!"

The colonel carried the message back to the general, only to return telling me that the general wanted me at the party as guest. I did not have to perform any hypnotism, but I was to bring along a pianist from the company. I was stuck! So long as I had to attend, I decided to make the best of it. I drove the jeep all the way to Naples, purchased a canary along with a small cage, and returned to my quarters in Presenzono. Then, I ordered Boris Barere, the pianist, and Arnold Belnick, the violinist, to accompany me to the party, but not until Burt Lancaster begged to come along on the pretext that the pianist would require someone to turn his music pages. So I brought him along.

Arriving at the Quonset hut, a prefabricated metal half cylinder cut lengthwise and plunked down on the ground, I left the canary in the jeep. We went inside and found some 20 odd American and Allied generals, plus a few colonels and some nurses. I saw real glass tumblers, ice cubes, and scotch whiskey for the first time since being overseas. My three men and I were served scotch on the rocks, and we promptly huddled into a far corner of the wall, feeling like wallflowers at a celebrity ball.

A few drinks later, Col. Porter walked to the front of the Quonset and announced that Lt. Goldblatt would now entertain with feats of magic. I had been promised I would not have to entertain! I was betrayed! I was shocked! I was also without alternative! I strode up to the front, adjusted the "mike" and with my senses in turmoil, started to perform.

For my first trick, I asked one of the generals to be kind

enough to lend me a dollar bill. I proceeded to read off the serial numbers and had the general write them down on a piece of paper. Then, I palmed the bill and made it disappear. Next, I asked a general to give me a cigarette. I lit it, drew a few puffs, and then gave the half–smoked cigarette to the general who had lent me the dollar bill. I asked him to unroll the cigarette, and when he did, he found his rolled up bill inside — with the same serial number that he had written on the piece of paper.

The audience enjoyed that one immensely, and I had by then mustered the confidence to continue with more magic. When I finished, relieved and ready to return to the corner from whence I'd come, the colonel appeared at the mike and announced that Lt. Goldblatt would now entertain with hypnotism. And, he added, as there were only two chairs in the place, would everyone please squat down on the floor to watch the show.

I went into a state of quiet desperation! I was brought up front again and looked out over the heads of a bevy of squatting generals, "Gentlemen," I announced "there is no mystery to hypnosis. I am not superhuman. Anyone of you can do the same thing, so rather than hypnotizing one of you, permit me, instead, to demonstrate hypnosis on a canary bird that I just so happen to have outside in my jeep. I am sure you will find it more interesting."

I then left for a moment and returned with the canary, grateful I had procured it. I placed it on its back on the palm of my hand, said my "magic words," and the bird went stiff. It was immobile and appeared to be dead. As further demonstration, I picked it up off my palm and placed it on the palm of one general, then another, and another. Having thus demonstrated its completely hypnotic state, I clapped my hands. The bird came to

Chapter XII Lt. Louis, at War with the U.S. Army

"life" and simply flew away.

It was all over! I was out of the woods, and rather successfully so, too. I felt relieved — no, reborn! But no sooner had this sense of elation overtaken me than a clamor arose out of the audience to see more. Now they were asking that I hypnotize one of them. I was cornered. My elation turned in a flash to sickening reluctance, and I asked for a volunteer to step forward — probably the first time in military history that a lieutenant asked for a volunteer from a group of generals.

In my heart, I was hoping a volunteer would not step forward. I just couldn't picture myself hypnotizing a general, particularly in front of Gen. Mark Clark and all the other generals. There came a rumble out of the audience; each urged another to volunteer, and just when an elderly general with white hair began to rise, Col. Porter stepped forward and said, "Hypnotize me! I'll be your subject."

I replied that one could not be hypnotized against his will. Porter had been standing in front of one of the only two chairs in the place, and when he said he was willing to cooperate, I gently pushed him into the chair behind him. "Open your collar," I instructed. "Be fully relaxed. Your mind a complete blank. You hear no sounds other than my voice. Ful–ly re–laxed, look in–to my right eye. A drow–si–ness is now over–coming you. Your eye–lids are now clos–ing. Soon, you will be sound a– sleep."

I continued this spiel until he fell into a somnambulistic trance, at which time I began the phase of having him do my bidding. The colonel, in his late 30s with a round face, weighed about 180 pounds, was five foot eight and dictatorial in manner, obviously one who took advantage of his rank. Yet, there he was, in effect, no longer a colonel but solely the obedient subject of myself, powerless and unhesitatingly submitting to my every command.

For my finale, I asked Burt Lancaster to help me lift him. We placed the backs of his ankles on the arm of one of the chairs and the back of his neck on the arm of the other. The rest of him was rigid and outstretched in between, with nothing else supporting him. I then proceeded to stand right on top of him, exerting my full weight on his generous paunch.

Before completing the performance, I left him with a posthypnotic suggestion: he would not remember anything that had occurred during his sleep, and every time he saw me scratch my right ear, he would shout out loud "Happy birthday General Clark!" To the hilarity of everyone, he most awkwardly did so throughout the duration of the party.

Suffice to say, Gen. Clark and everyone else were highly impressed with my performance. When it was all over, my sigh of relief was muffled only by the applause. I then called upon the violinist and pianist I brought with me, for whom Burt Lancaster turned the pages.

Now, all I had to deal with were the problems that came with success. It didn't take long. The very next day Col. Novotny advised me that headquarters had recommended I be promoted in rank from first lieutenant to major, bypassing captain, and that I be placed in command of all PX operations in the area. I was naturally flattered by the recognition, but was, nevertheless, compelled to tell him I did not want to be transferred out of the 21st Special Service Company, that I did not want to be separated from Lt. Buckley, and that, with his permission, I preferred to remain a first lieutenant. Since Col. Novotny had the authority to grant my wish, he consented.

Chapter XII   Lt. Louis, at War with the U.S. Army

# # #

In the spring of 1944, the battle for the hill of Monte Cassino raged full force. The site of a monastery founded in 529 A.D., it was then occupied by the Germans for the high strategic vantage point it represented. The abbey at Monte Cassino had been an influential cultural and religious center for centuries, and the Americans were reluctant to bomb so important an antiquity. Consequently, the Germans were able to hold off our forces for some time, but eventually, this World War II battle became the fourth time in the abbey's history that its buildings were destroyed.

One pitch dark night of the battle, during a blackout so stringently enforced that even the "cat eyes" of vehicle headlights were not allowed to be used — and no smoking outdoors besides — Buck and I drove in our jeep, as we had so many other evenings, to attend a poker game. The game, similarly, was by candlelight in a light- sealed tent.

We left the game at midnight, and as we had done time and time before, tossed a coin for who was to drive. Buck won and did the driving while I had to lie prone on the fender to warn him off the shoulder for fear of land mines and booby traps, and this night for ditches, as well, since he couldn't see his hand in front of him and was literally driving blind!

We crept along at a snail's pace and covered but a few miles. I was guiding him, much like the blind leading the blind — "right!" "left!" and "ahead!" my outstretched arms signaled. Soon, we couldn't help remarking, "Gee, the fireworks are getting closer. It looks like the krauts are gaining on us. No doubt we'll be ordered to evacuate tomorrow!"

Next thing we knew, we were stopped by an MP who,

upon seeing we were officers, motioned us on forthwith, evidently of the opinion that we knew what we were doing. Accordingly, entrapped by a classic misunderstanding, we continued to move forward. It seemed that in no time at all tracer bullets were flying overhead, and we realized we had made a terrible mistake! We were headed right into the heat of battle with all hell breaking loose! A sight to behold — Buck, still driving blind and me "navigating" us into a major battle perched up on a fender! Actually, we had been driving north right into the action, when we should have been heading south, away from it. We never managed to live that one down!

After the American capture of the hill and the Abbey at Monte Cassino, we were ordered to move the company up to the Anzio beachhead. There, Buck and I, along with several other officers including Col. Novotny, had billeted ourselves in a house with part of its roof bombed out. It was situated high on a hill overlooking a road and right along the waterway where many Liberty ships were anchored. Fortunately, the house was surrounded with bomb craters, which meant that the area was clear of booby traps and we were able to use it as a tent area for the men.

Army personnel had been ordered out of the underground shelters and the smoke screen had been lifted just a few days before we arrived. We were about to enjoy several weeks of peaceful living there when, suddenly, at midnight on June 9, part of the remaining strength of the Nazi Luftwaffe, about 18 war planes, came in over the harbor. They bombed and strafed where the Liberty ships were moored, only about a hundred yards from the house. They made a direct hit on an ammunition dump, and it kept exploding into the next day. We were ordered to keep away from the corners of the house we lived in as that was where we would be the most vulnerable.

When we joined the army, we'd brought along for laughs our pure–silk Sulka pajamas, for which we'd paid $100 a pair, and we'd never worn them. On this particular night, I said to Buck, "If we're going to get killed, what do you say we die in class! Let's put on our Sulka pajamas and get under the bed!" Throughout all the deafening noise of intensive bombardment, plus the continuous explosions of the ammunition dump, all for a full hour from midnight to 1 A.M., there we were under the bed, dressed, so to speak, either to kill or, more than likely, be killed!

The air attack by the Nazis was incessant. They'd fly in, drop their bombs, and fly out, only to come back with their death loads over and over again. We had been repeatedly told that there was nothing to fear so long as you could hear the eerie whine of the falling bombs. It's only when you can't hear them that your number is up. What they really meant was, you can't hear them at all when you're dead! Buck, momentarily losing his sense of humor, didn't think that funny at the time.

One of the men in the outfit went and found himself a machine gun and used it, not knowing that the ammunition he was firing was tracer bullets, like calling cards, giving away our position. By 1 A.M., the American planes had beaten them off, and we were happy to learn that the entire company had suffered not even one loss. The Luftwaffe was mainly after the Liberty ships and they did, in fact, sink a number of them. Although I appeared calm throughout the entire episode, my nerves finally gave out in the late morning when, while loading the trucks in preparation for moving out, my hands started trembling and I shook all over like a leaf in the wind. Several of the men did go to the hospital because they were so shook up.

At 9:30 that morning, the 21st Special Service Company joined up with a large convoy of vehicles and tanks headed north, traveling together the 40-mile distance to Rome. Quartered in that big, beautiful, and historic city, we felt calm again. Organizing a rest center for combat troops back from the front lines was our first task, and it took us to Lido Beach, only 16 miles south of Rome. As the Nazis had expected the Americans would make an assault there rather than at Anzio, they had mined, booby-trapped, and set barbed wire throughout the length of the shoreline. They had even put up warning signs *Achtung Mina* for their own protection.

Gluttons for punishment, Buck and I volunteered to inspect the area even before the army engineers got there. Lido Beach had always been a fashionable resort area. Fearful of the mines, we parked the jeep when we got there and carefully inched along the rest of the way where we could see dead horses, cattle, and overturned vehicles all around. We ventured into some of the houses where we found food still on the table, clothes in the closets, and various personal belongings scattered about, indicating that the populace had left in a hurry. In general, our inspection was foolhardy, as we had been warned neither to open any doors or drawers nor to step on any papers on the floor because of booby traps. When we reported our findings back at headquarters, it was decided not to use the area as a rest center after all.

Unlike their counterparts in southern Italy, the girls in Rome were fashionable; they used makeup, wore stylish clothes, and were generally prettier. The people in Rome seemed to have everything, except food. It was an easy matter for Buck and I to make a hit there. We would give the girls a loaf of bread, a Hershey chocolate bar, and some cigarettes; that

Chapter XII   Lt. Louis, at War with the U.S. Army

simply was all the requisites for a relationship.

During the time the company was quartered on the outskirts of Rome, I met a very pretty blond girl by the name of Countess Elly. She was German, looked very much like the movie star Doris Day, and spoke Italian and English, as well as German. Her husband, an Italian count, was young and handsome; they lived in a beautiful home.

I met with the countess frequently and even introduced her to various other army officers. I would pick her up several blocks from her home and take her to my quarters. Her husband happened to see me one day seated with his wife at a table in a restaurant, whereupon he gestured menacingly to me. Running his finger across his throat, he left no doubt as to his meaning. Fearful that he would catch up with me and make good his threat, I hoped for orders to leave the area. Having survived the bombings, land mines, and even the volcano, it would be the height of irony to die at the hands of a jealous husband! Fortunately, he disappeared soon afterward.

Later, a colonel told me that my girlfriend and I were being watched by army intelligence and that they knew every move we made together. He went on to say that the girl was a German spy, and that I wasn't to let on I knew. Rather, I was to continue seeing her and report back as to the questions she asked and the comments she made.

Shortly afterward, she was arrested as a German agent and placed in jail. I then received a letter from her, which read:

Dear Louis,

Many thanks for everything. Please do something for me when it is possible. I think to see you very soon. I thank you.

Elly

At the time, Buck was dating Elly's friend and she invited us up to Elly's home after the husband had disappeared. Where the rugs had been ripped off, we were astonished to see wires to radios for sending and receiving messages.

Subsequently, we were moved with the entire company up to Florence, where we continued to stage the "Stars and Gripes." As a satirical takeoff of the army's weekly newspaper, the *Stars and Stripes*, it had been growing in popularity among the men.

Chapter XII   Lt. Louis, at War with the U.S. Army

Though World War II was brewing abroad and we would soon be involved, my friend Herman Buckley (called Buck), my brother Joel, and I (supporting them at center) still had time to clown around on our yacht the Carolita during the summer of 1941.

Life is a game, play to win!

Another Maurice Seymour portrait, this time in my army uniform in 1042. During the war, Buck and I ran a Special Services unit, supplying troops in North Africa and Italy. Shortly before my 90th birthday, I posed again in this uniform.

While the Fifth Army worked its way up Italy, we were frequently under fire; in June of 1944, we arrived at Anzio while the Luftwaffe was still bombing there.

Chapter XIII
Coming Home to New Challenges

Then my European idyll was suddenly to end. In the latter part of September, my sister Rose wrote to tell me of Nathan's terminal illness. Cancer of the pancreas, it turned out to be. I started immediately trying to pull strings to get home to see him before he died. Although past 40 and overage, I still faced obstacles and regulations that prevented me from going home or getting a transfer. No full colonel or one-star general would sign papers allowing me to go back to the states for fear that Gen. Clark would be displeased. They worried that the general wanted Lt. Goldblatt to stay there entertaining the troops.

Finally, I got in to see the second in command, another general. Although he couldn't release me from the army, he did make me a courier assigned to deliver a package to Washington and then return. The general also told me that, once I got back to the states, I would have 21 days leave and could use them to see the Red Cross. Possibly, it could retain me there, or perhaps relieve me of further army duty.

The package the general wanted delivered was to his wife in Washington. It consisted of souvenirs Buck and I had collected when we first entered Rome.
Because of the package's weight, I was permitted only 35 more

Life is a game, play to win!

pounds, so there was very little I could take back as my own.

My orders in hand, I managed to board a plane to Casablanca, where I stayed for one day before going on. I couldn't believe all the changes that the inhabitants had undergone in the 20 months since I'd been there. The people were wearing western–style, civilian clothes instead of bed-sheets; automobiles and trucks had replaced the burros and horses. The next morning, I was shipped out on a cargo plane, having the distinction of being its only passenger. I sat fastened in a bucket seat among the cargo of freight all the way to New York.

Although I was delighted when we finally landed, I realized only too well the reason I had put in for my return to the States and for which permission had really been granted. But the first thing I did when I got to New York was to have a glass of milk, something I hadn't tasted for quite a few years. Then I took a train to Washington to complete my courier duties and visit with Joel. Once there, we received an urgent phone call from Chicago. Nathan, just 50 years of age, was dying and had only a few hours to live.

In Chicago, the first thing I did after checking into the Drake Hotel was drive out to Nathan's home in Wilmette. I could sense a morbid difference. Not too long before, the house had been an ostentatious symbol of drive and mastery. Now, it presented a pitiful scene. Its grandeur had become a mere hour-glass; the sands of my brother's time were rushing to the bottom.

I kissed and hugged him and then stepped back in shock. Except for his grotesquely bloated belly, he was a skeleton. When he raised his arm, the wristwatch he wore fell to his armpit. His first words, "What! No Purple Heart medal!" He seemed disappointed at the few medals my uniform bore, and

Chapter XIII   Coming Home to New Challenges

that I showed so little wear from army life.

"Did you see the new office I built? Did you see how beautiful I changed the State Street store?"

"No," I replied. "I haven't been to the store yet."

"You have a treat coming. You won't recognize the State Street store. It's so beautiful," he smilingly murmured as though describing a beautiful child.

He had not been told he had cancer. This was a time when that word itself was taboo; to be spoken only as a whisper. Then he said he was getting better and that when they pumped the water from his stomach, as the doctors had been doing, he would be well again. He boasted of how well he had been eating and that he felt fine. He bawled out Maurice in my presence for not getting the right doctors; he blamed them for his lingering illness. It was an ordeal to look at him with his sunken eyes and protruding cheekbones. He weighed no more than 80 pounds. Nathan! Always so quick to dream, to see, to make real! Now, everyone knew the hard, cold, irreversible fact — everyone, that is, except Nathan.

After the funeral and *shivah*, or mourning period, Joel returned to his duties in Washington, and I began taking steps to obtain a discharge from the service.

While in Chicago, I visited the Goldblatt's stores, mingled with most of the employees, and in general began the process of reorienting myself back into active business life. I was astounded by the many changes that had taken place, especially at the State Street store. I also saw the office Nathan had built for himself and that everyone had been talking about. It was immediately adjacent to my own, a 500- square-foot room. That was certainly large enough to accommodate the many meetings I would be holding there with buying and management personnel.

Life is a game, play to win!

I spent the entire month of December reacquainting myself with the general operation.

On the day before Christmas, all the buyers ran a combination birthday (I was 41) and Christmas luncheon party for me. I was pleasantly surprised to see Burt Lancaster there among all my well wishers. He was passing through Chicago on his way to Hollywood, where he intended to crash his way into the movies. He asked me to wish him luck. A few months later, I received an invitation from Mark Hellinger to attend a party and the showing of Burt's first movie, *The Killers*, at the Ambassador West Hotel in Chicago.

Shortly after Christmas, Joel and I decided to go on a vacation before reentering the Goldblatt business. He was already out of the service, and my honorable discharge was to be processed in Florida. We arrived in Miami Beach and checked into the Roney Plaza Hotel, both still in uniform. I was suffering from a bad case of arthritis in the shoulder, and both of us had trouble with our teeth, which we attributed to a bad case of nerves.

One evening, when Joel had gone out on a date and I didn't have one, I joined my old friend Eddie Bragno from Chicago and his girl, Molly Netcher, who was a niece of the family that owned the Boston Store on State Street in Chicago. After Eddie, Molly, and I had dinner, we went up to Eddie's penthouse across from our hotel.

There, I proceeded to drown my loneliness and frustration by getting drunk. Then, when Eddie and Molly went out on the terrace to be alone, I began to feel reckless and foolishly decided to surprise them in the midst of their lovemaking. By climbing out a window and jumping a three–feet span between Eddie's building and the one alongside, I could crawl up the

Chapter XIII   Coming Home to New Challenges

slant, shingle roof overlooking the terrace. I hadn't at the time calculated the risk of the sheer drop from the top of the tall building. And so out I climbed, made the jump, then clawed my way up to where the roof peaked. Straddling it in a strange and uncertain victory pose, I surprised the amorous couple right out of their skins!

Eddie, benumbed beyond words, became terribly fearful of my dangerous predicament and began slowly to caution me down. Quickly coming to my senses, I realized the danger in which I found myself. Still high up on the roof, I became petrified and at first froze beyond even hearing him. Knowing it was do–or–die, I carefully inched my way down, rejumped the abyss between the two buildings, and made my way back through the window, safe at last and much more sober than when I started.

# # #

As soon as that vacation was over, I found myself back on the job at the Goldblatt Bros. department stores. It was 1945, the year we created a radio program called "Let's Have Fun!" which was broadcast over WGN from the State Street store and starred Jimmie Costello.

The weeks and months of this dramatic year were alive with happenings and events, both within and outside the company. For Goldblatt's it was as if time were compressed. The relocation of administrative offices, new systems, changed buying policies and relations with vendors, amplified recognition of prime vendors, all were significant to the new operation being fashioned, we hoped, to suit the future.

Outside the company, rapid events throughout the world conveyed startling promise that a new era was beginning. On

April 12, the nation and the world mourned the death of President Franklin D. Roosevelt. April 30, Adolph Hitler committed suicide; eight days later all German resistance ceased. In this same month, Goering and Himmler were seized; both later committed suicide. As Germany collapsed, Benito Mussolini was tried in summary court martial and shot. On August 6, the United States dropped the first atom bomb on Hiroshima, inflicting a toll of 130,000 killed or injured; the second bomb fell on Nagasaki on August 9. On August 14, Japan accepted unconditional surrender.

Now, the postwar period, too, was plagued with severe merchandise shortages, as well as personnel unavailability. Price and quality controls were rigidly in force, and material for store remodeling was scarce.

Army surplus goods began to become available, and we joined in the mad scramble to get our share — and more! We bought 10,000 army blankets, which were a sellout in only 10 days at $5.00 each. All sorts of merchandise crossed our path, even two–and–a–half–ton army surplus trucks. We waged a price war with Mandel Bros. promoting them; our price was $1,900 each!

I continued to regard Sears as our foremost competitor, and a model of sorts. I continued to read and study its catalogue like the merchandising bible it was. I had already added bicycles, sporting goods, hardware, electrical needs, auto accessories, and more to the Goldblatt's family of hard–line categories, which enabled us to compete with Sears, and with Ward's, too.

With postwar scarcity still rampant, especially in hard–line big–ticket items, I couldn't help but notice that Sears was consistently advertising an electric motor at

Chapter XIII   Coming Home to New Challenges

$24.95. As a result, I instructed our buyer, Sy Fingold, to add this item in the hardware and electrical departments. His reaction was "It can't be done!" because Sears bought the item in large quantities direct from the manufacturer. He contended that Goldblatt's, buying five to 10 such motors, would have to pay more than $15 each and, therefore, could not compete with Sears price. Besides, the item was scarce and couldn't be had anyway.

Nevertheless, I ordered him to buy 20 motors from Sears itself at the retail price of $24.95, then to advertise them for $18.99, below the price he had paid. Sy was confounded! "How can I do that! I'll lose money. Besides, Goldblatt's hasn't even the reputation for selling motors and my department will be stuck with them!" he said.

I replied, "How can you lose money if the customer won't buy them from us! Besides, were you to sell them out, you can only lose $120 in all. Furthermore, if that were to happen, we could know we could sell them and you would be able to buy then in hundred–unit quantities and perhaps, then only pay a dollar or two more then Sears pays for them, in which case we would sell them for one dollar less then Sears and make a small profit. We would continue that way until we develop a real business on the item. Then too, if the customer won't buy them, we would advertise them at still a lower price until they're sold out." Fingold listened patiently to my harangue, then went out and did what I asked.

He bought the motors from Sears, advertised them at $18.99, and sold out in two days. Thereafter, Goldblatt's purchased the motors direct from the manufacturer in hundred–unit quantities, sold them through the ads at one dollar less than Sears, and made a small profit. It was the lesson I had learned earlier with Firestone tires and other products.

#

These experiences became the principle I applied to a variety of hard–line items and by which I was able to develop a business in items that other competitive department stores like Field's, Mandel Bros., and Carson, Pirie, Scott didn't even carry.

Then, in later years, I felt perhaps this principle wasn't that smart after all. Actually, what I learned is that it wasn't a universal rule. On the one hand, I felt that if I might apply the practice to apparel, our profits might be greater and solid growth in the apparel categories would follow. Yet, I remembered only too well the bad experience Nathan had in 1937 when he tried to compete with Marshall Field selling their identical $100 dresses at the Goldblatt's price of $69 dollars. We realized then that, although the idea may have been good, Goldblatt's had neither the patience nor the guts to stick with it. So I came to realize developing a fashion line was unlike hard lines.

Goldblatt's had always been saddled with a handicap in trying to develop fashion business. Unlike hard goods manufacturers, the fashion vendors would not sell to us, price cutters that we were. Another glaring difference was the very nature of the two: hard–line items remained basic for years; styles changed rapidly in fashion apparel.

In this situation, I likened Goldblatt's to the musician with the bass fiddle while his competition plays the harmonica. While we lugged around a large and cumbersome instrument to make our merchandising music, the competition carried the little harmonica — all it needed to perform — in its pocket. In other words, we always had to work that much harder for a "tune" in the hard lines we were known; in apparel, the margin of profit was greater, thus its tune sweeter and easier to come by. Accordingly, Goldblatt's had to produce more sales per square foot, because we were producing a smaller percent of profit than our competitors.

It was all a huge education process. We were educating the merchandisers, who would by their actions educate vendors as to our integrity and reliability as a company. I held many meetings with both the buying and management personnel, talking all the time along the same theme: buying the future with the present. I used only scant notes, never speaking from a fully written preparation. My objective was to excite the audience of several hundred buyers and managers, to instill each and every one of them a fierce sense of wantmanship, both individually and as a combined force. I was their coach, and they, the players!

For what the meetings accomplished, I was proud. By filming or recording, then studying them, I was able to develop subsequent speeches and further define future goals.

Every year, just before the beginning of the New Year, I called what I perceived to be the most important such meeting of the year. I made then what I called the "state of the union" address to some 300 company executives. Freely, with all of them as partners, I proceeded to share as much information as I had about the business, our direction and goals, the hurdles and pitfalls, too. My manner of delivery was natural, earnest, and animated. I waved my arms, paced, and thrust my first into my palm to drive my points home. I was ever so aware that I would not be alongside these wonderful people when they perform at their jobs, that they must know as I know, feel as I feel, and *do* as the goals I defined required. I philosophized with stories and sprinkled them with quips; I made them laugh. I paid tribute to the feats they had performed and to those who had participated in such performance; I expressed my faith in their surmounting the challenges ahead.

Never, in reviewing the past year, did I cite the "bad" without first elaborating on the "good." I outlined the budgets and plans for the year ahead and I prevailed upon them to recognize that the very nature of accomplishment — in any enterprise — was the almighty report card, the final result from the effort they apply in achieving plan!

Then, with all the sincerity I could muster, I saved a special part of my speech to glorify the people–power of the firm as being its secret weapon, the strength the competition did not have. With their power to want and thereby to actually achieve, only with their unique and outstanding "wantsmanship," did they transcend mediocrity into genuine ownership complex. "You, therefore, are the strength of what we are and what we are about to become! For this, I am indescribably grateful!"

# # #

During the war, while Joel was assigned to army quartermaster in Washington, he met a man who had invented a ballpoint pen and who sought after Joel to back him in its marketing. Joel turned the offer down, but did refer the inventor to his friend and mine, Milton Reynolds. Milt went on to develop and produce the radically innovative ballpoint pen and promoted it exclusively at Gimble Bros. in New York and at Goldblatt's in Chicago at $12.50. Sales of the Reynold's ballpoint pen developed into millions of dollars.

So we were still having fun as merchants, but after the

Chapter XIII Coming Home to New Challenges

war I realized that we were not only a thriving operation but a big business. Thus some new management techniques were in order. Nathan was gone, so there were now three brothers running the company. Some of the disagreements among us that surfaced during the 1930s had left Joel wondering whether he wanted to return, but we managed to work out an arrangement all three of us could live with. Maurice was chairman of the board; Joe was president and chiefly responsible for operations. I became executive vice president and general merchandise manager, as well as secretary and treasurer. We had become a public company in 1928, with Maurice and Nathan owning 50 percent of the stock. In 1945, our nine-member board of directors included Nathan's wife Frances, Abe Pritzker, as well as Joel, Maurice, and myself. We had 11 stores and around 2,000 employees. Though we had gone beyond being the store where hard-working greenhorn immigrants could count on getting a job, we were still known as a good place to work.

Our phenomenal growth during the 1930s — we nearly tripled in size — was due in great part to the extraordinary energy and loyalty of our employees. Knowing that our continued strength and growth would be dependent upon them as well, I made it my business to be responsive to employees and to motivate them on every occasion. To do this, we had frequent meetings, both to share information and to sustain spirit.

On one such occasion, I called everyone's attention to the untapped strength, knowledge, and skill that lies dormant within each of us. I urged their own self-awareness of potential capabilities for true professional, if not extraordinary, performance. To demonstrate my point, I used one of my old hypnosis tricks. If I were to ask any one of them to place his or her ankles on the arm of one chair and the back of their neck on the arm of another chair and thus be suspended with nothing in support of the center, and if I were to stand with my full weight on their midsection, they would probably say that it couldn't be done!

Yet, I told them I performed this many times through hypnosis. I realized that the analogy to hypnotism as an object lessen was far-fetched, but so was the very concept of "hidden" potential. I pressed on, the experience was a real one. And just as real was my point: that anyone could do it, but didn't know they could do it!

By the time I concluded this talk, I suspect the audience was divided into three schools of thought. To some it was a fun topic beyond full comprehension; to others, it provoked thinking in terms of true personal potential; and to still others, it represented a new and vibrant opportunity to search their inner drive and separate and evaluate their surface tools from the unexplored and latent ones, and then to begin to use them.

It was the latter two groups that I had hoped to reach; if they numbered many of our employees, all the better. But, even if I had managed only to expand the horizons of, let's say, two buyers, one merchandise manager, and one member of management, I may have significantly opened up daring new potential that, hopefully, could influence the entire company.

At my combination birthday and Christmas party a year later, those very same people presented me with an Hawaiian steel guitar. Their birthday card read: "Since you say you can do anything a professional can do, we would like to see you play this Hawaiian guitar for us on your birthday next Christmas." I accepted the challenge.

I immediately began to take lessons and practiced hard. Fairly soon, I had learned to play. Eventually I played well

Chapter XIII *Coming Home to New Challenges*

enough so that the following year at a similar party, I played six numbers in a duet with the talented and popular orchestra leader Lou Breeze. I strummed away on my Hawaiian steel guitar, and he, on his dazzling banjo. I hoped I had thus proven my theory. Anyway, a new talent in the company was uncovered, and we all enjoyed letting our hair down.

#

Viewing these first postwar years as a springboard to Goldblatt's future, I issued a steady flow of bulletins to our staff. I wanted to keep everyone posted as to my thinking and alert to the standards and requirements of employee performance. I knew full well that the scene of operations where we would succeed or fail was at the store level, more particularly on the selling floor. I made it a practice to visit all 15 stores during daytime hours and evenings, too, on the three nights we were open. I worked hard and enjoyed every moment of it, but I left myself little time for diversion.

I've always maintained that the total is no better or worse then its parts, and that in order to improve the bottom line, the profits, it is necessary to consider each individual department and put measures into effect for their improvement. Further, I advocated doing likewise with each classification within a department. We would break down the historical record for every phase of its operation: sales, margin of profit, sales per square foot, markdowns, stock turns, and more. We would evaluate the extent to which each contributed to the department's total operation. Thus we did, and the results of this study became the foundation for our future growth.

Goldblatt's success was also making it increasingly possible for these once greenhorn merchants to return something to the society that provided our success. Back in 1936, the members of the Goldblatt family had established the Goldblatt Trust Foundation, and 10 years later, the trust gave one million dollars to the University of Chicago. The grant's purpose was to establish the Nathan Goldblatt Memorial as a center of an extensive program for cancer treatment and research. At the time, this was the only university–based hospital in the country whose entire staff was engaged exclusively in cancer treatment and research. Maurice, no longer actively involved with the company, spent a great deal of his time building this facility.

Goldblatt employees also supported this cause, and in April 1947, they established the Nathan Goldblatt Cancer Research Fund. Employees of our Milwaukee Avenue store in Logan Square started this off by raising $600. In the years that followed, employees throughout the stores, the warehouses and offices alike, raised over two million dollars completely on their own, independent of any company assistance. This money was donated to several hospitals for research into the detection of cancer. Goldblatt's thereby became the only department store organization in the country whose employees raised money on their own to support cancer research.

# # #

Despite hard work and good works, we still managed to enjoy ourselves. In the late 1940s the "Let's Have Fun" radio show, emanating from the State Street store's eighth floor, achieved its peak of popularity. As Chicago was the major transfer point for train travelers at the time, which frequently meant delays and layovers, several Hollywood stars had time available to come on as

Chapter XIII   Coming Home to New Challenges

show guests. Among the first to appear was Eddie Fisher, passing through town on his honeymoon with Debbie Reynolds. Walt Schwimmer, a noted Chicago producer at the time, produced these shows for us, and they were a hit. More than 70 stage and screen celebrities visited Goldblatt's in 1947, including such famous starts as Joe E. Brown, Lauritz Melchior, Xaviar Cugat, and Roy Rogers to name a few. We even flew in the whole cast of *Carousel* for appearance at the Hammond store and that of *The Red Mill* to perform at the Gary store.

Goldblatt's continued to be the competitors' menace it always had been. We still advertised the most–wanted, everyday items at and below cost as leaders to build customer traffic. This intensified on the important holidays, when we would feature a few prime holiday items at prices below cost, thereby undercutting all our competition. The years hadn't changed this promotional philosophy. We still offered turkeys at Thanksgiving, eggs for six cents per dozen at Eastertime, plus chocolate–covered marshmallow eggs, ham, and jelly bird eggs. At Christmas, we had live trees at one dollar each. There were geranium plants for Mother's Day, American Flags on Memorial Day, noise makers for New Year's, and candy corn on Halloween — unheard of values that screamed "Only at Goldblatt's!" all through the year.

Goldblatt's was still the innovator. The years hadn't altered the fact that we were into classifications of merchandise that other department stores didn't even carry. There were, for example, our landmark pet department with its entire live menagerie, and complete departments of liquor, hardware, auto accessories, and horticulture, to name just a few.

Unfortunately, it became necessary for me to make some drastic personnel changes for the sake of adhering to our vendor relations policy, through which we promised not to cut prices on certain nationally branded items. Though we still regarded ourselves as maverick merchants, we had become part of the retailing establishment and we had to adhere to its practices. In other areas, the rules were changing and we had to change along with them. Most of our buyers went along with these new procedures, but some found it difficult to follow the new rules. While the majority dealt fairly and honestly with our vendors, there were a few who persisted in taking advantage of them by not living up to promises or resorting to the chiseling sometimes practiced in years past. The vendors, though, could be fooled only once. They would learn to prepare themselves for the buyer's next visit and be ready for him. Typical was a furniture buyer who, no matter what price the vendor quoted, would not place his order unless the price was chiseled down. Consequently, and in self-defense, the vendor would raise the price higher than that at which he sold his goods to other stores, then he let himself be bargained with to a price he had preselected and close the sale. Other buyers persisted in buying substandard goods, contrary to policy.

  One day when a carload of five-drawer bachelor chests arrived at the dock, the buyer promptly phoned the manufacturer in North Carolina, telling him he was returning the entire shipment because the chests were damaged. He added that he would refuse to accept the shipment unless he could get 50 percent off the price the order called for. Hence, the manufacturer, figuring it would cost him more to have the goods returned and believing, besides, that the furniture had actually been damaged in transit, agreed to the reduction.

  Upon learning of this, I went directly to the loading dock myself and inspected the furniture personally. The chests were slightly warped, but the purchase order itself had specified an imperfect condition. The purchase price was cheap, and I saw why, but the overriding fact was that the chests were not of the quality standard Goldblatt's should sell in the first place.

I was very disturbed at this blatant disregard of policy and chose the only course left open to me. I had the buyer phone the vendor to tell him that Goldblatt's would accept the full carload, that it had, in fact, arrived exactly as the purchase order specified. Further, we would pay the full price and not deduct the 50 percent off the bill. I told the buyer that the merchandise must be signed at the stores openly stating that the price was low because the chests were damaged. They were to be inspected by the customer and sold "as is."

But I could not permit the perpetuation of this disease in the company. I had to fire the buyer, who had been an employee for 30 years, and thereby serve notice to the rest of the buying division that this practice wouldn't be tolerated. Nevertheless, to guard against their overreaction, I preached that it is not wrong to negotiate a price and that it was right to buy at the lowest price possible. What was wrong was sacrificing quality for price; certainly, they didn't have to cheat to make a good buy.

I felt the meetings I had with the buying and management personnel held special meaning for three reasons: (1) this brash company of greenhorn immigrants had metamorphosed into a major establishment and we had to adopt new ways of doing business; (2) as we moved forward, it was important to detail our goals, budgets, and perspectives as I saw them; and (3) the staff looked forward to this communication with management, because it helped them understand the developing power and scope of the company. The meetings also provided an opportunity for them to ask questions and make comments.

My "state of the union" talk in 1947 was a good indication of how far the store had come since our days on Chicago Avenue, and I'm including it in full below. For this meeting, we had around 300 employees gathered in the auditorium of the State Street store. Power and scope were the twin themes of my talk.

> It has been said with more truth than humor that Goldblatt's is a place where anything can happen and usually does. Over the 1947 year, Goldblatt's derived and inspired its share of excitement, color, and human interest.
>
> In our mail orders, we actually filled and shipped Jeep motors to North Africa, fruitcake to China, an ash can to Norway, and a 10-pound loaf of pumpernickel bread to Nova Scotia. Our Chicago Avenue store gave a big party for GI war brides from all over the world and in so doing provided them their first official welcome to their new homeland. We leased West Madison and Crawford as a new Goldblatt's store site, and we opened the most modern warehouse in the country.
>
> Yes, Goldblatt's had a finger in every pie. As a matter of fact, we taught 2,000 women how to bake a pie and 3,000 women how to can peaches. We further looked after the housewives' interest when 40,000 diligent hens laid 6,000,000 eggs for Goldblatt's customers, and 100,000

Chapter XIII Coming Home to New Challenges

corn–fed pigs supplied tender, succulent ham for our meat departments.

Goldblatt's furnished 8,500 wedding rings to newlyweds and more than 190,000 diapers for newborns. If you enjoy statistics, 1,000,000 gallons of Goldblatt's brand motor oil has gone into keeping our customers' cars on the road. We sold 300,000 work shirts, approximately 1,000,000 handkerchiefs, and 4,720 diamond rings. Goldblatt's has given the "new look" in fashion powerful impetus by staging more than 150 fashion shows and style demonstrations. Our competition had publicly stated in a retail article that Goldblatt's was responsible for the big sales spurt in television sets and you'd be interested to know that there are 12,000 TV sets now in operation in Chicago, as against 4,000 a year ago.

Yes, Goldblatt's did its bit to keep the wheels of industry turning. We sold 2,000,000 yards of dress goods, more than enough to stretch from Chicago to New York. Modestly, we can lay claim to having made 98,000 women happy with Valentine gifts purchased at Goldblatt's. We sent 69,000 moppets back to school outfitted in our clothes, and 2,500 of them were entertained Saturday mornings with thriller–diller movies right in this auditorium.

We staged a fashion show for the blind, held Armistice Day services for the American Legion, "preached" temperance via a movie shown in our Liquor Shop, and even had such live animals on

Life is a game, play to win!

our premises as muskrats, deer, pigs, calves, and chickens.

Hungry customers devoured 500,000 Goldblatt's doughnuts, 1,300,000 hot dogs, 2,000,000 loves of bread, 2,000,000 pounds of cheese, 500,000 layer cakes -- and at Thanksgiving, we sold 25,000 turkeys.

You would hardly say we're small potatoes!

To publicize our Food Show last February, Catherine Fellmath, famous woman athlete, rode astride a steer down State Street; to open our Carnival Sale, we had a parade complete with cowboys and Indians!

1947 was also the year we averted a strike by our employees and welcomed back refrigerators, washers, stoves, and ironers to our appliance department; and, incidentally, we set a pattern for the country in the promotion of Thor gladirons. We staged the most sensational housewares show in America in January 1947, and the young lady who was our disc jockey on the selling floor at that time, the much-talked-about hidden voice in washers and lamps, now has her own network show.

More than once we've been given proof that our customers really like us. One man recently wrote us that the auto battery he had bought from Goldblatt's seven years ago gave him spectacular service, that it never needed recharging and was still going strong. Another man came into our Broadway store and raved about the blankets we had on sale. At first we were flattered. "I'll take seven dozen!" he said, admiring our offering.

"Seven dozen!" exclaimed the salesclerk. "Do you need that many for your family?"

"No," said the customer, "I need that many for my horses. I'm a veterinarian, and I can use them when I deliver colts."

Speaking of salespeople, a blond young woman from our 47th Street store won three city beauty contests and may soon be Hollywood bound. At 91st Street, an employee who was kind to an elderly customer was left $15,000 in her will. And our State Street Santa Claus was given a Benrus watch and an award for heroism on the "Kate Smith Hour" for leading out children in the December 20th State Street store fire. Oh, yes, we had a fire, but we also hung up a city record for emptying the building in 10 minutes without a single casualty, and were open for business again in 45 minutes.

At Christmastime, half a million people gazed with rapt attention at our Christmas mystery window, with its two santas and two dwarfs, and the mystery was solved by Hannibal Cobb in a two-page spread in *Look* magazine.

Goldblatt's opened more than 40,000 new credit accounts in 1947 and found on its roster such fascinating new names as Geraldine Turnipseed, Terlic Toliver, and

Life is a game, play to win!

Nathaniel Tootle. And even the law of coincidence works hard at Goldblatt's. We recently had two mail orders from an Anne Trickle and a Mrs. Floody who live on Wetty Street.

In advertising, we used over 10,000,000 lines of advertising in metro and local papers and published 800 pages of circulars, with a combined circulation of over 20,000,000.

Our men's furnishings department boosted masculine morale with the sale of 500,000 ties and 250,000 men's shirts, even in a year when shirts were hard to get.

We raised funds for La Rabida, the Community Chest, the Red Cross, and other major charities, and we furthered another kind of uplift — the sale of 150,000 brassieres!

On our "Let's Have Fun" radio show, 2,400 contestants vied with one another for the privilege of having pies thrown in their faces and bottles of seltzer water squirted down their necks. We gave away $20,000 worth of prizes on this show and, in our Mrs. Quarter Million Contest, turned away 2,600 women from our already jam-packed auditorium. This was the year we increased our listening audience from one and a half to two million, and we plugged 210 national brands on our airways.

This was the year, too, of flying saucers and you may remember we dropped our own flying discs from a plane and almost dropped our advertising controller from the plane in the process.

Chapter XIII *Coming Home to New Challenges*

We entertained 3,500 club women in our Home Service Center and played host to more then 3,700 teenagers at our Saturday Teens and Tunes Club. We took the show out to eight youth canteens and helped establish Goldblatt's as a youth center. And when the mercury soared to a hundred degrees, we passed out 120 gallons of ice-cold lemonade to our faithful employees.

We've been successful with our Unit Control system, but there are some things you can't control. Five percent of our female employees left us last year to become mothers.

We dispensed 7,200 aspirins to our employees, including executives; looked after 39 confused customers who persisted in going up the down escalator; and bailed out of jail the driver of our loud-speaker truck who had been booked for disturbing the peace. That was when we were conducting sidewalk interviews on the Star Sale. And our china department received a long letter ordering a set of dishes that began, "Dear Goldblatt's: Send me a set of your $9.98 dishes. I hope they don't break easy. I am a widower and having a terrible time raising my five children alone . . ." When we finished the letter, we were a little undecided as to whether to send him a new set of dishes or a new wife!

Yes, everything happens at Goldblatt's. But the one thing that happens the most is the ringing of the cash register. And the one thing that both our friends and our enemies comment on is that in this organization there abounds a surging, striving, reach-the-goal-or-bust spirit that galvanizes everybody into action. We're certainly on our way! We're going places, and the going is great!

#

Mr. Irwin Lowell, who had been in the operating end of the company for many years, was promoted to manager of Goldblatt's New York buying office soon after the end of the war. One day I asked him to go over to Macy's and buy every hot-selling item it had and send them to me in Chicago, so I could show them and discuss their selling potential with our buyers. He replied, "Louis, how can I do this; how am I to know which item is hot and top-selling when I'm not a merchant? I've been in operations these many years and was concerned only with the holding down of expenses. I know nothing about merchandise."

"It's easy to do," I said. "You don't have to know anything about merchandise. All you have to do is to put a blindfold over your eyes and walk through Macy's. Whenever you bump into a crowd of customers, take off the blindfold and buy the item the crowd is buying and send it off to me."

Irwin got the point, and shortly all sorts of bargain items were dispatched back to Chicago.

For most of my life, all my efforts and strength had been directed toward motivating, promoting, and staging sales events in a theatrical fashion. I always remembered, though, that I could do none of this by myself. It takes a team to perform teamwork, and I played the roll of coach. My job was to motivate people into "wantmanship" and to plant the seeds of promotion

Chapter XIII   Coming Home to New Challenges

in producing more sales.

Business to me was a game, a challenge, and I loved it. I was once asked, "Louis, if you could wake up in the morning and find you could go any place in the world, have anything you want, do what you like, choose your pleasure, what would you do?"

I answered, "I would go to work!"

At another time, I was asked, "Why do you work so hard? You don't need all that money; you can't take it with you."

I answered, "I'm not working, I'm playing and making money is the least of my ambitions. I can't help it if I'm making money by playing and doing what I love to do."

That zest for selling I'd had as a youth, which compelled me to run across town to pick up a B.B. gun for a customer or to hurdle the display tables in our Chicago Avenue store, hadn't left me. I was nearly three times as old as I'd been then and running a $100 million company, but I still loved to sell and to encourage other to do so, too.

In 1948, for the first time in its history, Goldblatt's rang up more than one million dollars in sales in a single day. The occasion was what had originally been known as the Nathan Goldblatt Day Sale, but was changed to the Star Sale of the Year after Nathan died. That year, the immediate postwar shortages being a thing of the past, a contest was held among all 15 stores. The store increasing its sales over the previous year by the largest percentage would win a banquet dinner, entertainment, and dance for all its employees. To further the Star Sale idea, the winning-store manager would be presented with a 20-inch tall, 14 karat, gold-plated statuette with his name inscribed on its base. We called the awards Nathan's and fashioned the entire affair and presentations after the famous

Hollywood Oscar nights. All of the company's top management was invited, and all the guests were encouraged to bring along a guest of their own.

A smaller version of the Nathan statuette was awarded to the one department manager for each store whose sales had increased by the largest percentage in that store. This enormous party was held at the Sheraton Hotel, and among the entertainers were Joe E. Bishop, the Grey Sisters, and the Ben Sharp's orchestra. The event was staged every year thereafter, with changes that evolved in response to the chain's growth.

Starting eight weeks prior to the sale itself, I held luncheon meetings in my office for 30 department managers at a time, representing all the stores in the chain. At these gatherings, the managers would put on skits involving customer situations that demonstrated extra–smart selling of extra–value offers. Other skits would reenact delightfully amusing episodes depicting enthusiasm, general aggressiveness, and boundless determination to bring glory to their department and store. These sessions culminated in their pledging daring sales budgets to me, vying at the same time with one another by showing up the "pikers" who weren't enthusiastic enough in their planned sales. Each left the meeting convinced that his or her store would win!

The buyers, too, came to meetings to show their samples of "great" buys they had made, so they could offer "sensational" bargains. Though we had become a major chain of stores, the enthusiasm to excel, to lead, to win still distinguished Goldblatt's. Great values were still the keynote! And naturally, the values were greater than we had ever had before, and greater, by far, than the competitions.

So the race was on for the Star Sale of 1948. Buyers

Chapter XIII   Coming Home to New Challenges

pleaded, even fought, for extra department space, for merchandise outposts, for "booth" tables. They competed for better, cleverer signs. They even stole the next fellow's sign holders as I had done back in the days of getting started in this business.

For the Star Sale, I worked a six and a half day week, providing an example for many middle and top management employees. I addressed everyone by their first name and they called me Louis or Lou. And this Star Sale produced in the Goldblatt's tradition.

#

We had always moved with the times in terms of merchandising opportunities, and shortly after the war, I began to foresee the oncoming explosion in the television business. Epoch changes in the manufacturing, retailing, and consumer market for this new item prompted my determination that Goldblatt's would be dominant in selling them. So one day, I gathered together all employees of the radio and television departments and not only described my vision of the years ahead but outlined plans for a target of $10 million per year in this business within the next five years. I was bent on Goldblatt's becoming the largest retailer and headquarters of television selling in all Chicago.

I lost no time shopping the market, visiting TV manufacturers from coast to coast. Many smaller ones had been bootleggers during Prohibition, and with its repeal began first to manufacture radios, then later TVs. As opportunists, they recognized that the consumer demand for nationally branded TVs far exceeded the supply, and they began to make unknown or private brands.

Life is a game, play to win!

Therein I saw opportunity and proceeded to create Goldblatt's own private brand, naming it Vision-Master. By this time, Goldblatt's had been accepted as a seller of big-ticket items in which we had developed our own brands, such as Freeze-Master refrigerators, Cook-Master stoves, Stitch-Master sewing machines, and others that competed with brands from Sears and Ward's. I knew that in producing our own private brand we would have to undersell the national brands by at least $100, but thereby we would expand the market to include the masses.

I went about purchasing the various component parts from different manufacturers: tuners from one source, chassis from another, and cabinets from still another. Then I had them all shipped to the one manufacturer whom I had contracted with to assemble several thousand sets at a time. They did it at a cost that enabled us to undersell the national brands by $100 and still make a profit.

The program had huge implications for our future and required support and steadfastness from every corner of our organization. The years rolled rapidly by, and in 1948, televisions sets produced sales of $1.5 million for Goldblatt's and in 1949, $4 million. By 1952, the $10 million mark had been achieved, and Goldblatt's became Chicago's largest TV retailer.

#

The events of 1949 flew by with Europe and the Middle East reorganizing and much of Asia still in upheaval. The year before, Britain had granted de facto recognition to the new state of Israel. West Germany was established as a nation when the United States, British, and French occupation zones

Chapter XIII   Coming Home to New Challenges

were transferred to German control; Konrad Adenauer, twice imprisoned by the Nazis, became the first chancellor of West Germany. The North Atlantic Treaty Organization was founded, and the next year the world learned that the Soviet Union had developed its own atomic bomb. The Chinese communists captured Chungking, forcing the Nationalist government's eventual move to Taiwan. A U.S. superfortress aircraft, the *Lucky II*, landed in Fort Worth after completing the first non-stop flight around the world. Mildred E. Gillars, the notorious "Axis Sally" of World War II infamy, was convicted of treason for her wartime broadcasts on the side of the Nazis. She was fined $10,000 and sentenced to 10 to 30 years, of which she served 12, in a prison in Alderson, West Virginia.

In May of that year, I sent a 25th wedding anniversary greeting to Gen. Mark Clark, then Sixth Army commander stationed at the Presidio in San Francisco. I still have the nice note I got in response. A few years later, I saw the general again when he came to Chicago for a reunion celebration. Our family lost another member in 1949 when my sister Anna Handelsman died at age 60. There were still six of us, and I was the only one who hadn't yet married. Two years later, I found myself the lone bachelor of the Four Must Get Theirs as well, when in 1951 Buck married a pretty girl named Lil who worked for Goldblatt's as a lingerie buyer. Now it was two down and one *not* to go. (Eddie Simon had left the group long ago, marrying and moving to California.) I continued to live at the Drake as sort of a reaffirmation of my commitment never to marry! "Why not?" people were almost sure to ask; to which I was just as sure to reply, "Why buy the book when the public libraries are full of them!"

When Joel and Lynn had married, it no longer made

sense for him and me to maintain our joint bank account. Convinced that my own bachelorhood was absolutely an indestructible condition, I said to Joel one day, "I don't need and have no use for money now. I could never spend what I have in my bank account. You're raising a family and can use the money. I'd like to give it all to you, and hope you'll accept it."

"Don't be a fool," Joel replied. "There will come a time you'll need it. Besides, I will not accept it; but thanks anyway." In later years, I realized how right he was. I had been a fool to make the offer.

In the early 1950s, supermarkets were on a rampage, obliterating mom and pop grocery stores everywhere. Goldblatt's, too, found it difficult to compete with them, and so we discontinued our food operation.

Chapter XIII   Coming Home to New Challenges

Brother Nathan had died of cancer in 1944, which brought Joel and I back into the store shortly before war's end. Here Maurice, myself, and Joel pose at a company function a few years later. Though we were all smiles here, our public faces were increasingly having to mask private differences.

The success of our stores attracted a great deal of national attention, from celebrities as well as shoppers. In 1946, comedian Sid Caesar was a guest; before getting dressed up, we'd gone for a swim in Lake Michigan.

Life is a game, play to win!

I'd met comedian Joe E. Broen during the war and attracted him to participate in several store promotions after that. Here he acts up with an actress (whose name, alas, I can no longer recall) playing ditzy cowgirl.

Goldblatt's also developed homegrown talent for some of our promotions. Here two of our buyers in drag help rouse others' enthusiasm for the 1951 Star Sale during a meeting in my office.

Chapter XIV
Goldblatt's Goes Establishment

In March of 1951, I was especially gratified to be the honoree at a dinner sponsored by many of the national brand manufacturers with whom Goldblatt's did business. At that time, I was presented with a large bronze plaque, upon which all the represented brand names had been inscribed. As I stepped up and gazed out into the assemblage of vendors, I could not help but think back to more than a dozen years earlier, in the late 1930s the days when I realized we had to change our thinking, our tactics and become a part of the nationwide name–brand community of retailers.

Considering our greenhorn origins, it was a momentous decision at the time. It was also one I made with considerable opposition from Maurice and Nathan, who still saw themselves as immigrant merchants, as outsiders in American retailing. Once that decision was made, we had to climb into respectability. We had to practice integrity in pricing, with our word becoming our bond. Our bad habits had to fall away to good ones. We had to upgrade our quality standards. First, I had to make personal pleas to vendors all around the country and then police our buyers in markets everywhere.

The applause of this audience brought me out of my reverie. Never one to relish the public spotlight, I approached the podium with a clenched fist — I better be sure, darn sure, that I had something to say, the lesson I'd learned as a bar mitzvah boy.

I cannot recall what I did have to say on that occasion, but in May that year, the *Chicago Tribune* invited me to deliver an address before its Second Annual Distribution and Advertising Forum. The talk was later published and distributed in booklet form, and I've restated below, in essence, what I said then. My talk still speaks to many issues faced by retailers and offers historical notes on how retailing has changed in this century. Vendor relations concerns the interrelationships among the supplier, the retailer, and certainly the consumer. At the time this talk was given, name brands were still establishing themselves. Retailing nationwide was about to make the big switch from mainly independent stores selling branded and unbranded merchandise to chain stores selling the same goods in branches all over the country and promoting them in national media. With the introduction of name brands, the manufacturer rather than the retailer became responsible for quality. It was a momentous switch, and Goldblatt's played a part in its happening. The talk was called "Forging the Retail Link" and rereading it 40 years later, I think I did have something to say.

>Forging the retail link has not been completed, but it is in process. There is much toil ahead. It must yet go through a heat blaze of trial and error for the link to be sufficiently pliable. Nevertheless, in the past 25 years, there's been much progress in the relationship between retailer and vendor. Some have already fused their interests. Others have made some progress in doing so, still others hardly have an iron in the fire. But

Chapter XIV Goldblatt's Goes Establishment

the growth of mass distribution we are seeing today is dependent on retailers and vendors being linked in the same chain.

Not so many years ago caveat emptor (let the buyer beware), was the rule. Its implication was that the manufacturer's sole intention was that of selling to the retailer, who, in turn, depended on his salesmanship in selling to the consumer. Today, the successful vendor manufacturers with the *consumer* his sole concern, providing the most serviceable product, the best value for the money. He even engages in research and testing.

Then, with the best possible product, he proceeds to sell it directly to the consumer through national advertising. He even guarantees the consumer's satisfaction! He also labels the product showing contents or ingredients. All this, plus conforming with federal safety and legal requirements of every kind. A number of years ago, determining the quality of grass seed other than by its price was impossible; only a laboratory could reveal the ingredients. Our customers were helpless and had only our word to take for a product's contents, and we could only accept the vendor's word to take for a product's contents. Not so today. It's printed right on the package.

I remember our own crude technique in determining the kind and quality of a simple item like feathers. Today, there's a National Association of Bedding Manufacturers organized by the manufacturers themselves that, among other functions, verifies quality and labeling. This, in turn protects the retailer.

Progress towards educating the consumer through such information shown on products — be they the wool content in a sweater or the chemistry of a vitamin tablet — has contributed toward vendor–retail harmony. And the consumer, knowing thereby what to expect for her money, continues to buy the satisfactory product. Accordingly, the vendor has performed a preselling job; he has "sold," in effect, the product before the retailer buys it. So that, if the product has true value, the consumer will buy — regardless of how the retailer may feel about the item.

The links between the manufacturer and the consumer having thus been forged, the remaining retail link need only be added to complete the interdependent total chain, a chain being no stronger than its weakest link. That weakest link has been the retailer. On the other hand, he is rapidly becoming strong, but now as a distributor! He no longer depends solely on his salesmanship. No longer need he bargain for deals. He need not verify quality. His role becomes that of striving to be a top retail distributor. The old ways of selling have been replaced.

He requires systems that enable merchandise control and trend detection. Buying is performed through information, not by personal whim. He no longer need be a genius. He targets

Chapter XIV Goldblatt's Goes Establishment

being a top distributor by purchasing from top prime resources. As for buying and selling at Goldblatt's, when we buy from top prime resources, we automatically become an important "distributor." Our sales job depends on our support of the vendor's selling programs. We avail ourselves of his national advertising in all the media. We, of course, provide effective display and orient our personnel with all the product information, often including contests and prizes. We are concerned with the long-range potential, with reorders and certainly with customer satisfaction — all for a stronger customer bond.

We must also provide conveniences and service. It follows that our employee teams receive every known benefit and consideration.

As there are prime resources, there are also prime advertising media. We spent $3,250,000 in advertising last year [that would be 1950] in metropolitan, community, suburban, and foreign newspapers, as well as through shopping news, radio, television, billboards, direct mail, and more, 69 percent of which was concentrated in metropolitan prime media. The largest part of that was in the *Chicago Tribune*.

We do not buy linage or pages; we purchase sales return! Our concern is for the lowest possible percentage advertising cost, which we derive from a prime medium, and which in turn, affects our profitable distribution of merchandise.

Since time immemorial, the retailer has asked, "Will we make our day?" It's our measuring rod. If we do no more than a year ago to support a given day, we can only expect to equal the sales figure of a year ago. Now, we confront the challenge with the questions "What did you buy?" and "How much did you buy?" We've even changed the proverb "As Ye Sow, So Shall Ye Reap," to the retail connotation "As Ye Buy, So Shall Ye Sell!"

Some years ago, I launched Goldblatt's vendor relations policy and listed by department and even by item all the vendors with whom we do business. We then began the herculean statistical task of determining our profitability by vendor, even the vendors responsible for our markdowns. We sought to know the advertising cost, the percentage of inventory, square footage devoted to product, stock turn — all by vendor! But most importantly, we wanted to know what percentage of each department's total purchases was made from each vendor.

The process went on to sift out all the vendors that proved to be prime resources, just as we review our buyer's showings periodically. We have certainly come closer to achieving the goals of our vendor relations program over the past several years. At the close of last year, we found that we had purchased merchandise from 8,686 vendors and that only 557 of them, or six and a half percent of the total, accounted for 53 percent of

Chapter XIV Goldblatt's Goes Establishment

our total purchases.

Our objective is to increase the number of prime resources and to reduce the total number of vendors from whom we buy. We have further proven that we took fewer markdowns on merchandise coming from these prime resources. The 557 vendors improved our inventory turnover and were directly responsible for our customers being more pleased and causing less returns. These prime resources produced a large enough profit to offset a multitude of buying mistakes by purchases from thousands of other vendors. I call these resources My First Love possibly because I happen to be a bachelor, and just as a bachelor has a first love among many, so does the retailer.

The layman sees a sales volume of $100 million and envisions our selling thousands of items in quantity. Not true. Actually, there are some items that sell in such huge quantity they make thousands of other items appear to be standing still. Take linens, for example. From a huge variety of classifications, Cannon towels do 31 percent of this department's business. Yet Cannon does not occupy 31 percent of the square footage or account for 31 percent of the markdowns. And the inventory turnover and dollar profit with Cannon towels is far greater, too.

All the more, we don't "sell," we "distribute." Cannon made their towels a preferred product. From laboratory testing to national advertising, they virtually took the customer by the arm and brought her into our store. Then, with display and assortment, we did a top distribution job. All we did was take the customer's money and wrap the package.

These prime resources are the distributor's teacher, and we are the material with which they work. If one does not value the other, they cannot together build a growing business or produce a satisfactory net profit. It is as important that our buyers be respected by the vendor as it is for those same buyers to be so regarded by us, their employer. We purchase the future with the present and a coming success is dependent on what we do today. By building a strong vendor relationship, we will be repaid in the future with growth in our business.

In forging the retail link, it is as important for vendors to know who their retail distributors are as it is for us to know who our vendors are. The vendors hold the advantage in this respect. We do not know the names and addresses of most of our customers. We only know what they buy and when they buy it. The vendor not only knows what he sells and when he sells it, but he knows to whom he sells it.

Therefore, he must be as anxious to sell to top prime retail distributors as we are to buy from top prime resources. He should know if we produce a profit for him and whether we are increasing over a given period. This information is a clue to future sales trends with the retail distributor.

I am confident in the progress being made in forging a strong retail link worthy of its position, placed as it is between the consumer and vendor. Let us, together, strive to make the future even stronger and more harmonious.

The concept of "first loves" continued as part and parcel of the Goldblatt's vendor relations policy, and I asked our buyers to carry the list of these prime resources around with them at all times. This was not only an instrument of good public relations (as our prime vendors knew they were listed in our "first loves" book), but we also found that the purchases from prime vendors increased and our cause moved forward all the more. To my knowledge, no other department store either treated or conceptualized the subject of vendor relations as we did.

In later years, I inaugurated the GVP or Goldblatt's Vendor Partnership. Honoring this, we hosted individual private luncheon meetings; to these came the management of the prime vendors, members of our buying division, and Goldblatt's top management.

The meetings were incredibly productive. First, they gave the groups an opportunity to know and understand each other's mission. Next, they gave us an opportunity to objectively discuss mutual plans, untapped potential, and even problems. Invariably, we would target a new, ambitious, yet highly doable sales goal, then proceed to detail step-by-step implementation of the elements required on both sides of the table to achieve it. The results that generally followed in the form of increased sales were dramatic. Increasingly, the national brand vendors put aside their old vows and began to do business with us.

#

Those days, back in the early 1950s, were when parakeets, or budgies and known by the Chicago consumer as love birds, were popular. As pets they were generally kept a pair to a cage, a male and a female, and the average customer was not even aware that they could be trained to talk and do tricks. The only retailers in Chicago who sold them were pet shops, Woolworth's, and Goldblatt's.

With our cost of $2.50 each, we made a good profit retailing them at $5 to $10, depending on color and general appearance. Goldblatt's bought them from Max Stern, owner of the Hartz Mountain bird food firm, at an average of six per week. Early in 1951, I told Max I would buy a thousand instead of the usual six if he would give me a lower price, as well as pay for a full–page ad in the *Chicago Tribune*. He agreed, but said he would need some time to accumulate such a large quantity.

While it was not a profitable deal for him, he felt that, as a result of the Goldblatt's promotion with its ensuing sales, a strong market for the birds was bound to open nationally. He could then become the biggest distributor for birds and bird food in the country. In the years to follow, that did, indeed, come to pass.

The budgies simply fascinated me, and while Max was still getting the thousand– bird quantity together, I decided to prove for myself that their talent for talking and doing tricks wasn't a myth. I brought a young male back to my apartment at the Drake, intending to better shape the forthcoming ad from my own experience.

I kept the bird in a cage on my dresser, although I let it fly around the place freely. When it wanted to be fed, it would come

Chapter XIV Goldblatt's Goes Establishment

back and go into the cage. "Dink" and I soon became friends, and I was able to train him to talk, although very little, as well as to perform all sorts of tricks, such as to roller skate, push a miniature baby carriage, hoist a thimble full of water to drink, and even perform "magic" tricks. That was, I trained the little fellow to lift a particular playing card that was face down among an entire deck spread across the table; my trick was to slightly turn up the card's corners then, I perfected the trick, making it audience–worthy by asking a guest to pick a card, which I "palmed" or otherwise "forced," and then I would call upon Dink to turn up the card my guest had chosen.

The bird never failed, and when he was totally trained I knew our advertising claims would be legitimate and, in all good conscience, went ahead with the ad stating that parakeets could be trained to talk and were truly loving house pets.

I advertised them at $10 and offered a written guarantee that they could be trained to talk. We had a complete sellout of the thousand birds. Thereafter, Goldblatt's advertised parakeets very often and our parakeet business boomed, although it wasn't long before many department stores began to carry them, too. A number of customers did complain their birds couldn't be trained to talk, but they wanted neither a refund nor an exchange because they had grown so fond of their bird as a pet.

In the meantime, my roommate Dink was growing impossible to live with. He would perch on my shoulder as though he were glued there, bathe in my sink while I shaved, and perch on my dinner plate while I ate. No matter how I tried to trick him in order to escape from my apartment when I had to go out, he would come zooming across the living room and land on my shoulder before I could open the door to get out. When we two bachelors had finally had enough of each other, I gave Dink away to the hotel housemaid. In my own mind, I since often questioned which of us held the other captive. I only knew that, at long last after 10 months, the lone bachelor was free again! Dink may have gone, but there was for me a source of satisfaction that I helped bring the parakeet to the status of a common household pet.

# # #

My newly restored bachelorhood did not last long, though. In January 1952, I met Roberta Pernecky on a blind date and promptly fell in love. Her stage name was Bobbie Richards, and she had won the Chicago Miss Photoflash and Miss National Press Photographer beauty contests and appeared on the "Lucky Strike" television program as a singer. She had worked as a model, singer, and actress, appeared in the movie *Rhubarb*, and was seen in many films, TV commercials, and programs.

After going out with her a few times, I asked her to marry me. She turned me down, arguing that she was Catholic and I was Jewish, that I was about 30 years older than she, and above all, that she wanted to remain single and never marry.

I was determined and wouldn't take no for an answer. I continued to court her, wooing her with greeting cards, notes, phone calls, and even stunts. One midnight I phoned her in Chicago from New York, and when she asked what I was doing at that hour, I told her I was enjoying listening to her voice while eating a banana split. She answered, "I could enjoy a banana split myself if it weren't so late." After we said good night, I phoned Yellow Cab in Chicago and ordered a super banana split to be delivered to her home at once.

It was close to 2 A.M. when the cab driver rang her

Chapter XIV   Goldblatt's Goes Establishment

doorbell and handed her the banana split, along with a loving message from Lou. Although she couldn't help being impressed, her parents and three brothers told her I was crazy.

I persisted in my drive to win her over, and we were finally married on November 12, 1952. We then left for a glorious honeymoon in Hawaii and lived happily ever after — but only after a perplexing, one-in-a-million beginning.

Before leaving for the magical islands, I had contracted a bad cold, was on penicillin, and had been advised to continue the medication when we got there. I planned to do so. But no sooner had we checked into our hotel in Honolulu than the phone in our room rang.

"Hello. Mr. Goldblatt, this is Louis Goldblatt!" The caller with his illogical opener blew my mind. From being startled at first, I quickly settled into believing this was just a honeymoon prank and decided to play along. But it wasn't a prank at all.

"I just got out of jail," the caller continued, "and I want to advise you of some big misunderstandings ahead. Go buy a newspaper and see for yourself; I look just like you. What's more, even our wives look alike. Go buy a paper. You'll see what I mean," he repeated.

No sooner had I hung up than I went down to the lobby, picked up a paper, and sure enough, there it was: a photograph of "Louis Goldblatt," my surprise caller, walking out of jail, no less. The article, a feature story, described his role in some labor-involved prosecution and mentioned Harry Bridges, the well-known union leader. "Okay. Remarkable coincidence and all that, but so what." I amused myself thinking about it while I headed back up to the room.

The very next morning when the hotel nurse didn't

respond to my call to come and give me a penicillin shot, I thought I'd go down for the mail and try reaching her again later. When I got to the desk clerk, I noticed a nurse standing nearby who couldn't help overhear my asking, "The mail, please, for Louis Goldblatt." I could see she took on a look of utter confusion, and I looked straight at her, quietly saying, "I'm Louis Goldblatt from Chicago."

"You're Louis Goldblatt!" she kind of murmured.

I could see a look of profound relief in her face and she went on to explain, "Oh, forgive me, Mr. Goldblatt. I thought you were the notorious Louis Goldblatt." Then she snapped, "Lucky thing! When I thought you were the other one, I wanted to give you poison!"

My life thus being "spared" and our honeymoon back on course, Bobbie and I headed for the enchanting nearby island of Maui. Before we left Chicago, our friend Marshall Field III had asked that we convey his best regards to his good friend, the manager of the hotel where we were staying. We were assured he would take special care of us. Unfortunately, he was off the island at the time. I was somewhat disappointed but nevertheless felt our greetings could wait, and we resumed pursuing the joys of our honeymoon. But, not so fast!

When we sat down to lunch, people asked to change their table. Some even left the dining room. It was the same at every meal. We found ourselves the victims of the most awful service, besides. It was the same story when we went to the beach. Of course, honeymooners normally want to be alone, but this was too much! Everywhere we went, we were treated as though we had the plague.

Finally, at the end of our stay there, when we were checking out, the assistant manager came up to me and said,

Chapter XIV   Goldblatt's Goes Establishment

"Sure was nice to have you with us again, Mr. Goldblatt. I hope everything was satisfactory."

"Again!" I said. "I've never been here before in my life!"

Sheepishly, he inquired, "Oh, Mr. Goldblatt, aren't you associated with Harry Bridges and all that?"

"No, no," I insisted. "I'm Louis Goldblatt from Chicago. From Chicago," I drilled it into him twice.

"Oh, Mr. Goldblatt, such an error. But, that's why everyone has been avoiding you! I'm so very sorry, I . . ."

Sorry! I thought, as we left with indelible memories of the friendly islands of Hawaii. And with all that, our ordeal still wasn't finished!

We went on to Mexico for the second (and final) phase of our honeymoon. Mexico because, when we were still in the planning stage for this trip, Bobbie couldn't quite decide which of the two she preferred the most. It was my decision, therefore, that we "do" them both. It turned out a fortunate decision, too, because in Mexico, we had no "identity crisis," no headlines, and no shunning of the newlyweds.

However, when we got back to Chicago, there it was again! An article in the *Chicago Tribune* with a picture of me, really me this time, but with a full story, including all the sordid details, of the "other" Louis Goldblatt. "How could this happen?" I asked. It was really too much, and here in my own hometown.

Of course, I called the newspaper and it printed a retraction the next day. No more were Bobbie and I to be harassed, and we settled down to being ourselves, finally, without any mix-ups, truly to live happily ever after!

# # #

Life is a game, play to win!

Over all these many years in retailing, I continued to study Sears" merchandising techniques, ever increasing my respect for its catalog. I sent a copy of the 1953 issue to each of our divisional merchandise managers, with an illustration of a huge diamond pasted over the front cover. Because the catalog weighed four pounds, I titled the new cover "The Four Pound Diamond."

It had become a practice of mine to tear pages out of the catalog, sort them by merchandise classification, and send them on to all our buyers. I was relentless in trying to extract the wealth of information these pages contained. This was the subject of many meetings with our buyers, whom I also instructed to visit Sears and report on their findings.

In 1953, Sears produced sales of $3 billion. I devised a method of getting a rough idea of how much business they did per page of items by dividing their sales by the number of their catalog pages. Further, I fine-tuned my estimate. If an item was either pictured in color or occupied a full page, I would conclude that it was a major selling item and all the more profitable.

That year, Goldblatt's, along with many retailers around the country, found itself heavily overstocked. Sales had grown sluggish, expenses were rising, and the competition was keener, by far. This marked the beginning of a new era and unless the retailer would change with the mainstream of the times, he would be doomed to suffer the consequences later. Department stores throughout the country were expanding into chains. Discount stores had come into the marketplace and they, too, were expanding by leaps and bounds.

Goldblatt's ran its annual Star Sale and rang up another record high in sales. Our star values that year were: ladies'

Chapter XIV Goldblatt's Goes Establishment

summer leather play shoes for $1.97 and summer dresses, $5.00; nylon curtains were $4.99; a 92-piece dinner set, $18.88; a two- piece living room furniture set, $139.00; 21-inch console TV with a 21-tube chassis $139.99.

Prices and goods had changed somewhat since the thirties, but Goldblatt's was still into bargains. Other items we sold in that sale were motor oil, a two-gallon can for 74¢; peanuts, 25¢ a pound; six-foot windowshades, 24¢; bedsheets, 99¢; men's workshirts, 99¢; golf balls, 18¢; and parakeets for only $2.99. We would completely install auto engines for $43.88, sell a round robbin sewing machine for $29.99, a foam rubber lounge chair for $39.88, and a box of 50 cigars, $1.49.

Maintaining our competitive balance meant I was constantly busy, promoting aggressively. I also made the time to respond to several speaking invitations, in which I tended to expand on the same theme: the retail link. One of these was an address before the Merchandising Executive Club of Chicago in September 1954; my subject, "The Missing Link." As the talk was an exposition of the development of brand-name retailing in this country and Goldblatt's role in it, as well as an interesting history of how we started in business and how I devised our statistical purchasing and merchandising plan, it is included in an appendix at the end of this book. Readers with a particular interest in retailing may still find it informative and may read it there.

The months of 1954 passed quickly, but sales and profits showed only a slight improvements over the previous year. A price war was in full swing, and price cutting on nationally branded items, mainly minor appliances, took competitive prices to slightly above cost. At times, they were forced lower, causing the discontinuance of the Fair Trade laws. Goldblatt's, like many other stores around the nation, was looking for its particular niche in the post war consumer economy. We knew that many of the ways we were used to doing business — and which had brought us great success — were in need of change. We were searching for a new strategy, for a new niche, an effort that was complicated by the Goldblatt brothers" increasing inability to agree on what that new strategy should be.

Since our marriage, Bobbie had accompanied me on my buying trips, both in and out of the country. On one trip to Paris, I managed to enjoy the sights, temporarily leaving the burdens of the company behind. It happened that we met up with the head of the Taittinger champagne company, Monsieur Claude Taittinger himself. A bachelor, he asked us to join him and his girlfriend one night for dinner and show at a smart Paris nightclub. Patrons there were characteristically greeted by a fellow holding a wine pouch made from a pheasant's belly; holding it high, he would squirt a long stream of wine direct from its tiny spigot into our ridiculously wide–open mouths below.

I was especially frisky that night and longed for an opportunity to pull off a prank. With the wine episode, I'd reached the height of playfulness. I was ready to seize any opportunity to perpetrate hilarity. And I did!

Once inside, I told my three dinner companions to go to their table, that I'd join them in a while. I left, presumably to go to the men's room, but instead I dashed backstage to the entertainer's area. There I quickly located the head man, and in halting English with lots of gestures and mock motions, I was finally able to cross his palm with a $5 bill. That prompted him to hand over a costume, which actually was a long flowing robe affair complete with staff and a beard that was held taut to my face by a rubber band. Yes, I was to play the role of God and

Chapter XIV   Goldblatt's Goes Establishment

the rest of the entertainers were my followers. The scene we were to depict was a bullfighter's funeral procession that God alone appeared to be leading.

I quickly put the costume on and, smothering in billows of beard, stood panting and giggling in the wings. In the meantime, Bobbie, M. Tattinger, and friend, couldn't imagine what had happened to me. When their curiosity had just about turned to worry, on came the act. The processional moved slowly to the center of the floor, majestically led by the Almighty himself.

From behind the beard, I could see concern written all over Bobbie's face. She was looking in the direction I would be coming from, still somewhat watching the act. I, of course, walked as I had been instructed, careful not to get too far ahead of my followers. Then I veered over to the vicinity of their table, coming closer and closer. They all looked at me, uncomfortable at my presumptuousness. I bent forward, now just about face to face with Bobbie. Then, in a quick flash of motion, I stretched my beard on its rubber band, and Bobbie saw that "God" had changed to Louis!

"Oh, my God," she managed to utter, not realizing how right she was. When she recovered, she and our friends broke into hysterical laughter. Good trooper that I was, and with all due reverence, I finished the act. But I never finished making Bobbie laugh every time we recalled the antic. Furthermore, she never once said to me, "Who do you think you are? God?"

Life is a game, play to win!

Though I had long declared I'd never marry, dancing-eyed Roberta Pernecky caught my attention in early 1952, and we were married later that year. Though our wedding, a union between merchant prince and young singer and actress, led to a few raised eyebrows, it's been a remarkably enriching union for over 40 years.

Chapter XIV   Goldblatt's Goes Establishment

Promotions on State Street included winking elvesd marching across the windows and mannequins on a similar track whose clothes were changed as they disappeared behind a curtain. Once, in 1957, I rode on the back of an elephant for a State Street Council promotion.

Life is a game, play to win!

Though Goldblatt's had begun as a price-cutter, by the 1960s when we had grown to a 30 plus-branch store, we were a leading retailer of brand-name goods. Here, I joined Ed Broyhill and other executives of the Broyhill Furniture Company at a Drake Hotel luncheon during the 1960s.

Chapter XV
The Sixth Sense of Retailing

A question I was often asked is what's the most important element in a successful business? I would always answer the question in a single word — manpower! People are the most important factor in any business, but especially in our business. By manpower, I meant our employee team, a very special kind of manpower. Our employees, I always thought, were better than any other company's employees. They had imagination and vision, they were creative, and they had the ability to dream — and then make their dreams come true!

Our annual Star Sale came into being when our employees staged a Nathan Goldblatt Day — the predecessor of Star Sale — as a surprise for the Goldblatt brothers. After that, it became a tradition with an amazing record of achievement. Each year, the employees managed to beat all their past performance records. They were able to do this because they had their hearts in their work and a strong spirit of determination, a spirit I call wantmanship.

By wantmanship I mean an "I will" attitude, a conviction that you could accomplish almost anything by wanting to do it strongly enough. How else could we explain the almost unbelievable record of the Star Sale? It was a promotion originated by employees, and each year that it was held, it shattered previous records through the enthusiasm and sheer determination of employees.

As the foregoing indicates, I had become known for giving inspiring talks to Goldblatt's employees. These had come to the attention of outside organizations, which were increasingly requesting my services as guest speaker. There wasn't time for them all, but I did accept a few. One I am particularly fond of was given to the Executives Club of Chicago in September 1957. I called it "The Sixth Sense." In the talk, I presented some of the principles I'd developed in nearly 50 years of retailing, beginning with watching my parents in the Polska Skalp, then working for Alex, and eventually joining Nathan and Maurice in the Goldblatt Bros. Dry Goods store.

Selling, I said on that occasion, is the foundation of everything in life. Whatever we are doing — conversing with friends, pleading, debating — usually involves selling, but business always involves selling, especially when we wait on a customer.

In the days of my parents" Polska Skalp, I recalled to that audience over 35 years ago, customers would come into a store to buy something they needed. Today, in an era of consumer abundance, customers are sold something. Products are presented to be seen, touched, smelled, tasted, even heard, through the five senses. But the really successful merchant sells things using his sixth sense — a combination of his own vision, imagination, and planning.

I spoke of the importance of national brands, how they presold the customer, and I reiterated one of my favorite rules: we buy the future with the present. To this end, I spoke of the importance of a budget, which I think of as a pledge, a goal, or a vow. A budget requires vision and imagination, but it also

Chapter XV *The Sixth Sense of Retailing*

requires planning, the ability to make one's dreams come true. If there was a secret to the Goldblatt brothers" success, it was having that sixth sense. We knew where we wanted to go, we were creative in getting there, and we did adequate planning so we wouldn't run into insurmountable obstacles on our way. "We will never become any bigger or better than our budget," I concluded, "and likewise, we will never be any bigger or better than we have prepared ourselves to be." Though privately I felt that we brothers were no longer doing this as well as we once had, I didn't tell the audience that. Instead, I stuck to my public role of putting a positive face on our affairs. (The entire text of my talk is given in an appendix.)

#

There was a method I had applied in merchandising a classification for greater sales and profits, which always seemed to work. An example of it was the change I brought to the small business we were doing with a throw-rug manufacturer.

One day I asked the vendor what it would be worth to him to hire a general sales manager who could guarantee more business than his factory could produce. I then proposed a rug promotion by saying, "I will be your sales manager. I will give you a huge order if you will come down in price, as well as pay for a full-page ad in each of the metropolitan newspapers, plus a page in our circular. One more thing. I want you to contribute a mink stole to the wife of each rug department manager who achieves his sales quota — one that's large enough to cover your cost for the mink stole. In return, I will display the rugs throughout our store and, in addition, I'll trim a full window with your rugs in each of them.

I felt confident of the hidden persuader I had with this promotion. I was sure the wives of the department managers would spur their husbands on. In my framework of healthy domestic psychology, I envisioned the wives checking their husband's sales progress every night when they came home, aiding in the formulation of a "catch–up" strategy when sales might be lagging, or urging them to retain, if not surpass, their on– target position when succeeding.

I said to him, "I will guarantee the success of this gigantic promotion, and I predict that department stores across the country, seeing these ads and hearing of the sales response, will want to buy your rugs and duplicate it."

The manufacturer consented to my proposition. The subsequent sale was so huge a success that when Goldblatt's attempted to phone in its reorders, the line was continually busy. When I finally reached Mr. Lichtenstein, the owner of the factory, he told me he was being deluged with phone orders for greater quantities than his factories could produce.

Thereafter, not only was this sale event set as a precedent at Goldblatt's, and repeated in years to follow, but the same sales promotional strategy was applied later to many additional merchandise classifications, always producing exceptional results.

# # #

The early 1950s were eventful, in and outside of Goldblatt's; some events closed an era; others opened new ones. In 1954 Ellis Island in New York, through which 20 million immigrants (I was one of them) entered the United States since 1892, was closed. A year later, Richard J. Daley became Chicago's

Chapter XV   The Sixth Sense of RETAILING

mayor; consolidating power locally and wielding it nationally, he was destined to influence the upcoming election which made John F. Kennedy president in 1961. Also in 1955, after word that President Dwight Eisenhower had suffered a heart attack, the New York Stock Exchange registered its worst price decline since 1929. That same year Col. Robert R. McCormick, publisher of the *Chicago Tribune*, died at the age of 74; this, four years after the death of competing publisher, William Randolph Hearst in 1951.

In 1955, Disneyland opened in Anaheim, California; Arco, Idaho, a town of 1,200 people, became the first community in the world to receive electric power from atomic energy. In 1955, British Prime Minister, Winston Churchill, submitted his resignation to Elizabeth II. In 1956, *My Fair Lady* starring Rex Harrison and Julie Andrews opened on Broadway. In 1956, British troops completed their withdrawal from the Suez Canal, turning the waterway over to Egypt after operating it for 74 years. The same year American actress Grace Kelly married Prince Rainier of Monaco.

Though the 1950s were times of peace, prosperity and bliss, there was little peace and seldom any bliss in Goldblatt's executive suite. Problems we had had before resurfaced in the same and different guises. They would continue to dog the company until its bankruptcy in 1981, two years after I left for good and a year after I had sold my stock.

My brother Nathan was usually credited with being a merchandising genius, always able to spot trends and opportunities before anyone else did. Brother Maurice was the financial wizard. He had long ago figured out that if we brought goods in and sold them within 10 days, we would have money to pay the bills and even earn a two percent trade discount. To sell these

Life is a game, play to win!

goods out within 10 days our prices had to be lower than the competition, thus Goldblatt's was one of the early discount, cut-price retailers.

The country's economy during the depression of the 1930s caused manufacturers to be hard-pressed to keep their plants running. They were anxious to sell their goods, even at prices below their cost, and particularly to Goldblatt's because we were willing to pay cash for large quantities of merchandise. This enabled us to make incredibly good deals. Our customers had little money, so our reputation for the lowest prices in town brought an increasing number of them to us. They included not only the blue- collar immigrants we had always served, but others who a decade earlier had been more accustomed to shopping in traditional full-price department stores. Further, we prospered for the same reason the movies did during the depression — our retail showmanship offered cheap entertainment; a trip to Goldblatt's was an escape from dreary poverty and enervating unemployment.

We also had another advantage that neither the upscale traditional department stores nor the mail-order merchants had. Goldblatt's was in neighborhoods all over the city, where our customers were. In days when postage and streetcar fare took scarce pennies, one could shop at Goldblatt's without needing either.

Family cohesion and ability to work together were most decidedly not one of the reasons for our success. Though initially Maurice and Nathan's strengths had complemented each other rather like Simon and Hannah's had when they worked together in the Polska Skalp, the brothers extraordinary success soon brought out the differences between them.

In many ways, our purchase of the State Street store in

Chapter XV   The Sixth Sense of Retailing

1936 set in motion a series of conflicts among us that would intensify as the years went on. Marshall Field & Co. had never been able to operate the Davis Store on State Street profitably, and Goldblatt's found it difficult to do so as well.

Our policy of cutting prices on nationally branded goods was tolerated by the stores on State Street so long as we were doing it out in the neighborhoods. But when we introduced price cutting on branded goods to State Street, the stores there told the manufacturers they would discontinue their lines if they sold to Goldblatt's. So a year or so after we acquired the State Street store, I dropped my general merchandising functions and took over the downtown store. I proceeded immediately to change its merchandising policies so they would conform with the rest of State Street. This was quite opposite the policy of all our other stores.

By reorienting the State Street store toward fashion, doing clever window displays, and hiring my own staff of buyers, I was able to turn the store around so it could compete with others on State Street. My brother Maurice opposed all of these moves.

After I had turned the State Street store into a profit-making operation, my old friend Eddie Simon left Goldblatt's and his job as advertising manager, so I took over the advertising functions. But this led to more conflicts with my brothers. After a terrible argument with Nathan, I quit and left the company. Shortly afterward, a meeting was held among Maurice, Nathan, and myself. As a result of that, I returned to Goldblatt's as the general merchandise manager, replacing Nathan who resigned. He then opened four community discount stores named Gold Bond, but during the war he reentered Goldblatt's and worked there again for a few years before dying of cancer at the end of the war. When Joel and I returned to Goldblatt's after the war, we discontinued the Gold Bond stores because they hadn't been profitable.

In the extensive correspondence we conducted while we were in service, Joel and I heard reports of problems back home. Goldblatt's had difficulty getting goods because war shortages were more severe for the off-price vendors we were used to doing business with than they were for more established vendors. In addition, many of our most talented staff members were in the service along with Joel and me.

During the war, I received hundreds of letters from Chicago about the many conflicts and arguments going on between Maurice and Nathan and that business was going poorly as a result. Joel and I made a pact that when the war ended, we would reenter Goldblatt's but only with the understanding that he would be president and in control of operations, and I would be merchandise manager and executive vice president.

In his letters, Maurice kept telling Joel and me how disgusted he was with the business and that he could hardly wait for us to return to Goldblatt's. He wanted to retire and take it easy, but in January 1945 when Joel and I were ready to reenter the business, Maurice reneged and insisted that I be president and not Joel. I wanted harmony, brotherly love, and respect for one another, and I wanted to prove that love between Joel and myself could make Goldblatt's grow into an important and successful chain of stores. This was something Maurice and Nathan had not been able to do because of their egos and constant fighting.

Despite our attempts to change his mind, Maurice was adamant. He would not budge and because we couldn't return

Chapter XV The Sixth Sense of Retailing

under our terms, we decided to go on a sit-down strike and not return. After several weeks, during which time I vacationed in Florida, Walter Heymann of the First National Bank and Maurice begged us to return. We did when he agreed to our conditions.

For several years thereafter our business was progressing smoothly and successfully. Maurice kept himself busy running the cancer research foundation. He began to interfere again when, in his seventies, he started a company that imported artificial flowers from the Orient. Naturally, he wanted Goldblatt's to buy them and in prodigious quantities. The dispute with him over this issue and others sapped my strength and that of several top staff members.

If life inside our family at work was increasingly discomforting, my life at home with Bobbie and our children was increasingly satisfying. When we were first married, Bobbie lived with me at the Drake Hotel — in the same suite where, 40 years after our wedding, we had an anniversary party in 1992. Our first son was born on November 29, 1953, and several days before then, I had sent an announcement card to some of our good friends. It read, "Our baby will be born at the end of November. It will be a boy and will weigh 7 pounds, 11 ounces. His name will be Gary Louis Goldblatt." As fate had it, this prank turned out to be a reality.

Our middle son Stuart joined Gary in September 1955, and soon after they were born, Bobbie and I moved to a large apartment on Commonwealth Avenue near Belmont Harbor on Chicago's north side. On the last day of February 1959, youngest brother David joined them. Though Bobbie had given up her career as singer and actress when we got married, she kept herself very busy with our boys, many community activities, and listening to my stories in the evening about office disputes.

For the 10 years from 1953 to 1963 my life at Goldblatt's was miserable. The three of us argued constantly with each other, and we could not seem to get our business going as well as it had the decade before. Finally, in May of 1963 during a palace revolution, Joel and I were ousted from the company. That year, when Maurice was back in the saddle in full command, was also the first time in Goldblatt's history that it lost money. During the nine months I was out of the company, Nathan's son Lionel, who was one of our buyers as well as a board member, continually asked me to come back. He and Maurice were fighting, he said. When he did not agree to my terms, I refused.

In December of 1963 I accepted an invitation from Maurice to have dinner at his home. After an evening of listening to him plead with me to return, I finally agreed to come back, but only if I were to be president, chief executive officer, and chairman of the board. Maurice was not allowed to interfere with me or other members of the company, and I was to have a three–year contract with these terms. Eventually Maurice agreed, and I rejoined Goldblatt's. When we had left the company earlier that year, Joel pledged never to have anything to do with Goldblatt's again. He kept his word, started an optical company, and ran it until shortly before his death in 1981. Soon after, Bobbie and I moved to our own home in Wilmette, a comfortable lakeside house just south of where Nathan's mansion had been. We've lived there now for over 30 years, and almost every day in each of those years my life with Bobbie and our children has become richer and more satisfying than ever before.

Chapter XV   *The Sixth Sense of Retailing*

# # #

Just before the start of the second World War, one Goldblatt's employee, Frank Folsom, had gone on to work for the government in Washington, D.C., and in 1961, we were equally proud when Philip Klutznick, the developer who was a member of our board of directors, was appointed ambassador of the United States Mission to the United Nations by President John F. Kennedy. But though I never had quite such an august appointment, I was still sought after, more than time and inclination would fully allow, as a speaker. Though talks about the fighting in our executive suite might have kept members of the audience buzzing for weeks afterward, I instead chose to talk about the retailing business than our family's business. One of the talks I am still most proud of was given to a management seminar at the University of Chicago's business school in February 1962. I had been asked to talk about what retailers expect from manufacturers and their products, but I was uncomfortable with that topic as, to my mind, the relationship has to go both ways. Therefore, I called my remarks "To Get, You Gotta Give, or Give and Take."

    The statistical relationship I had established a dozen years earlier between prime vendors and the amount of space and other resources retailers invest in selling their products was, in those days before computers were widely available, still regarded as a pioneering effort. By this time, in the early 1960s, the role of national brands — largely through television advertising — had become far better established than they were a decade earlier. Retailing had changed, so we had become distributors more than salesmen; we relied on the manufacturers of national brands to bring customers into the store as much as they relied on us to get their goods to customers. As the talk summarized my attitudes about being a merchant — or what I'd learned through 50 years in the business — it's included in an appendix. But the astute reader will already have gleaned much of its accumulated wisdom by reading this far.

Despite my public image as successful merchant full in charge of the vast enterprise he had helped found, the reality of my days was far different. The struggles within the family for control of the business continued and frequently interfered with my ability to mind the store. Nevertheless, I forced myself to attend to my functions, and most of the time the daily merchandising excitement crowded out the sad state of affairs behind the scene and restored my pace. A merchandising event began one day in 1962 when a rotund fellow by the name of Bud Welch brushed aside my secretary and barged into my office, unannounced, demanding an order for his Welch baby buggy.

"You must see the buyer or the merchandise manager," I told him.

He replied, "I saw them several times but they wouldn't place an order with me; and I will not leave your office until I get one and Goldblatt's is willing to sell my line." He stressed that he would accept Goldblatt's terms because, once he had an order from us, he would be able to sell his item to all the other department stores.

It appeared that he had invented a most innovative buggy, and one that could be sold at a low price. He was sure it would replace all the high-priced baby carriages on the market. As it turned out, to a great and revolutionary extent, Welch's buggy was destined to do just that.

"All right, I'll give you an order for a carload of your

Chapter XV The Sixth Sense of Retailing

baby buggies under the following terms," I said, thinking he would not accept my conditions and leave. "I will buy the carload on consignment and will only pay for the portion sold. Also, you will have to pay for a full-page ad in each of the metropolitan newspapers, plus a page in our own circular." And I kept on, adding, "I will devote a full State Street show window to display your buggies, and I want your wife in the window to demonstrate them. Furthermore, I don't intend to pay the invoice for 90 days, and I want a greater trade discount for paying the bill."

He agreed to all of it. I was so stunned, I called for one of our lawyers in the legal department. He drew up the contract, and I placed an order for a carload of Welch buggies.

All the terms of the contract were lived up to and in only a few days we not only had a complete sellout but we ordered another carload. It wasn't long before department stores all across the country were selling the Welch baby buggy. Bud Welch had proven he wasn't so dumb after all. In time to come, he would become a close friend of mine.

It was natural for me to repeatedly make similar deals, advancing merchandising firsts, dropping bombshells in the market. At this point, there would be no doubt that we were first-class, powerful promoters, and we mixed ideally with ambitious, promotionally inclined vendors. Together, we created awareness, demand, and a dynamic market for their products.

This was the year of the Cuban missile crisis, when President Kennedy ordered a naval quarantine of Cuba in an effort to force Russia to withdraw its nuclear missiles from the Communist island nation. Lt. John H. Glenn, Jr., piloted a spaceship three times around the earth, becoming the first American to orbit the Earth, and the Telstar Communications

Satellite was launched into orbit, relaying television and telephone signals between the United States and Europe. Johnny Carson took over as host of NBC's "Tonight Show." The following year, 200,000 people heard the Reverend Martin Luther King deliver his "I Have A Dream" speech during a civil rights rally in Washington. Millions more heard this dramatic event over television, as they were also to do three months later when Jack Ruby shot Lee Harvey Oswald two days after the assassination of President Kennedy.

I had that year more time to watch such things on television as, in February 1963 when Bobbie and I returned from a trip to Israel, we learned that the board of directors had decided to vote Joel and myself out of the Goldblatt company. The decision was to take effect at the next annual board of directors meeting, set for May of that year. Maurice had aligned himself with Nathan's heirs and, winning control of the company, forced out Joel and myself. Then, after being absent from the company for seven months, I was asked to come back. I said I would, but only on my terms. They were accepted and I returned in full control in January 1964, as president, chief executive officer, and chairman of the board. Joel never again worked for Goldblatt's.

Chapter XV The Sixth Sense of Retailing

Frank Graham, an official of the American Stock Exchange, celebrates with me the listing of the Goldblatt Department Stores on the exchange in 1967.

Bobbie and I chatted with Gen. Mark Clark at a dinner in his honor in 1968. I had served in the forward echelon under him in the Italian campaign during World War II.

Life is a game, play to win!

CHICAGO TRIBUNE, TUESDAY, SEPTEMBER 22, 1970

Goldblatt Honored

[TRIBUNE Staff Photo]

Louis Goldblatt [left] speaks after receiving decoration. Dr. Giuseppe Avitabile looks on.

The Knighthood of Merit of the Italian Republic was presented to Louis Goldblatt, president and chief executive officer of Goldblatt's department stores during ceremonies yesterday in the State Street store auditorium.

Knighthood was conferred on Goldblatt by Dr. Giuseppe Avitabile, consul general of Italy in Chicago.

The award was presented to Goldblatt for his long interest in the cultural and economic life of Italy and his work in improving Italian and American relations.

22 Chicago today, Tuesday, September 22, 1970

Italy honors Goldblatt for 'friendship'

LOUIS Goldblatt, president of Goldblatt Brothers Inc., has been awarded the highest civilian honor of the Republic of Italy.

Giuseppe Avitabile, consul general of Italy in Chicago, presented Goldblatt the Knighthood of Merit in ceremonies yesterday at the Goldblatt's State Street store eight floor auditorium.

Lawrence X. Pusateri, Gov. Ogilvie's special counsel; Anthony Bottalla, president of the Joint Civic Committee of Italian-Americans of Chicago; and Francesco Quadrio, Italian trade commissioner in Chicago, paid tribute to Goldblatt.

"I ONLY hope my three sons who are here believe everything that was said," Goldblatt quipped after getting the award.

He has traveled widely in Italy, and Goldblatt's featured a "Festa Italia" at the State Street store in 1968.

Avitabile said the 1968 event "popularized products of Italian industry and hand crafts in America."

He added, "this award, however, is especially to the

LOUIS GOLDBLATT

man who contributes so much to the bonds of friendship between Italy and America."

OTHER Knighthoods of Merit have been given to Chicagoans Charles C. Cunningham, director of the Art Institute; and the Rev. James F. McGuire, president of Loyola University.

Goldblatt, who is president and chief executive officer of the firm which operates 40 department stores in Illinois, Indiana, Michigan and Wisconsin, called the award "another Italian masterpiece, a masterpiece of generosity."

During the late 1960s, I was honored with a "knighthood of merit" by the Italian government, in recognition of both Goldblatt's long reputation of providing employment opportunities for immigrants and or our record of importing goods from Italy: countries that traded together could make peace together.

Chapter XV   The Sixth Sense of Retailing

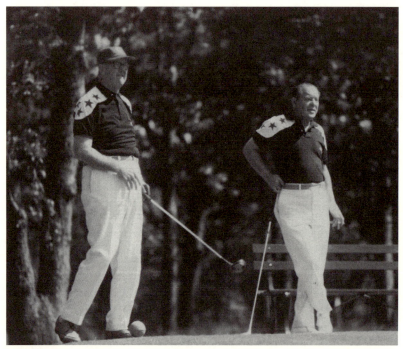

In 1966, sportscaster Jack Brickhouse and I participated in a golf tournament sponsored by the Chicago Tribune.

Life is a game, play to win!

Chapter XVI
Taking Charge

During 1964, my first full year at the helm, I made 115 visits to the 30 Goldblatt's stores, inspecting — touching, in fact — every merchandise classification at every store. I met and talked with all the store management personnel, motivating them to produce greater sales and profits. The arduous routine demanded 14 hours a day, extending into the evenings. I saw too little of our three young boys.

I created an organization chart for a company that had never functioned with one before. Members of top management I called chiefs of staff, a remnant of my army background, and I demanded that every move be channeled through them. I virtually plunged into every phase of company operation, coded by a defined organization scheme that provided me with both knowledge and control.

When the news of my new post became known, there followed an endless barrage of congratulatory letters and phone calls from our vendors promising fullest support and cooperation. Although my days were structured by an all-inclusive, precision-like calendar, I nevertheless insisted on personally reading every customer complaint directed to my level. Rather than hire an outside firm at a large fee to point out the company's failings, I reasoned we should have this service performed

Chapter XVI   Taking Charge

by those who could do it best: the customer herself. I preferred this direct, often emotional, customer communication; thereby, I'd get the facts and feelings from the source itself.

I was pleased when, a few months after I'd assumed the presidency, there were signs that the company was beginning to turn around. With a flow of letters to all our employees, I expressed my appreciation for their cooperation and support and predicted a successful year for the company in 1964.

Goldblatt's had had a profit-sharing plan for employees since the early 1950s, and for years participating in this was one of the chief benefits of working for Goldblatt's. Shortly after becoming president, I became aware of an unfortunate reality. For the first time in the history of the plan, members had not received a contribution from the company for the 1963 fiscal year. That year the company had made no profits. I requested our board of directors to do something about this. The board responded by authorizing a contribution to the plan in the sum of $20,000 to be made, *over and above* the amount the profit plan would receive as its share of the profits of the company for the fiscal year ending January 1965. I always felt that the key to Goldblatt's success was its partnership with its employees. To make our goals for 1964, we were going to need in great abundance their efforts, continued loyalty, and support.

We must have gotten it, because after the first five periods, sales were markedly up. In June 1964, I sent a letter of thanks to all employees, announcing with pride the results of their efforts thus far: "The score for the first five periods — sales up 7.9 percent over last year on the basis of comparable number of stores; profit performance improved 70.3 percent ... and continues to trend upward." We were, I thought, on the way to improvement, when we had another blow, bringing the collapse of the Louis store to mind.

In November of the year, right before the Christmas business peak, a terrible, huge fire broke out at Goldblatt's warehouse, burning it completely to the ground. The entire city of Chicago, as well as the surrounding cities, stopped in awe to sympathize with us at the enormity of the catastrophe and to recognize the many acts of heroism displayed in the course of coping with the disaster.

Newspaper headlines, airview photographs, front page feature stories and editorials in all the metropolitan and trade newspapers, as well as radio and television, captured the incredible scene of destruction for the greater part of the week. A headline in the *Chicago Sun–Times* read: "City Calls for Aid as Fires Rage; 44 Injured" and the story went on to say "Forty-four firemen were injured Saturday . . . part of the 450–man force that battled for 16 hours before dousing a $2,500,000 fire at Goldblatt's furniture warehouse. The fire was the biggest in number of alarms sounded since 1957."

The warehouse was a picture of utter devastation. "The heat was so intense, its curved steel support beams bent into bows," another story read. All the merchandise in the Goldblatt's warehouse was destroyed or heavily damaged by the flames, smoke, and water. The Chicago *Sunday American* in a front–page headline declared: "41 Firemen Injured in Fires. Fear $5 million stock damage." "Nearly 500 firemen were at the scene with 60 pieces of equipment," the story began. There were numerous other descriptions of the grueling 17–hour fight with the blaze.

Ironically, the *Home Furnishings Daily*, a trade newspaper, published an article on November 17 that read in part: "'We will have one of the greatest years in profits and sales in

Chapter XVI   Taking Charge

our 50 year history,' according to Louis Goldblatt, president." In a separate article of the same issue, the news of the warehouse fire was reported that included the reference, "Goldblatt Bros., Inc., is scouting the city for a site to erect a temporary warehouse and eventually will rebuild a new one at the site of the 400,000–square–foot building destroyed." The fire was so intense, a *Sun–Times* story said, "The magnitude of the Goldblatt's warehouse fire was responsible for temporarily exhausting the Chicago Fire Department's supply of fire–smothering foam!" The *Tribune*, I was pleased to see, told of how I lauded the heroism of employees and firemen. "He said a number of his truck drivers risked their lives when they drove their trucks out of a concourse adjoining the burning warehouse. The executive lauded city firemen. Goldblatt said that because of so much generosity from countless sources, service will not be interrupted."

On November 18, the *Chicago Daily News* reported that we had already acquired an interim warehouse. "Goldblatt's has temporarily leased 500,000 square feet of warehouse space," the story said, "and intends to rebuild a new permanent warehouse on the Kedzie Avenue site."

Following the fire, I published large notices in the newspapers entitled "We Are Thankful." They noted that the losses suffered were material ones, that all lives were spared, and no serious injuries were sustained. In them, I thanked both the Chicago Fire Department and those of suburban towns that had rushed equipment to our aid, also the police department, civil defense units, the Salvation Army, and the Red Cross. I also thanked our employees for their loyalty and the many generous people — competitors, manufacturers, and distributors — who had come forward to enable us to continue

Life is a game, play to win!

to serve our customers.

I saw to it that I personally replied to every communication of sympathy we received from friends, civic officials, the many denominations of religious representatives, medical exponents, and business organizations. On November 20, I wrote every employee stating there were no words to express my admiration and appreciation toward those who were at the warehouse during those appalling hours. I coined the term "Go Goldblatt Spirit" for all their faithfulness.

Fortunately for our Christmas selling season, the warehouse that burned had housed furniture, major appliances, and rugs. Our main warehouse contained the thousands of other products we sold, and they were not touched. I knew, as did many of our employees, how important this Christmas season was going to be, and I told them our plans were to move forward resolutely. "Now [we are] at the threshold of the Christmas selling season, planned to be the greatest in our history," I wrote. "I am grateful and proud to be a coworker of yours."

Of the many replies I received, one was especially meaningful. It was sent by the secretary of one of our buyers. "It was inspiring to see everyone making room for all the representatives from the various companies," she wrote. "First, the whole buying floor was in a state of chaos; then [we] proceeded in an orderly fashion. Teamwork . . . that's what it was! I would like to speak for myself, for my boss, for the buyers, assistants and clericals. We too, are thankful, Mr. Goldblatt, to be working for you and to be a part of the "Go Go Goldblatt's team." It was signed Dorothy Kelly.

In the *Home Furnishings Daily* articles dated November 17, one outlined Goldblatt's strides in several areas of operation

Chapter XVI   Taking Charge

since I had assumed the presidency. "Among them: [it had] increased average sales per-transaction figure; added higher profit lines and offered better quality merchandise; set up departments within departments, thus providing departmental treatment; concentrated efforts on changing non-selling to selling area to accent sales and profits per square foot; improved merchandise display; improved communications; set out to improve customer service and image; stepped up the national brands program while adding certain private labels; traded up its fashion image in soft goods and furniture; increased its import volume; broadened its stocks while improving inventory turnover and reducing out-of-stock conditions; eliminated small gross margin purchases on fringe items; improved employee schedules; tightened up costs and expenses in truck deliveries by loading during nighttime hours while speeding up those deliveries; shifted its modus operandi around the district manager concept rather than operating specialists with strong managers now reporting to district chiefs; reappraised its study of legal costs, interest on loans, selling payrolls and other financial facets; trained personnel for use with the IBM 1440 computer; stepped up buyer's visits to its stores; liberalized its program of employee benefits. Although the company is expanded within the structure of its 30 stores, it will expand externally with new stores during the months ahead." I'm still proud of that record of accomplishment.

The dramatic improvement in sales and profits of 1964 represented the most outstanding record in the history of the company, and it was a record we had achieved in spite of utilizing the same advertising expense — $5.5 million — as the previous year.

Life is a game, play to win!

#

The year 1964 was eventful on the international and domestic scene as well. President Lyndon Johnson signed the Civil Rights Act, Ranger 7 spacecraft sent earth the first close-up pictures of the moon, Gen. Douglas MacArthur died at age 84, and Indian Prime Minister Jawaharia Nehru died in New Delhi. Premier Nikita Khruschev was ousted as head of the Soviet Union, succeeded by Alexei Kosygin and Leonid Brezhnev. Sidney Poitier became the first black to win an academy award as best actor for his performance in *Lilies of the Field*, and *Hello Dolly* starring Carol Channing opened on Broadway. Elizabeth Taylor married her fifth husband, Richard Burton. We had yet to begin realizing what the 1960s would come to mean in later years.

A year or so after I took over, I received a letter from Walter Heymann, who was still our banker as he had been nearly 40 years earlier when the Louis store collapsed. I'd been to visit with him earlier that day. He said he was pleased to confirm an unsecured line of credit for $15 million; that the bank was, indeed, pleased with the results for the year to date, and that he, too, joined in the expectation that another banner year was in store for the company. I maintained a smooth and successful pace with the board of directors, holding a record for having passed resolutions on all the motions I brought before them. They complimented me on the job I was doing, and they expressed their pleasure that Goldblatt's stock dividends had been raised twice since I had taken office.

All the while, I energetically pursued my fervent belief that the bottom line of the statistical statement could never be better or worse than the pieces of which it is composed, that its

Chapter XVI   Taking Charge

weaknesses must be individually ferreted out and corrected for continued improvement. By applying this same thinking to the employee work force, that is, that the level of motivation and application on the part of everyone must be inspired to the fullest, I came upon the idea of creating the "Gold Nugget" program. It recognized that the company was virtually a gold mine of 10,000 ardent, ambitious employees, many among which were the "corporate treasures" that the program name implied.

Therefore, it behooved management to "mine" for these employees and communicate the virtues of all these representatives of upward mobility. They deserved greater remuneration as well. Subsequently, the program brought forth no end of positive response. Recognition of new-found strength in performance and news of zealous individuals throughout the company was reaching me daily and was one of the most gratifying experiences I encountered.

In a letter sent in March 1965, Paul Nagle of the Office of the Postmaster General in Washington wrote to our vice president and personnel director, Chester Malin, a commendation we were both very proud of: "in a report of a review of your employment practices, only very rarely is it thought to be appropriate to express word of commendation for the way in which a company has implemented the Equal Employment Opportunity Programs. Our people . . . were enthusiastic about the circumstances found . . . and the high standard you have been following in extending employment opportunity to all, without regard to race or similar consideration."

A new record was set for 1965 with sales climbing to $162 million as compared to 1964's $153 million. And we accomplished this with no additional new stores. Profits increased an astounding 58 percent to $2,404,186 after tax, compared to $1,520,389 the previous year; this too, for the same number of stores. We were doing so well that, in early 1966, I recommended to the board of directors the third increase in two and a half years in the stock dividend. The stock was also split, two-for-one. At this time, our employees owned about 20 percent of the company.

That April, in a talk I gave to the Illinois Retail Merchants Association, I noted several developments that would soon consume that nation's attention. One was the first hints of the Yuppie; the other, the effect computers would have on business.

"Dear Children, Eggheads and Well-to-do-ers!," I began, noting that: "we find ourselves in an era of youth, wisdom, and wealth. Five percent of the nation's population are in their mid-twenties, or younger." I compared figures on education: at the turn of the century, 13 percent of all children from ages 14 through 17 were in high school; at that time, 95 percent were, and more than half of them would go to college. I referred to unprecedented disposable income, which aided by government programs and company pensions bolstered the middle class while shrinking the poor, and I noted the increased availability of leisure time for outdoor activity and consumer appetite for better products. "The greater part of the population never knew a depression and wants better things," I said.

"What, then, is to be the retailer's attitude and participation?" I challenged. My response was the revolution of inventory control with electronic data processing. It was not only a necessity of the times due to the incredible varieties of merchandise, but it also made possible what came to be called classification merchandising. In Goldblatt's, we implemented this as DWAD or "department within a department." What this meant, essentially, was that we would control inventory by individual classifications of items rather than by department. We began looking toward the time when the computer would balance, order, and adjust open- to-buy on these. The greater degree of accuracy the DWAD classifications of items made possible also enabled us to provide greater return for each dollar invested in inventory.

I predicted that present trends then spelled an era of fewer vendors, more important national brands, and many private brands. The customer's selectivity had matured and was bound to shape it so.

This was a period when there were more jobs than people to fill them, so I addressed the manpower shortage as well. This reminded me, I said, of Eve's question to Adam, "Do you love me?" and Adam's answer, "Who else?"

"You see," I said, "even the Bible tells you that you have good people when there are no others; so love them! But, at the same time, exert more effort to train them."

I concluded that along with everything else reaching new highs, so were opportunities, and I told one of my favorite stories. "A businessman was asked the reason for his success. He replied that he jumped at opportunities. He was further asked how he knew when the opportunity was there. He replied that you don't know; you just keep jumping!"

That September, the *Chicago Daily News* devoted a full page to the story of my turning the company around. The piece set me to wondering what if the public knew the story "behind" the story, too; of the intrigues, the battles, and betrayals within the family. There had been pitfalls in my just attaining the opportunity to create this success. There had been hostility toward my ability and ambition. Even in our family of brothers with a common heritage of hard times and hard work, petty jealousies and resentments had made their destructive presence felt. Blood, I began to note, could be thin, thinner even than water.

As president, however, I would not let that unpleasantness keep us from growing. In 1967 Goldblatt's opened its first Home Center — 100,000 square feet devoted to home furnishings. That year, we remodeled or enlarged 19 of our 30 stores, and began stressing imports that enhanced our fashion image.

Tigers, that year, were big. The gasoline companies were "putting a tiger in every tank," and the feline became a symbol of power itself, so Goldblatt's, ever quick to spot trends, created a new and major sales event called A Tiger of a Sale. We even brought live tigers into the State Street store, caging them on the eighth floor. When we ran full–page ads in both the *Sun Times* and *Tribune* depicting tigers as on sale at Goldblatt's — "your choice, Bengal or Siberian" — news of the stunt spread throughout the country. Although none were sold (we wouldn't dare!), the theme enhanced all our Tiger of a Sale advertising, created an almost uncontrollable customer response, and accompanying sales.

We'd rented the animals from the Bernie Hoffman Animal Kingdom and treated them as considerately, if not lovingly, as we could. On the evening before the sale, about 100 mobile patients of a local children's hospital were brought to Goldblatt's for a private showing of the tigers, narrated by Bernie Hoffman himself. Goldblatt's provided all the children with dinner and a wonderful time was had by all.

I had been told on the side that one of the tigers had no teeth and was, in fact, quite old and gentle. When dinner time came for the tigers, I proceeded before the entire audience to

Chapter XVI   Taking Charge

take large hunks of raw meat and hand feed one of them — the wrong one it turned out! The few who knew this rushed toward me in near panic: "No! Mr. Goldblatt! Louis! For God's sake! Not that one!" I could well imagine headlines reading I'd been attacked by a Siberian tiger, in a Chicago department store, no less!

When 1966 came to a close, sales had increased to $170,066,521 from $162,220,909 in 1965; profits were $2,951,012, compared with $2,404,186 the previous year. Earnings per share before the two-for-one stock split were $3.96 compared to $3.25 per share the previous year. And I was particularly proud of the fact that we'd had this splendid performance again without opening additional stores.

For the State Street store's spring opening in 1967, we created a real impact. Each of the store's main-floor columns displayed a breathtaking assortment of live potted plants, adorned with colorful, oversized bird cages, each containing live, singing canaries. Overall, the sight of this flora and the sound of nature's song proved to be a stunning array. Goldblatt's was a magnet to traffic on the street. Some of the birds did manage to get loose, and flew wildly about the main floor, but they were readily retrieved once they got hungry.

I continued to drive the company to increase sales and profits, further growth and expansion. Saturdays, Sundays, evenings — I spared no effort in learning the plans of the departments and seeing them function in actuality at each of the stores, plus I was seeing to the nonmerchandise-related administration of the company.

Later that year, Goldblatt's bought the eight Wasson's department stores out of Indianapolis, Indiana, and the magnificent Goldblatt's Furniture Home Center was completed and opened in the Scottsdale area on Chicago's southwest side. Featuring 100,000 square feet of dreams for the home, it was a first of its kind. Goldblatt's then operated 39 stores, and we had extensively remodeled many of the older ones.

The March 1967 issue of *Chain Links*, our company newsletter, carried a message that I found particularly gratifying. It began "Dear Boss" and went on to say how much "the team" liked having me come to the stores and work alongside them. They liked the fact that I wasn't a president who stayed in his office all day. "It's good knowing you want to listen to us . . . and then take action," the letter read, and continued: "We're proud to see the name of Goldblatt's so often in the financial pages . . . how we've broken new records; . . . that our progress reflects so in our Profit Sharing returns." I never knew quite who was behind that letter, but I did appreciate it.

Invitations to speak continued to come in, and I obliged them when I could. In May 1967, I talked to some 800 high school seniors who had participated in the Chicago Public School's Distributive Education Program. The 700 business representatives who employed them also attended the affair. The talk was called "Brass Tacks with Love," a reference to one of my early memories in retailing. I imagined they were thinking what I thought about at their age: What should I do? Where am I going? Where am I now? Where will I be 10 years from now when I will be 28 years old? What do I have a flair for? I repeated my motto: "We buy the future with the present. We will never get more out of life than we put into life now. Your future is being determined right now," I told this group of bright, ambitious seniors, and suggested they get down to "brass tacks" — measuring their prospects and ambitions carefully.

"The first requisite for making a success of your life is to

Chapter XVI   Taking Charge

do what you love best. For only when you love what you are doing, can you do it well. So, in thinking of the future, consider strongly to undertake that which you love the most— that for which you have a flair," I continued. And I realized how lucky I had been to have figured that out at an early age.

The year 1967 produced sales of $185 million compared to the previous year of $170 million; profits increased to $3,176,488 from $2,951,012 in 1966. Cash dividends were increased to 60 cents per share for the year compared to 37.5 cents the previous year. Profits for 1968, however, proved disappointing; although sales climbed $24 million over 1967, our profits increased only slightly.

Our promotional calendar was already more replete than that of any other retailer, but we added still another event in 1968. We called it Goldblatt's Great Sale and persuaded the *Chicago Daily News* to provide tens of thousands of a special printing of the newspaper that carried a three-column announcement of the huge event right on the front page of an otherwise normal edition. The announcement included my photo and an excerpt of the remarks I'd made earlier, charging our executives with the uncompromising task of gathering more extraordinary, money-saving values than ever before.

In addition to distributing enough copies for all our employees and supplying each store with stacks of the paper for their take-one stands at the entrance doors, we came up with an old Goldblatt's style gimmick to add drama to our sale — we hired an army of newsboys to hand out copies of the newspaper, free, throughout the neighborhoods, shouting, "Extra! . . . Extra! . . . Read all about it! . . . Goldblatt's biggest! . . . Goldblatt's best! . . . The Great Sale! . . ." Politics and the youth revolution may have been the biggest news that year, but Goldblatt's could still pull off a sale that got people's attention.

Still, over the years, I just couldn't shake the bass fiddle syndrome — we made music by lugging around that large instrument, while our competitors seemed to do well on their little harmonicas. I would tell my close friends that in running Goldblatt's, one had to work like a horse and, by all appearances, our competition didn't really work that hard. It didn't stage that many huge sale events, but it still made a profit! It was the damnedest thing. I attributed this to the image the company started with back in 1914, that of the cost cutters, the value givers. We had to make our money on volume. That took more work, but was, of course, the reason for our growth to 39 stores by 1968.

I confided to my own family and friends the apprehensions I harbored about replacing myself one day when I got older; in 1968, I turned 65. I felt I would never find another president willing to work around the clock. To my mind that was essential if the company was going to continue to be successful. While my feelings ran the gamut from despair to elation, I would frequently switch the focus of my concentration, reminding myself of a little ditty I'd learned somewhere: "Early to bed, early to rise; work like hell and advertise!" I frequently wondered why I worked so hard, knowing, of course, that you can't take it with you. In my heart, though, I never felt I was subjecting myself to self–abuse or punishment. How could I be, doing what I enjoyed?

The many years of the company's existence were punctuated with more than it fair share of violent happenings: fires, holdups, floods, killings, extortion attempts, and accidents. Then, in 1968, a crazed man managed to conceal a bomb that exploded in the basement housewares department in our South

Chapter XVI Taking Charge

Chicago store, causing several customers to be seriously hurt and maimed for life. He was later apprehended.

That year, too, my brother Alex passed away at the age of 82, only a few years after retiring from the company. For nearly 40 years, he had managed one of our stores on the South Side. Of the eight children, there were now five of us left. The country was tragically aware of death on the national scene that year, too. Rev. Martin Luther King, Jr., was shot and killed on April 5; only two months later, Senator Robert F. Kennedy was also shot and killed.

During the mid-1960s, beginning with the year I assumed the presidency, Goldblatt's had turned around from a money-losing into a profitable operation. I was frequently asked how the company had managed to do this in so short a time. So at one point I put together an article, called "On Your Mark," in which I isolated the ingredients of leadership as I believed them to be, and the challenge of communicating their meaning to even remote corners of the company. Its themes were those I've stated before — that I saw myself as a leader of team leaders, communicating standards, heritage, and personality, and I encouraged employees to communicate with each other. The people a leader chooses as his closest associates must be aware of the reasons we chose them. Then, the leader must work through them, never around them.

When any leader thinks he's made it, he's had it. There is no standing still. He may smile at success, but only as a stranger. If he fails, he must reorganize his efforts. If results do not follow, the program is wrong. There can be no author's pride! "Morale" is a mere term, and using the word won't make it happen! It can't be programmed like a refund policy. It doesn't start yesterday, nor is it apt to end abruptly. It's woven at every level.

When our company was small, we trained ourselves to think big. Then the bigger we grew, the greater the importance of thinking in terms of collective small businesses, all under one flag. The larger we grew, the more important was my walkout into the field. Retailers must always see their operations from the customers' perspective. They determine what we are, what we might strive to become. Trends and styles may change, but the concept of value from the customers' point of view never changes.

The president must always be like a sponge, absorbing the headlines and the back–page squibs for their impact on the retail scene. He is ever aware that everything carries with it seeds of its own obsolescence; we secure the future with leadership that is on its mark today.

In another article written about the same time for the magazine, *Retail Overview*, I talked about the merchandising methodology that had enabled Goldblatt's to turn itself around. Important to us was the concept of classification merchandising, what we called DWAD, for department within a department. This concept channeled our thoughts into updating fixtures in order to increase sales by cubic and square foot. This, in turn, led to a scientific space–allocation program that coupled increased margin potential with fashion. At one store, the margin mix had improved one and a quarter percent immediately simply by a small change in fixtures.

Our visual merchandising program included greater use of glass in showcases, seasonal versatility in fixtures, and greater use of "gondola" (or hanging) fixtures, which multiplied the merchandise impact by far. We accelerated merchandise exposure via narrower but higher shelving. This not only quickened merchandise turnover, it provided more accessible aisles throughout the store. Our space– allocation program also led us to calculate existing utility, or nonselling, space for possible conversion to selling space without sacrificing efficiency. Then we enhanced decor, bringing on the shop within a shop concept, and we increased lighting throughout. We sought to bring attention to national brands, private brands, and imports.

For the president himself, time allocation was supremely important. He must know how much attention to detail is enough; how much, too much. In the late 1960s, it was also important to note the shift toward youth, who were saving less than their older counterparts. Our major sales alone would not suffice to attract these customers. Controlling expenses was also essential. The habits with which a company may have been living for years can become prohibitively costly. At one of our stores, for example, by simply removing a partition between "receiving" and "marking," we consolidated the jobs of two supervisors. We came to "see" what was always there!

The president, in my view, must always be an avid reader, consuming company reports of every kind, trade journals, business and news publications, plus everyone else's advertising. If there's a potential gold mine somewhere, it's the president who must do the digging, who must uncover the nuggets, be they particularly creative people or other untapped corporate resources. In conclusion, whenever I thought about leadership, I came back to my notion of the sixth sense: vision, planning, and wantmanship.

#

In 1969, Goldblatt's built and opened its second Furniture

Home Center. Located in Downers Grove, Illinois, it was a mammoth 167,000 square–foot, ranch–house styled installation — the largest of its kind in the country. The grand opening went far beyond our expectations and drew home furnishing retailers and manufacturers from everywhere in the country, as well as from abroad. To announce the opening, we took out special rotogravure sections in all the metropolitan and suburban newspapers, and we also started doing ads in the electronic media. Thousands upon thousands of free gifts were prepared, customized, and imported a full year in advance. I like to recall that highways to the western suburbs were snarled for miles around, jammed with curiosity seekers and shoppers alike. Everything new and traditional, as well as "avant" — in furnishings, home entertainment, and gracious living — was included in this store. It was a long way, I thought, from Goldblatt's days of selling 10 cent dishpans as loss leaders.

The Goldblatt's chain at this time consisted of 40 stores. That year, we again had a two–for–one stock split, and again we increased the stock dividend, this time to 72 cents per share from 60 cents the previous year. I still believe that one of the reasons for our continued success was that our employees were stockholders. Through our profit–sharing plan, they owned 407,624 shares of Goldblatt stock. So they, too, benefitted when sales and profits were good.

At this point, after over a half century with the business, I was able to enjoy a certain amount of gratification from our success. Seeing, at long last, the credo I had refined out of a lifetime of grappling, often at incredible odds, come to fruition, provided me with some satisfaction. It was like taking a sigh of relief after a long ordeal. This sense of having arrived provided indisputable proof for the cynics. It was an ecstatic feeling, one associated with no thoughts of money or gain, but it was as much my own as my fingerprints. Thus did I revel in what I was doing for the company I loved, fortified by marriage and family, particularly Bobbie's and my abiding love for each other.

#

As the 1960s came to a close, I began to take cognizance of a vital, new, onrushing trend, virtually a revolution, in men's fashion wearing apparel, and I knew we had to be prepared for it. A brand-new fashion era was upon us and it would leave very few retailers and manufacturers unaffected.

To me, the signs were clearly perceptible. To my dismay, young men were wearing their hair longer. There was a general swing away from convention, and with it a need to assert one's own fashion identity. Thinking of the dazzling plumage with which the male peacock mesmerizes the female, I dubbed our effort at Goldblatt's at least within the company, the peacock revolution.

Preparing for this meant interpreting an amorphous "mood" and "movement" into an appropriate environment of new merchandise, new fixtures, and new attitudes. I embarked upon a thorough investigation of both the national and international men's fashion scene — reading all the magazines, going to the many markets, and then isolating the fashion clues that seemed to be emerging. When I felt satisfied with my homework, I called a special meeting of the relevant buyers, all the store managers, the planning department, advertising and display, security, other administration, and top management to get set for The Peacock Revolution!

At the meeting I launched the complete program for the men's and boys' departments for all our stores. I'd decided that the entire south half of the State Street store's main floor, 25,000 square feet, was to be devoted to these departments. In order to provide the increased space, departments such as notions, stationery, toiletries, tobacco, and others were relocated elsewhere. We ordered new walnut fixtures and paneling, carpeting, special new-action mannequins; all evoked a feeling of masculine elegance. Customers could even see into the shop from the street. Semi-strobe and marquis-like lighting provided the necessary drama. We wanted customers to visualize ensembles and accessories — the wardrobe as a whole for that total look.

We created the Today Shop featuring the very newest for young men, counterpart to the female Young Juniors, which had earlier become a traffic-getting department. National brands were favored, and we strove for bigger sales transactions to be derived out of coordinated purchases. To draw further attention to this new merchandising scene, we had the Board Room, in which we set off the high fashion, higher-price apparel for the middle-aged, executive-type customer. We even had an Un-Barber Shop, where instead of removing hair, Goldblatt's would add hair in the form of sideburns, a moustache, even a toupee.

Thus did we hail the sizzling 70s in male apparel. Beginning with the fall season of 1969, the male of the species became a clotheshorse. With varied colors and styles, he was finally able to individualize himself. In sharp contrast with their former uniform style, men would no longer be just another face in the steamroom where they all look alike. The post World War II babies, the takeover generation, had become a high percentage of the total population. Their wants were to greatly change the American scene in housing, lifestyles, and clothing.

Chapter XVI   Taking Charge

It was a sociological and marketing revolution.

No longer would men wait until they wore holes in their garments before buying new. They would change with the fashion. No two men need look alike. We had stripes, checks, see-throughs; long sleeves selling in the spring, the Spanish look, the Western look, the Edwardian look. Pants came in hip huggers, bell bottoms, flairs, pleats, cuffs. Colors! Prints! Florals! The shaped sport coat, the drizzler, and peacoat were all still with us, but now we had to add the leather look, the CPO, the bush and safari jacket, and belted outerwear. Fur, real and fake; metallics, vests, jump suits, underwear in purple, yellow, deep blues. We sold toiletries and jewelry in our new men's department, hardware kits, flashlights, and barbecue utensils.

"I foresee your being in the market very frequently," I said to our buyers. "The patterns of your buying will change as often as the fashion pendulum swings. Menswear will be no less volatile than ladies' ready-to-wear. Yes, it's a couple hundred years late in happening, but it's here. And it's here NOW! Goldblatt's will serve the male customer as he requires throughout the sizzling 70s!"

Outside, in the winter of 1967–1968, Chicago was to experience the second greatest snowstorm in its long history of severe storms. The snow was piled so high that the streets throughout the city were closed. Many of our employees had no way to get home. I, too, slept at the store overnight for two nights, in fact. Little did I know of the drama unfolding back at my home in Wilmette.

Bobbie and the children were out of town at the time; the only person in the house was our Polish maid who spoke no English. With the storm's ferocity becoming quite evident to her, she went to the garage adjoining the house to feed our two Belgian sheepdogs and bring them into the house, but inadvertently she'd let the door close behind her. As there was a huge snowdrift blocking the garage door, she had trapped herself in the garage, leaving no possible way for her and the dogs to get out.

Considering the havoc of the storm, I kept calling the house to check the general condition of things, knowing, too, that I would have to speak with her in Polish. But, there wasn't any answer. Finally, after almost two days, I was able to make it home. Then I discovered her, huddled with the dogs in the garage, inside the car but with neither food nor blankets for warmth. Both she and the dogs were in a semiconscious state, near frozen and weak from hunger when I found them. I managed to take them into the house and eventually revived them. Just a little longer and it would have certainly ended in a horrible tragedy. I was very glad when Bobbie returned home and the storms abated.

# # #

This was a year for watchfulness, and it being my nature, I was constantly on the lookout to step–up employee effort with some unusual motivation. Thus, when I came across some ESP reading material, I dreamed up a handle: ESP for Extra Special Push. The Christmas season was coming, the time of the year when retail stores produce 80 percent of the year's profits, and we needed a particularly good year. In a letter to buyers and managers, I reiterated that the greater profits are derived from those sales *beyond* the budget. That extra special push in terms of competitiveness meant extra special surveillance of the competitor's pricing and values. We were still urging our employees to give their all, and then some.

That year, too, I was very proud to be appointed a director of the Chicago Better Business Bureau and delighted when it published the following as part of an introduction for me: "Louis Goldblatt is principally self-taught, with a passion to know. With energy and wise counsel he seeks to achieve the most difficult goals first, and then goes on to achieve the less difficult. His concept of management is to afford equal opportunity to all in the company and to find, with patience an sincerity, qualities in people that they themselves do not believe they possess. . . . Like his stores, he is a vital part of the city and its people."

In the fall of 1969, a recession began to be felt and the country's economy slipped; inflation set in. Analysts were viewing the coming months with gloom. Nevertheless, sales for the year reached a new high of $215 million compared with a past year of $208 million; profits, however, decreased to $2.6 million from $3.3 million in 1968. I had, to my dismay, proved prophetic in the article written in March 1968, in which I said, "sales alone will not suffice."

But gloom was nowhere to be found when on July 20, 1969, the world heard that the Apollo II astronauts became the first men to set foot on the moon. That same weekend we learned, with a sense of consternation, that Sen. Edward Kennedy had left the scene of an accident in which a campaign aide had drowned. Vietnam war protesters continued to demonstrate across the country, which that year included a candlelight march around the White House. Doctors in Houston, Texas, implanted the first complete artificial heart in a man from Skokie, Illinois. Judy Garland, who gave so much heart to others, but seemed never to have enough of her own, died at the age of 47. Sirhan Sirhan was sentenced to death in Los Angeles for the assassination of Sen. Robert F. Kennedy; his sentence was later reduced to life imprisonment. The trial of the Chicago Eight began on charges of conspiring to incite riots during the 1968 Democratic National Convention. Britain's Prince Charles was invested as the Prince of Wales. His subject John Fairfax arrived at Ft. Lauderdale after having rowed across the Atlantic alone, the first person to do so.

###

During the late 1960s, our overall import programs had been increasing considerably. We had been particularly successful with the huge quantities of fashion apparel, as well as exciting gift goods, that our buyers were bringing out of Italy. Our buying office there was combing all the major markets, and our buyers were traveling back and forth with newfound items from all the major Italian cities, many of which Buck and I had lived in during those hectic years of the war. While there, we had developed personal relationships and a strong attachment to Italy.

I had no idea that our company's long dreamed of trade efforts with that country were being so closely monitored by the Italian Trade Counsul, nor did I realize they knew of my own Italian experiences. Thus to my surprise and delight I learned that, at the conclusion of an elaborate import fair called Festa Italiana, I was to receive the highest honor the Republic of Italy could bestow on a foreigner. I was deeply touched when Italy's consul general in Chicago, Dr. Giuseppi Avitabile, along with a retinue of other Italian government officials, officiated at

Chapter XVI   Taking Charge

a most auspicious affair. In a colorful ceremony held in the flag-bedecked auditorium of the State Street store, I was awarded the Italian Knighthood of Merit for "increasing world understanding through trade."

The evening was attended by a host of local civic officials, including my long- time friend, Judge Saul Epton, many other friends and business associates, plus Goldblatt's executives and employee representatives. In the many speeches that were given, I found particularly gratifying an expression used by a member of the Illinois General Assembly, Lawrence X. Pusateri, who was there representing Gov. Richard Ogilvie. I was, he said, "a man who squanders himself in his giving."

But of all the praise I heard that evening, the one I treasured most was being commended for the opportunities created by Goldblatt's for Italians as well as all other ethnic groups. A surge of nostalgia gripped me hearing those words. I couldn't help but think we, too, were once the same greenhorns, just looking for work and with it success. I didn't kid myself that evening — I was neither a statesman nor a politician — but I came away reassured that an indisputable fact of life, trade and prosperity, was also the fact of peace for time to come.

Around the world that year, Alexander Solzhenitsyn was awarded the Nobel Prize for Literature, and Wladyslaw Gomulka resigned as head of Poland's communist party after a week of rioting over food prices. Elsewhere in the world, Palestinian guerrillas blew up three hijacked airliners in Jordan, and an earthquake in Peru killed more than 66,000 people. President Nixon signed a measure lowering the voting age to 18 from 21; the Ohio National Guard fired on a crowd of antiwar demonstrators at Kent State University, killing four students. Hot pants were the fashion rage in 1971, as was the high slit skirt. It was also the year I had a brush with death while on vacation in Jamaica with Bobbie and our three sons.

One day, while the boys were throwing golf balls into a swimming pool and diving to retrieve them, I decided to join in, diving off from the diving board. Upon surfacing with one of the balls in my hand, I shouted to my sons to hold out the long net pole so that I could grab on, and they could pull me over to the edge of the pool. But the boys didn't know that I had never learned to swim! After all, they'd seen me dive many times before and swim under water, never knowing that I could stay under just as long as I could hold my breath, then I'd have to take hold of the side of the pool or stand in shallow water. Not this time, however! Not in 10 feet of water and nowhere near the edge!

So, I shouted, "Help," but they thought I was clowning. Nevertheless, they handed me the pole — I was saved! — Then they let go. — I wasn't saved! Instead, I sank out of sight, drowning at the bottom! Fortunately Bobbie heard the commotion, and knowing I couldn't swim, dived in and rescued me. It was only then that Gary, Stuart, and David came to know that their father was probably the only man in the world who could dive, but couldn't swim a stroke!

Well how, they wondered, had this come to be? It was, I had to admit, pride, and false pride at that which might have stood between me and staying alive. The tale goes back to when I was a youngster in grammar school, during a beginning- term swimming class. The instructor asked that those of us who could swim stand on one side of the pool; those who couldn't, on the other. I was too ashamed to admit I couldn't swim, so I naturally joined the swimmers.

I dove well enough, for sure, and always did it close to the edge of the pool, so I could grab on when I surfaced. Yes, I had pulled off my little deception, and my classmates, like my sons, were none the wiser, until then. I had always thought that with a sense for diving thus developed, could swimming be far behind? But this experience gave new meaning to pride cometh before a fall, or more aptly before you sink! We can't live, I was again reminded, by what we ain't.

# # #

Though I couldn't swim, I did still relish diving into big ponds — thus when Emmett Dedmon, editor of the *Chicago Sun–Times*, asked me in May 1971 to contribute my thoughts on the nation's economy to a conference he was to participate in with President Richard Nixon, I was happy to oblige. At that time, the economy was behaving sluggishly and the administration was looking for causes and solutions. Among my comments were that: "adverse psychological influences [are] inhibiting the American consumer. The customer, sensing the climate nonconductive to spending, [has] put off his buying and restricted it primarily to the everyday needs."

Then I predicted that "while consumer confidence is [still] fragile, increased spending will hold throughout [the year]. As employment and general growth were the president's chief concerns, I went on to say that "retail sales in the past three months for our company are, on a comparable store–for–store basis, 8.5 percent above the same period last year. In the coming months we expect that even those sales percentage increases will rise. At the same time we, like most businesses, are operating with stringent expense controls which, in turn, do cause a greater rate of unemployment."

I concluded by commenting: "We in retailing did not experience the unemployment cutbacks that occurred in manufacturing, especially in certain geographic areas. Employment in our industry expands as sales volume increases." In a little more than a week, I received a gracious acknowledgement from the White House. And, naturally, I have saved it, too.

In 1972, the Goldblatt's chain consisted of 46 stores throughout the Midwestern states of Illinois, Indiana, Wisconsin, and Michigan, and we were justly proud when it was announced that Goldblatt's had won the Brand Names Foundation 1st Place Award as National Retailer of the Year in the Department Store Class–One Category. This was an honor I had never expected Goldblatt's to earn, considering the distrust manufacturers of national brands had held for so many years. Achieving this recognition had been the grand effort of my lifetime: the countless programs to indoctrinate and undisciplined, unwieldy, buying force; my ceaseless espousing of quality as a factor even before price; my own trips to brand vendors in all the markets across the country pleading for their trust — and then making certain we earned it. To have established this code and practice in our company where there had been no code at all was prize enough. But for Goldblatt's to earn national acclaim for in this practice for me was especially meaningful. And to achieve this acclaim in the form of such testimonial was icing on the cake.

Later, Goldblatt's was to run a special and colorful promotion which we called World–Wide Patterns for Living '72. The national brands award, plus our foreign buying exploits, had evidently caught the attention of some U.S. government agencies interested in international trade. I was asked to address a special group of American ethnic leaders to share my views on selling

Chapter XVI   Taking Charge

imports and special country promotions. My talk stressed that whatever the diversity of the cultures of the world, and conflicts between them accelerated trade among nations was the truest binding force for peace.

Throughout my life, I never felt I had adequate opportunity beyond some scattered public statements to fully express the depth of my feelings for the city I had adopted as a child and which I had since come to adore — Chicago! Not until *Markets of America* requested that I write an article describing Chicago as a marketplace did I put into words something of what I thought about the city. The editor had asked for an "on-the-spot informative study," which was to be "a timely forecast to be used by manufacturers and businessmen who advertise their products nationally and regionally . . . and by site seekers, among others." Published in the 1970 edition (*Markets* was an annual publication of the *Advertiser* magazine), my article appeared along with those of others, including Cincinnati retailer Fred Lazarus III, Indianapolis mayor (and later senator from Indiana) Richard Lugar, and Quebec's then prime minister Jean-Jacques Bertrand. Later, the Chicago City Council added it to the city's archives as an "official love song" to Chicago.

In the piece, I compared Chicago to a mackerel, the fish that must keep constantly swimming to keep from sinking to the bottom, surely an apt metaphor for Chicago, a city of extraordinary growth and vitality. The competition of being on a fast track kept us constantly improving. At the time I wrote this article (1970) Chicago was still only 135 years old, making it then the youngest of the world's 10 largest cities. No one business dominated our economy — instead, it was the nation's leader in a dozen or more diverse industries, from commercial printing to candy making, industrial machinery and die–making to meat–product manufacturing. Chicago was a transportation hub, convention center, and the nation's largest exporter, I discovered in process of writing the article. It still, 25 years ago, manufactured more TVs and radios and household appliances than any other city, and did 93 percent of the nation's mail order business.

Though Chicago can no longer claim leadership in many of these fields, it still is a city of villages and neighborhoods. This I pointed to as one of Chicago's major virtues, along with its marvelously hard–working people — which I always said was the greatest factor contributing to Goldblatt's success. I reflected on the number of outstanding colleges and universities, that our medical schools helped train one–fifth of the physicians in the world, that we had one of the largest lakefront parks found anywhere, the world's largest commodities market, as well as its tallest buildings. "Holy mackerel," I concluded, "Chicago is on the go." The city had been good for the Goldblatt brothers and for hosts of other families. I was to be one of these fish.

# # #

The fiscal calendars within the procession of the passing years took precedence, certainly by my own corporate–oriented outlook, over another concept of time. I would think of personal events, like birthdays, in terms of the "period" in which they fell, or the sale event that heralded their coming. In 1973, the steaming cauldron of events in the company was matched only by those to be uncovered at the White House. The Watergate scandal rocked the nation, dismayed the world, disgraced the administration, and brought down a president. Though the

Chapter XVI   Taking Charge

Goldblatt family intrigues never became part of the public record in the way those of the Nixon administration did, they were surely sufficient in quantity and drama to fill several pot-boiling novels. The roller-coaster course of the Goldblatt's stock on the American Exchange — from a high of six dollars and as low as two and five-eighths during the 1974 — was mirrored by fluctuating passions inside the executive suite.

Despite this, the Goldblatt's employees' support of the cancer research effort hadn't faltered for an instant. In 1973 alone, they raised $150,000. In the nearly 30 years since the fund had been established, Goldblatt's employees had raised $2 million for this work on their own, contributing it to leading universities and cancer research hospitals throughout the country.

Chapter XVII
Disengaging

In 1974, Africa beckoned more than company intrigues, so Bobbie and myself, Gary, Stuart, and David took off on a photographic safari. We shared some unforgettably thrilling, even hazardous, experiences with elephants, laughing hyenas, and lions, all the while mercilessly shooting every animal we encountered with our cameras.

Naturally we had to do this trip our own way. Rather than join an organized tour, we hired a "white hunter" along with his land rover. With us were three Masai tribesmen and their truck, which was loaded with tents, supplies, and food since we would camp in the open field along with the animals of the wild.

We started in Nairobi, toured Kenya, and got our share of adventure. At one stop, Bobbie and I shared one tent; the others were in other tents around the fire. Because it was cold, we slept fully clothed in our cots. A lantern lit the entrance to our tent, and one night, having to use the facilities (such as they were), I forgot the warning we'd had about laughing hyenas, an unfamiliar animal whose amusing name led me to regard it as harmless. I learned otherwise. Hearing their yelping sounds get closer, I rushed back to the tent. Then Bobbie and I saw the canvas move; the hyenas were rubbing against it. Our safe

Chapter XVII Disengaging

haven did not now seem safe enough. We peered through the slit in the front flap and by the light of the lantern saw an ugly, snarling creature, just inches away. What to do? We had no guns. So I yelled at the top of my voice, "Get outta here!" Every sneaking hyena turned and bolted. Bobbie said I should "retail" that voice.

In Tanzania, we came across a heard of elephants, and learned that lumbering isn't the way to describe their movement. A baby was among them, and we hadn't known how extremely protective the grownups are. Parked in four-foot tall grass only 100 yards from them, we relished the sight. But not for long. Suddenly, one of the elephants let out a deafening shriek, signaling the herd. It started thundering toward us. Because of the rough terrain, our land rover could go only about 15 miles an hour. If we could get to the smooth road, we could speed up. Would we make it? Our bodies bounced around the vehicle along with all our stuff until we reached the road — and yes, just in the nick of time.

On still another day, we came across two lions in an affectionate tryst. We parked about 50 feet away and rolled down our windows, all set to watch. The lions moved. We followed. Again they moved. Again we followed and parked. Then without warning, the black-maned male raced for us. We quickly rolled up the windows as he kept swiping at the windshield. The five of us feverishly clicked our cameras, reaping dozens of pictures — all blurred.

#

In the mid-1970s, Goldblatt's had taken to staging spectacular semiannual sales of top designer dresses with original values of up to $1,000. We sold them for a mere fraction of their original prices. The sales, which were run in the State Street store bargain basement, required extensive planning: hiring additional sales people, more security guards, and even police to control the mayhem of the crowds of customers. It was like the old days — bargain seekers after rock-bottom prices: chaos, flying elbows, the continual ding of cash registers. The crowds competed for the $100 to $350 dresses selling as low as $29.99, with labels like Geoffrey Beene, Halston, Donald Brooks, Oscar de la Renta, and others.

Whatever agonies I was fated to endure at the hands of the fellow board members, the assorted intrigues, clashes, and heartaches in between, there was still the ecstasy of sale extravaganzas such as that one. I also relished opportunities to address gatherings of our employees, particularly when the occasion was honoring them with special awards. One such event I recall with particular clarity was when employees representing all our stores gathered to honor one of their own. "All the powerful things in the world are invisible — honor, character, love, charity," I said to them. "They are lights within, casting their rays around you so that you can find your way."

On this occasion, Joan Vant, who worked in our visual merchandising division, was being honored by the National Retail Merchants Association. She had been given its 1974 Lazarus Award for outstanding community service, an honor presented to just one individual from the 30,000 member stores, in recognition of her efforts for the Goldblatt Employees Cancer Research Foundation. When the award was given, Joan spoke to 2,000 people gathered in the ballroom of the New York Hilton to recognize her and other award winners. She told them what she had done to raise the funds, and all the time tears were

Chapter XVII Disengaging

streaming down her cheeks. Many members of the audience reached for their handkerchiefs to dry their own eyes. They gave her a standing ovation. I was so proud. She brought to the foundation and to the Goldblatt company the power of those invisible attributes. I liked to think that we ran the type of company that enabled people like Joan to thrive.

Truly, I loved these people, and hoped their hearts were able to sense the feelings of my own. I hoped they understood how hard I had worked to maintain a rhetoric–free, united, and secure family sense in both my personal and business lives. Over my entire lifetime, I had longed to engender the "special people" quality to my administration that no amount of money could buy. I also hoped this could be passed on to the persons replacing me, but this was not to be as simple as I had hoped. There were challenges to deal with outside the company as well as in.

During the late 1970s, the board of directors of the State Street Council, of which I was a member, made a decision I felt was very unwise. The board voted to convert State Street, That Great Street, from all its glories and tradition of traffic and excitement, into a shopping mall. Although converting downtown streets into malls had developed into somewhat of a trend across the country, I felt it was not the right thing to do with State Street. Though this effort to compete with suburban malls had met with considerable success in some towns, there had been failures, too, and even more of them, as the years unfolded.

I implored the top men at Field's, Carson's, Weiboldt's, Charles A. Stevens, Sears, and Ward's, who were also directors of the council, to reconsider. I stated my feeling that changing State Street into a mall without a contiguous parking facility was a serious mistake. All but David Meltzer of Evan's Furs (and myself) thought otherwise, and the mall became a reality. Naturally, it far exceeded the originally budgeted cost and was, at best, doubtfully successful overall. More than 15 years later, as I write this, plans are underway to deconstruct the mall and bring cars back onto State Street. In the meantime, all but Field's and Carson's are no longer on the street, which is reviving again with stores like T.J. Maxx, Filene's, and Toys R Us. The old Goldblatt's store, which was once considered as a site for Chicago's public library, was later remodeled and taken over by DePaul University as part of its Loop campus.

Throughout the rest of the 1970s, there continued to be arguments and much dissention between my brother Maurice, my nephews, and me; and as a result, the business was neglected. In 1976, Stanford Goldblatt (Maurice's son) replaced me as president and CEO. When the company began to show a loss, Stanford resigned one and a half years later. I resumed the presidency until our company hired former Wal-Mart executive Harold Smith. As president, he held this position until September 1979, at which time both he and I were voted out of the company. We were replaced by Louis Duncan, a Sealy mattress company executive who was voted in as president, CEO, and chairman of the board. In 1980, he resigned and Lionel Goldblatt became president until 1981 when Goldblatt's went into Chapter 11.

The end finally came for me on September 14, 1979, a Friday and Bobbie's birthday. I was told I had 48 hours to clear out of the building. Two days to get out of a lifetime. Unfamiliar bad feelings are tough to sort out and handle, as are undigested tensions and worries. I barely recall getting into the chauffeur-driven company limousine the following morning and

Chapter XVII   Disengaging

driving down to the mammoth Goldblatt's State Street store. But I did arrive in my ninth floor office by 7 A.M. just as I had for decades. Questions. These ungodly feelings, how to handle them? Would that day bring an end to my anguish or only mark a new chapter with its own kind of grief? "Get hold of yourself," I said to myself. "There are almost 76 years of wisdom that will just have to come to your rescue."

That memory of Bobbie's birthday over 25 years earlier flashed through my consciousness — the day when I had surprised her by showing up at the door of our hotel suite wearing only my overcoat and shoes. It was a silly prank, but the memory brought on a smile as the limousine turned off Lake Shore Drive toward the store. Would some sorcery transform my attitude? There had to be smiles ahead, just had to be, I muttered reassuringly. There was life after Goldblatt's! It felt good to think it. Perhaps the sorting out had already started, and my wife Bobbie was the catalyst. Our home, children, friends, new interests, all this was in store for us. Everything came rushing too fast. I wasn't sure what I was supposed to be feeling.

What could be waiting out there? In three months I would be 76. That morning I had at least managed to scatter a big bunch of greeting cards around for Bobbie before leaving the house. If quantity of cards alone portrayed my love and devotion, it would have taken a carload. Loving her more because I needed her more seemed one-sided. I'd have to think about that.

Over all the months of squabbling and frustrations in the company, just one look at Bobbie when I got home was an uplift. The contagion of her spirit never failed. She called it total happiness and kept saying we just had to reach out for it, that my hands and mind would find fulfillment, new focus. I just had to take a good hard swallow. I'd said it a thousand times in business, "One door closes and another opens wider." Now, would it work for me?

That morning I did not perform the retailer's usual ritual, tearing out all kinds of newspaper advertising. I really couldn't, although I would have wanted to despite my new status, or lack thereof. My mind was too cluttered, and I had begun to feel a welling anger that overtook my sense of worry and stress. It stayed with me. I was oblivious to the traffic, even to the surface condition of Lake Michigan, which ordinarily I never failed to check.

I started packing things up on Friday, and the next day the moving out process began. My middle son, Stuart, and the chauffeur, Norman, labored with me all of Saturday and Sunday. We packed 61 years of memorabilia, the amassment of a lifetime. We were a kind of assembly line. More like disassembly. I sorted and grouped the keepables from the junk until I couldn't tell one from the other. It seemed that every twentieth item or so gave me pause to recall a time or incident that rendered it a keepsake in the overall collection.

Oh, the torrent of milestones in the company's history that come to mind when you're packing it up. The memorabilia resurrected people connected with this episode or that. Most of them are dead now, and though many had been valuable for all the years we worked together, some were capable and productive only for a particular period of development. They were right for the time. Others turned out to be scoundrels. There were photos by the fistful. And what a zealous kid I was. Those funny clothes! I was not more than 17, I recalled, looking at a picture of myself in knickers.

Chapter XVII Disengaging

From time to time I caught myself giving prolonged attention to one thing or another, entranced. In the corner of my eye I could perceive Stuart and Norman's empathy while they patiently waited for me. I would resume abruptly.

It was months before I got out from under the load I so painstakingly brought home. First, I organized much of it by year, then I prioritized it by a blurry standard of relative importance. Size and frangibility soon made that impossible. Bobbie had cleared and provided a room for my office and eventually the project settled in, but my reminiscences and inner turmoil would not be stilled.

Flashbacks would come in no chronological order. The Goldblatt Bros. Dry Goods Store. Momma's stories of the early years in Poland. As a kid, I had kept notes of the countless harrowing experiences of my parents, brothers, and sisters. They were stories of sheer survival, and I needed no notes for vivid recall. There, in that room I reached a peak of agitation.

First, there were the heroic hard years and many tender thoughts of the family adjusting, struggling, and emerging. Then the wrenching bitterness, the depressing overview of how our family had self-destructed. Thoughts of what might have been I could never dispel, but I would try. I had to try. I had to somehow put an end to reliving the past. It seemed even Bobbie couldn't help me with this pain, with the obsession my having been fired had triggered. Besides, it was endangering my health. It was a double-edged sword. By diabolic design I was out of the company, and I found myself wallowing in unmanageable thoughts. Like a moth to a flame, I was drawn to that upstairs room full of memories. I managed to rationalize my obsession. It was like something I'd once heard about judo, that if you would stop resisting and get it all out, the overload of the psyche would run its course, and then there could be peace.

Then it dawned on me. I realized that it would take a book to unload my psyche. It would be a Goldblatt's history, but more than the rise and fall of a family. I thought of how my book could trace much history of the department store industry and the great city of Chicago by marshaling the lifetimes of immigrant merchants, our successes and failures, and the phenomenon of family enmity that developed within the dynamics of our environment. I only knew it must be told and then I would be free.

Even after I'd acquired some peace with myself, I realized that revenge and jealousy, love and hate, as well as ambition, would always be with me. They are with all of us. Somewhere in the back of my head there is an ancient volcano where the years of my life boil and bubble. The random bits of things seen, felt, experienced, heard, and done or discussed were all tumbled together in this mental inferno. Until I wrote this book, I felt my volcano had never erupted, and I frequently worried when and how it would. Putting it all down in some sort of orderly progression of events and themes has stilled somewhat the boiling. But sometimes the old arguments resume with all their former power and intensity.

I've watched what's happened to Goldblatt's over the past 15 years mainly with detachment. I sold my stock as soon as I could legally do so, and since the company declared bankruptcy two years after I left it, I've had nothing more to do with it. While I was still there, I struggled helplessly to right what I saw as wrongs, but still the business went from bad to worse. Interestingly, what was left of the firm was purchased in 1982 by Jerry Wexler, who with the Pritzker boys had been a teenager Joel and I spent weekends with at their summer home in Wisconsin during the 1930s. A successful real estate developer, Wexler was one of the visionaries who dreamed what North Michigan Avenue could become back when it was still a rather relaxed neighborhood boulevard.

My brother Maurice died in 1983 two years after Joel's death. Unfortunately we never really reconciled, though I did remain close to my sister Sarah until she died in 1993, at the age of 103.

Even at 90 I can say that life is short enough as it is. Reliving how the business suffered and eventually succumbed to bankruptcy would only darken the bright side of a life blessed with good fortune. It's been a separate road, buoyantly traveled.

Life is a game, play to win!

Frank Graham, an official of the American Stock Exchange, celebrates with me the listing of the Goldblatt Department Stores on the exchange in 1967.

Chapter XVI   Taking Charge

All these boys joined Bobbie and me at my 90th birthday party, a festive brunch she organized at the Tavern Club in early December 1993, a few weeks before the real event on Christmas Day. Standing behind us are David, a keyboardist and composer in Los Angeles, Gary, who is a retailer in Chicago himself, and Stuart, a food broker in Florida.

Life is a game, play to win!

Afterward

When I retired from Goldblatt's Department Store, I was 75 and had had over 60 years in the business. Today I regard that long episode as little more than an illusion. I traded in its reality so as to grasp the truth of my life. To be worthy of all I have found, I must never bemoan the past. I have no more mountains to climb, no more worlds to conquer.

And that's particularly so now that I have completed this book. There was some point, indeed, in the diaries I kept all my life, as they have been my prime references. Also useful was all the correspondence I had saved, especially letters written during the war. In the years since then, I made notes of the arguments and dissensions within the family, the verbal battles I had with my brothers and nephews. I also kept notes on the disagreeable negotiations I had with union representatives in the early 1970s. Particularly in the 10 years prior to my retirement, I kept recordings of debates and arguments within the family. When I first sat down to write a book, my intention was simply to compile a record of my life in story form for Bobbie and our three sons. While material from my diaries and word-for-word records of family arguments are included in the original manuscript intended for them, I've tried to dance rather quickly over the parts of this

Afterward

story most derogatory to others. Writing this book has been therapeutic for me, and there's no constructive purpose in telling much of the rest of it.

It's hard now for me to realize that 15 years have gone by since I left the company. I wonder frequently how the 10,000 employees we had then have fared. I'd always thought of them as my team, my partners, my associated, even my family. In all the postmortems of our store and however much our business judgment may have come under criticism, we were always praised for how well we treated our employees.

These years of retirement have freed me of tension and stress. I'm a full-time citizen of the world, now. On the job, I smoked three packs of cigarettes a day. That being just another way to self-destruct, I quit cold turkey. My home office is my sanctuary, my study, and my writing place. I keep hours there from 5:30 A.M. to mid-afternoon. Other times I venture out to ride my bicycle, play with our dogs, travel, or run errands. During these years, people have asked me what I do and how I spend my time. I always say, "I'm just a playboy." I play golf, poker, backgammon, the stock market, and go on the world cruises with my wonderful wife.

Our three sons consult me on their business ventures, and I enjoy visiting them. Gary has three retail gift stores. With a son, a daughter, and his beautiful wife Denise, he lives near Chicago. Stuart lives in Tampa, Florida, where he is a food broker; his pretty wife Deborah is a capable business executive in the health field. David lives in West Hills, California, and is building a career as a musician, composer, and keyboardist for films and TV. Above all, I've retained my health. Every day is a romantic adventure in my 42-year love affair with Bobbie. She is not without writing talent herself and has worked for the

Chicago Sun-Times and *North Shore* magazine as a columnist and feature writer.

As for the past and the challenges I've faced, I draw upon George Bernard Shaw who said, "The reasonable man adapts himself to the world; the unreasonable one persists in trying to adapt the world to himself. Therefore all progress depends upon the unreasonable man."

As for the present and future, I quote May Lamberton Becker who wrote: "We grow neither better nor worse when we get old, but more like ourselves." In conclusion, I must say, the angels have done a good job watching over me. I applaud their ability.

Louis Goldblatt

Appendices

"The Missing Link" (1954)

"The Sixth Sense" (1957)

"To Get, You Gotta Give, or Give and Take" (1962)

Chapter XVI Taking Charge

The Missing Link
by Louis Goldblatt

EXECUTIVE VICE-PRESIDENT, SECRETARY AND TREASURER,
GENERAL MERCHANDISE DIRECTOR,
GOLDBLATT BROS. INC. CHICAGO, ILLINOIS
AN ADDRESS DELIVERED BEFORE THE
MERCHANDISING EXECUTIVE CLUB OF CHICAGO,
SEPTEMBER 20, 1954

When I was first requested to talk to you tonight, this little booklet entitled "Merchandising Executives Club of Chicago," was given to me. On the cover, I noticed and illustration, which appears to be a picture of a link. It, therefore, strikes me that this must be the Missing Link that holds together the important requisites for improved merchandising and promoting. Let us carefully remember these last two words, "Merchandising" and "Promoting"

Any business, be it a resource, a retailer, or an advertising agency (all of which are represented here tonight), must depend upon a chain of elements-each element and important link in the chain for progressive merchandising and promoting.

Every business that has been in operation for even one day, automatically becomes concerned with three important elements-those of past history, present trend and budgeting. These three elements shape our future performance. We already know what a present trend is, we are presently experiencing it. But we do not know what the future holds, and sop we prepare a budget.

All in all, the quality of our budgeting determines the quality of our merchandising and promoting. A business, like a human being , lives on hopes and desires. A business, like a human being, sets itself a goal, makes a pledge, takes a vow. In business terms we call these acts budgets.

A budget when finally created us composed of a chain of elements-each link in that chain a very important one. I will refer to each of these link as follows: the Prime Resource, the Prime Salesmanship, and the Resource. You will observe that I have two resource links on this chain. One is a prime resource, and the other is just a resource and nothing more. For every resource link in this chain that we can convert into a prime resource link, we automatically strengthen the entire chain that has to do with our future plant, wishes, goals, vows, pledges and budgets. All of these links put together shape our merchandising and promoting functions. The word "Merchandising" comes from the Latin word "mercor," which means "to buy and sell," The word "Promote" comes from two Latin words, "pro," meaning "forward move." In buying and selling and in moving forward, our budgeting must be properly applied to each link in this important chain. We must not have a single missing Link. Unfortunately, the present trend seems to indicate a future shortage of prime resource links. Of this trend continues, we will find the prime resource link missing from this chain,

The Prime Resource Link

Not so many years ago, expression, "Caveat emptor" was common-"Customer beware," The manufacturer primarily made his goods with the sole intention of selling them to the retailer. Today, the prime resource creates his product with the consumer as his sole concern. His primary object is to give the consumer all that her money can buy, and the most serviceable product he knows how to produce. To do this, he engages in research, laboratory testing, experience and know-how. When he has finally created the best possible product, he sell is directly to the consumer through his national advertising program. Then, to further complement his already successful accomplishment, he stands behind each purchase of his product by guaranteeing the consumer's complete satisfaction.

Today, unlike the custom of not so many years, ago this prime resource also protects the consumer by properly labeling his products. Today's products now plainly show the contents and describe the ingredients, whether they pertain to style, color, shape, size or durability. The resource provides this information on his product in addition to conforming with such provisions as may be required by the Federal Food, Drug and Cosmetic Act, the Trade Practice Rules, he National Bureau of Standards, the Wool Products Labeling Act, the Advertising Standards Committee, the Name of Woods Code,

Chapter XVII Disengaging

the Better Business Bureau, and many more.

I can remember a number of years ago when the only way to determine the quality of a pound of grass seed was by the price, unless we sent the seed to the laboratory to learn what ingredients it contained. Then our helpless customers could only take our word for it. Today, when the customer buys a package of grass seed, she knows the percentage of red top, blue grass, white clover, timothy, inert matter, etc. It is printed right on the package.

I can also remember that when we opened a sack of feathers we would blow into the sack to get a better idea as to what portion of these feathers were goose, duck, turkey or chicken-whether it was part feathers and part down, or all feathers, or all down. In those days feather frequently were not even washed. Today, there is a national association of bedding manufacturers organized by the manufacturers themselves. They constantly make purchases in retail stores and send them to laboratories to check whether the contents are properly labeled, and if all feathers are washed and sterilized. They do their own policing, thereby protecting the consumer from paying for something she doesn't get. This, in turn, automatically protects the retailer.

The progress toward educating the consumer through information contained on products-be it the wool content of a sweater, the filling of a mattress, or the ingredients of a vitamin tablet-has helped to a great degree in placing resource and retailer relationship on a more harmonious level. In this way, too, the consumer has been educated as to what she has a right to get for money, and she has continued to buy when she has found the product serviceable and satisfactory. Accordingly, as far as the retailer is concerned, the prime resource has already performed a pre-selling job. The prime resource knows that if his product is sound, and if it is what the consumer wants, the consumer will but it-provided, of course, that he supplies the retailer with the necessary sales policy and incentive for felling the same way about the product.

In this manner, a prime resource never stops perfecting his product. He continues to pour more efforts and money into further perfecting his product, and, accordingly, the consumer continues to enjoy a better, more luxurious and easier way of life through the use of these constantly improving products.

The Retailing Link

And now for the retailing link. The average retailer who buys from prime resources no longer depends solely on his own salesmanship. He no longer requires laboratory testing equipment to check up on his resources. He merely requires the ability to be a top retail distributor of merchandise to the consumer. To do that, old ways of selling have been replaced by modern methods. The average large retail distributor functions in the following manner in distributing his resources' goods to the consumer. He requires a system of basic stocks, unit controls and selling trend statistics. Thee systems tell him what the customer wants, when she wants it, and how much she wants. Based on these systems, the retailer's buyers purchase their requirements through information compiled by clerical personnel, and not by their persona whims, moods, likes or dislikes. Through these systems, the retailer no longer needs to be a genius or a master-mind. His most important requirements now are to purchase from top prime resources, and to promote the goods he purchases.

Allow me to portray the working of Goldblatt's in both the buying and selling fields. In most cases, when we buy from top prime resources, we automatically become an important retail distributor of nationally known branded items. Our success in doing a good sales job on this kind of merchandise depends upon how we back up the selling program as laid down by the prime resources. We make use of their national advertising in the newspapers. magazines, radio and television. Our presentation of the product to our customers requires effective display on our selling floors. Most often our displays include window back up plus store-wide displays. We orient our personnel with all the facts pertaining to the products through a series of meetings and bulletins. Very often we make the selling of the item a game, through the means of prizes and contests. We include all of our stores on such a program at one time, thereby creating maximum impacton the consumer. Of course, all of this is done only if we have certain incentives.

Just what incentives do we retailers look for when we take on a resource's product? We are concerned with the re-order business on the item, not just a hit-and-run, sell-and-forget event. We must be fully sold on the item. We must know that our customers will get their money's worth; that the item will be serviceable; that they will be pleased with their purchase, and, as a result, will continue to shop in our stores. No-I did not leave out the very important incentive-the item we take on must be profitable. With all of these incentives, we build a stronger bond between our customers and our prime resources.

Of course, this, in itself, is not the complete story of what is required to retail a resource's products successfully. We must also provide our customers with the necessary conveniences, and with courteous service. Naturally, we must also have a powerful and loyal team of employees who receive every known employee benefit and consideration.

Allow me to further elaborate on Goldblatt's buying habits, and our relationship with our prime resources. There is one salient signpost the retail distributor has today that

Chapter XVII   Disengaging

he has had from the beginning of time-the one signpost that has not changed even to this day. For years, the retailers, ourselves included, were concerned with this one question, "Will we make our day?" That seemed to be our one and only measuring rod. Strange as it may seem, past history, plus present trend statistics, permit us to plan future sales budgets that come very close to actual sales. We know that if we do nothing more for a given day than we did for the corresponding day a year ago, we can expect nothing better than to equal our sales figures of a year ago.

The ever common expressions in the retail business are, "Will you make your day," "Did you make your day," and "What percentage did you increase or decrease?" We have attacked this age-old sales attitude with counterphrases. Now we say, "What did you buy?" "How much did you buy?" and "From whom did you buy?" You have often heard the proverb, "As ye sow, so shall ye reap." To paraphrase it in the retailing business, It's "As ye buy, so shall ye sell."

Some years back, we launched a program known as "Goldblatt's Vendor Relationship Policy." We listed all the resources with whom we do business, by departments and even by items. We began the tedious and   herculean task of breaking down our findings into a series of statistical figures. We wanted to know which resources were responsible for our markdowns. We wanted to know such things as what our advertising; costs were by resources; what percentages of inventory were by resources; what our square footage was in a given department for a resource's product; what percentage of a department's total business was done by each resource; and what our rate of stock turn was on the product of each resource. Most important, we wanted to know what percentage of each department's total purchases was made from each resource.

After this information had been compiled, we sifted out all the resources which proved to be prime resources, and these prime resources have become an important part of our company. Just as we rate the ability of our buyers in the course of a year, and review their showings periodically, we now rate review these prime resources with whom we do business.

In the recent years we have made great strides in furthering our resource relationship policy. We have come closer to achieving our ideals and our goal. At the close of last year, we found that our company had purchased merchandise from 6,702 resources. We found that only 600 prime resources, or 9.1% of all the resources with whom we did business. It is our further objective to reduce the number of resourced, which are nothing more than resources.

The average layman sees a chain of department stores like ours, doing

$100,000,000 worth of business annually, and sees thousands upon thousands of items. The impression he gets is that we sell quantities of each of these items. That is not true. We don't sell all the items we carry in quantity. There are some items, and only a relatively few of them, that sell in such huge quantities that they make the thousands of other items we carry look as if they standing still.

For example, we have a domestic department that comprises many brands of bed sheets, pillowcases, muslins, sheetings, ticking, mattress covers, and all other such domestic textile items. Yet, in this department one brand, Pepperell, does 50% of the department's total business. I assure you that it does not occupy 50% of the square footage, nor does it account for 50% of the markdowns in this department. I assure you that its rate of inventory turnover is far greater than all other items in this department, and that our total dollar profit on it, too, is far greater than all other items.

We buy this brand from a resource whose product's performance and whose program for merchandising classify it as a prime resource, and as the ever-present link-not the missing link.

A little later on in this discussion, I will try to portray to you the kind of resource that I refer to as the "Missing Link." The Pepperell Company made a bed sheet, and they made it most excellently, and created a consumer demand because of their know-how, based upon many years of experience and research. They have given it every known kind of laboratory test. They put it on the market and then they sold it to the consumer through a good job of national advertising. Then they protected their policy program of distribution, which included the necessary incentives for the retailer. Then they virtually took the customer by the arm and brought her into our store, so that all we had to do was display it. Since our display was effective, and we carried it in the colors and sizes the customers wanted it, through our system of unit control, had it when the customer wanted it, in the quantity she wanted, and conformed with the Pepperell Company's policy for merchandising this item, we, of course, did a top retail distributing job on the product. No sales person stood at the counter and used any high pressure salesmanship in selling a Pepperell bed sheet to the customer. It was the customer who demanded the Pepperall bed sheet. All we did was take here money, ring up the sale on the cash register, and wrap her package.

This prime resource and his retailers work harmoniously, thereby giving this prime resource the necessary tools for further perfecting his products in the interest of bettering the American consumer's way of life.

The prime resource and the retailer are partners. If two partners don't get along, a business cannot grow. A top prime resource is the top retailer's teacher. The top retailer

Chapter XVII   Disengaging

is the material upon which the top prime resource works. If the one does not value his teacher, if the other does not live his material, then, despite their individual abilities and capacities, they cannot build a growing business or produce a satisfactory net profit. It is important that a resource and retailer work very closely. It is important that they be concerned with each other's success. Both together purchase the future with the present. Our future will always be dependent upon what we do today.

In holding a successful chain together, it is just as important for the resources to know who their retailers are as it is for the retailer to know his resources. In this respect, the resources have a greater advantage then the retailers. The retailer does now know the names and addresses of most of his customers. He only knows what the customers buy and when they buy it. The resource not only knows what he sells and when he sells it, but to whom he sells it. So the resources should be as anxious to sell to top prime retailers as the retailer is to buy from top prime resources. He should know which of his retailers really produce a profit for him and do a satisfactory distributing job. He should be concerned whether a retail distributor's purchases are increasing or decreasing over a given period, because this information is the clue as to what his future sales trend will be with that given retailer. A prime resource should also know which of his retailers conform with his costly and elaborate merchandising and promoting policy.

The Advertising Link

And now for the important advertising link. Take Goldblatt's for example. Our advertising expenditure last year was $3,500,000. This sizeable sum was spent in such media s=as metropolitan newspapers, community and suburban newspapers, foreign papers, our own shopping news, radio, television, billboards, 'phone, direct mail, etc. In spending this vast sum of money for advertising, we did not aim to buy lineage, space, pages, circulation or media. Instead, it was our objective to purchase the greatest amount of sales returns per advertising dollar spent.

Buying advertising differs considerably from buying merchandise. When we purchase a product we want to know what it is made of, how well will it serve us, are we buying it at a fair price. However, when we purchase advertising we are concerned with its end result, dollar sales returns. We are good buyers of advertising only when we purchase a low advertising percentage cost. The greater the sales returns, the lower the advertising percentage cost. Low advertising cost and large sales returns are realized purely through the quality of the copy, composition, illustration, timing and position, rather than the price per line or page. There is no such thing as a perfect ad, There is always one that could be even more perfect and product even more sales.

Display Link

Here we have another important link in the chain. I can well remember some 42 years ago when my brother Maurice was a sales clerk at Iverson's Department Store on Milwaukee Avenue. After working many hours and late into the evening he would come home and right after dinner would practice showcard writing. He was preparing himself for a future day when he would be in business for himself. He felt that the most important thing necessary to succeed in business is to know how to display merchandise on a table, how to trim a window and how to paint a sign. When you have no money to spend for advertising, you have to advertise your wares the hard way, which, by the way, is the most effective.

Forty years ago this month, my brothers Maurice and Nathan, with their total savings of $500, opened up for business. Their ages were 22 and 20. With the after school help of their two younger brothers, Louis and Joel, one 10 and one 7, they started off a business that was to grow into the present Goldblatt Bothers Department Stores. For several years after we had been in business, my brother Maurice made all the signs and did all the display work. Today, of course, we have machines that make signs and we employ professional interior and exterior display men. Signs must have informative coy. The sign on the item must be, not only the silent, but the salient salesperson to our customer. The display must stop and tempt our customer. Just how does this important link strengthen the total chain of links? You may be selling the product that a top prime resource produced, but you will sell much more if you display this product intelligently. You may spend money for advertising and it will produce a certain sales return, But the percentage of advertising cost will be lower for the same advertising dollar expenditure of advertising cost will be lower for the same advertising dollar expenditure if you do a plus business on this advertising item through your display efforts.

I remember how my brothers and I got up at the crack of dawn on cold wintry days to climb a stepladder and hang underwear, blankets, sacks of feathers, etc., to our awnings on the outside of our store. Around midnight, we would again climb the ladders to take down the stiff and frozen garments. Was it more important then than it is now to display your wares? Of course, it is much easier now. At least our fingers don't get frozen along with the underwear, but business generally is missing the aggressive mental attitude that makes use of the many tools in our possession-especially the tool of display and the backing up of a product. This display link cannot afford to be missing from the chain of

Chapter XVII   Disengaging

merchandising and promoting.

Salesmanship Link

Just what does the word "salesmanship" mean? The dictionary defines this word as follows: "The art of selling, or especially successful selling methods." I fell that all sales personnel have the art of selling, and have the ability to apply especially successful selling methods. What the greatest majority don't have is "wantmanship." What they know and have the ability to do is one thing, We need to add wantmanship to salesmanship.

There is nothing wrong with our sales personnel of today. Whatever may be wrong is wrong because of poor supervision, interest, direction and training. The resource knows how this product was manufactured. The retailer, too, knows all its virtues. The advertisements, in many cases, rave about the product. Very often, the display indicates the products many good features-but, too often, the sales personnel are kept ignorant of the romance connected with the manufacturing and distributing of this product. It is important for them to be informed about a product's features. Sales personnel need a personal interest in the selling of the product. This very often is done through prizes and contests, meetings, lectures and training programs. It is also necessary that selling personnel get the maximum of employee benefits. For them to be interested in their work, they must be happy in their work. They, too, must see a future for themselves. They must want to sell the item. Their desires rest in their employer's hands. An employer will get no more from hid employee than he gives. The mere giving of a salary is not the total requisite. The employer must give of himself. He must be concerned and interested in his employee's welfare. An interested sales person will make an added sale, will produce a greater sales transaction, will sell something to a customer that the customer did not come in to buy, and plus sales of this type represent a greater net profit than regular sales, since rent, light, heat, power and other such expenses remain stationary, regardless of sales volume. It takes an added push on the part of the salesperson to step up his or her selling efforts, but that added push requires wantmanship, which the heads of business have not instilled in sufficient measure.

Mental Attitude

Now I feel that I have covered the important links that make up the successful chain of merchandising and promoting. I have talked about the prime resource link, the prime retailing link, the prime advertising link, the prime display link, and the prime salesmanship link. This entire chain of links, when put together, produced a past history produces a present trend, and, finally, produces a future performance. All these elements are derived from the mother chain, mental attitude.

It is very rarely that we humans ever accomplish more than we set out to accomplish. It is also very rarely that a business is better than it had planned to be. It seems we are creatures of habit. It seems that our minds are cluttered with last-year-itis. We have the tendency to plan to do what we did last year. In projecting a budget, we analyze last year's results, and our present trend. If we project an improvement over our previous performance, usually it is merely a trifle, and so we do improve, but only a trifle. Mainly, this is because we don't know our own abilities, our own skill, talents and strength. If I were to ask any one of you to place your ankles on the arm of a chair, and the back of your neck on the arm of another chair, with nothing supporting you between your ankles and neck, you would say that you could not do it. You truly believe you cannot do it. Yet, if you were hypnotized and put in that position, you not only would find that you had done it, but could even do it with 200 pounds of weight on your stomach.

Subconsciously, we very often are powerful and strong. Consciously, we don't do a certain thing because our mental attitude tell us we can't. We think small, and, as a result, produce small. A business looks at its last year's records. Last year on a given day it did X amount of business. This year it projects a budget to do the same amount of business, with possibly a small increase or decrease, and it actually will produce what the budget calls for.

If we were told that we must produce 50% sales increase-that it was a matter of life or death-I'm positive we would come through with our 50% increase. Mainly, I'm finding fault with the business man's method of budgeting, in that it lacks the proper mental attitude elements, which, in turn, comprises many elements, such as the links in a chain that I have portrayed. For a budget to be sound, every small port that makes up the total budget must be sound in itself. Actually, we get no more of a future than we pay for. In simple words, we purchase the future with the present. A budget, in itself, does not produce a successful future performance. The future will never be any better than what we are doing about it today, nor will it be any better then the quality of our mental attitude today.

The Missing Link

Now, what has all this got to do with the Missing Link? An important link, if it is missing, stops progress. A missing link has a chain reaction effect. A missing link may

Chapter XVII Disengaging

very well be the very roots for changing the meaning of the two important words, "Merchandising" and "Promoting". It could very well mean "Buy, sell and backward move," instead of "Buy, sell and forward move."

A missing link is that prime resource who has scientifically perfected a product that the consumer wants. He has promoted and advertised the product nationally. He has educated the consumer on its merits and has created a consumer acceptance. He has established a price that provides a fair profit to him, a fair profit to the retailer, and a fair price to the consumer, and then in a moment of greediness, he has in one swoop destroyed all of these virtuous elements. I am referring, of course, to certain classifications of nationally branded merchandise-mainly appliances, television, furniture, rugs and various isolated individual items from all other classifications of goods. These particular resources (notice I no longer refer to them as prime resources-instead I am referring to them as resources and nothing more) no longer care who their retailers are. They are mainly concerned with distributing more goods, and in doing more business for the moment, rather then the future.

This had to develop into a dog eat dog business. The first thing that happened was that the price policy structure has been destroyed. Along with that, the profit incentive has been killed. Without a uniform policy designed for the future, and without a profit incentive, the retailer no longer stresses that nationally known brand. In many cases, the retailer has told the customer not to buy the item, that it is not good, and has tried to switch the sale into a competitive item that is more profitable. In still more cases, many important prime retailers have discontinued the item completely. Consumers are no longer rushing to buy these nationally branded items at retail stores or discount houses. The customer no longer knows what a fair price should be on the product, nor what king of service she will get for the price she pays. The customer, as very many years ago, has had to become a shrewd and sharp buyer.

Hooray...once again we have in certain classifications of goods the term "Caveat emptor"-customer beware. Are you getting the service? Are you getting your money's worth? Are you buying from a reliable and dependable retailer? Is the product you're buying guaranteed? How do you know that your are buying it at the lowest price? Are you buying the brand that you read about and heard about, and that you set out to buy?

Eventually, this nationally branded item will regress in sales. This goes on and on until the item in question is laid to rest six feet under. When this happens, the manufacturer won't have the money for research, laboratory testing and improvement of his product, and he will discover that he no longer is a prime resource. Instead, he is just a resource and nothing more-he is the Missing Link.

I am quite confident that a backward merchandising condition cannot last long in this country of democracy and free enterprise. I fell that business in this company's future will greatly benefit from our mistakes of today, and that the resource, retailer and consumer links will find themselves on a stronger and more powerful chain of unit in not so long a time from now, with no Missing Links.

Chapter XVII   *Disengaging*

The Sixth Sense

by Louis Goldblatt

Executive Vice-President, Secretary and Treasurer Goldblatt's Chicago

An address before The advertising Executives Club of Chicago

at the La Salle Hotel, Tuesday, September 10, 1957.

Reproduced Through the Courtesy of The Chicago Daily News.

Fortune Telling:

I am not going to talk to you on the subjects of inflation or the consumers expendable income, nor will I talk about the fact that there are 800,000 automobiles that must be disposed of prior to the new models coming into the market. I am not going to discuss shopping centers or the price of steel or that bacon and pork have hit a new all-time high in price, nor do I intend to predict the future. All of this is left for you to read in the trade papers that has been brought to you by economists, professors, predictors and fortune tellers. Rather, I will talk to you on a subject that is equally intangible-the sixth sense.

Selling:

Selling was, is and always will be the foundation for everything in life, but especially for business. Even when we converse we are selling, whether it's explaining, describing, pleading, debating or just chit-chat. Especially we sell when we wait on a customer.

In my opinion competition today is keener and more intensified than at any time in our history and will continue to grow as it has since the creation of this country. Today the mere selling of a product for less money, or the selling of a better product for the same money, or giving the consumer more for money is only a part of the total requisites for doing more business on these items. Today many other elements must be sold in addition to the selling of the product and here is where being competitive takes on a new garment.

In the early days a customer came into a store and the store sold her something. It might have been something from behind the counter, from a drawer, from a shelf, or from the showcase. Today when a customer comes into a store, most often she is not sold something-instead, she buys something. Just what causes her to buy today?

Aside from the fact that the item is what she wants and at the right price, she buys because the item practically sells itself to her for the following reasons:
1. Its visual and sometimes animated display;
2. Its tempting presentation that creates on-the-spot impulse buying. This is especially true at a time like now, because as the buying power of the American consumer expands so does the number of products which tend to become impulse items;
3. The manner is which the article is packaged, which very often raises a single item sale to a multiple sale:
4. The label and information on the package as to specs, description, contents, size, etc.;
5. The legible sign pointing out its salient features;
6. The most important reason of all-the salesperson-if, when, who, why and where there happens to be one.

Accordingly, in these present time selling techniques, the merchant is applying his God-given five senses. This he has accomplished through improved merchandising methods of self-service, self-selection, packaging, radio, television and newspapers.

Merchandise products are now presented so that they can be seen, can be touched, can be smelled, can be tasted and can be heard. Now that we use our five senses in selling I suggest we add the sixth sense.

The sixth sense:

Just what is the sixth sense? I choose to define it as follows: It is made up of three parts:
A. Vision;
B. Imagination;
C. Planning;

When this important sixth sense is applied to the selling of a product the sales are realized in accordance to the degree that this sixth sense was applied: however, bear this in mind-too often we have tendency to copy the average businessman's sixth sense, rather than exert or create our own. When we do this, we become average and when we are average, we are as near to the bottom as we are to the top. Therefore, the creative sixth sense that you yourself possess in turn creates vision, imagination and planning.

Facts:

Let us inculcate in our minds a fact that we business people are, or should be, aware of. The bulk of the retailer's business is done on only a handful of items, and approximately one-half of the retailer's business is done in only twelve hours out of the week. The bulk of the retailer's purchases is done with only a handful of vendors. Take Goldblatt's case as an example-of 8,264 vendors from whom we buy, less than 500, or approximately 6% of them, sell us 53% of our total purchases. These facts are so mainly because the manufacturer, with the consumer in mind, has laboratory tested, researched, perfected and guaranteed his product to the consumer. Then he's gone a step further by nationally advertising it, thereby creating a consumer acceptance so that the article is practically pre-sold even before the retailer stocks it.

Here is a typical example: For many years we sold automobile tires exclusively made for us under our own brand name, Apollo Tires," The quality was competitive and our prices were much lower than other brands. Two weeks ago we discontinued this private brand of tire and replaced them with the nationally famous brand of Firestone. Our sales zoomed up very suddenly. We discovered in one quick flash that we suddenly had what the customer wanted-a national brand that they could rely on, a brand of tire they could feel more safe on, when driving their car.

All this can be defined in two words-"national brands," These words are important to Goldblatt's, as they are to all retailers across the country. They mean simply that you are selling what the customer wants, when she wants it and at a fair price. Now let us keep these facts in the back of our minds so that we may connect them with the following comments:

We buy the future with the present:

We buy the future with the present. There is nothing you can do about today. Today is only something you spend to buy the future with. Our interest should be only in the future because that is where we are going to spend the rest of our lives. For this future we apply our sixth sense; however, we merchants in the business world have been calling this sixth sense by another name-we have been referring to it as "budgets."

And just what is a budget? Surely it does not differ from a goal, a vow, a pledge, a promise, a will. How do budgets come about? Budgets come from past experience, present trends and the immediate future outlook. This I choose to call the sixth sense, and I would like to describe these three parts of the sixth sense as I see then:

Vision-Imagination-Planning:

Vision-Imagination-Planning. Considering the word "vision" brings to mind a deity of ancient Greek mythology named Janus, for whom the month of January was named. Janus had two faces, one in front and one in back. He could not see the future without seeing the past. He could not see the new year without seeing the old year. In business, to get on the forward we have to get off the behind.

We are all gifted with the power of imagination. We are all capable of dreaming, but to make a dream come true we must wake up. As an example, we once dreamed that we could sell a quantity of outboard motors in the winter time when the Chicago lakes were frozen over with ice. We once dreamed that we could sell a large quantity of Christmas greetings cards a week after Christmas. These dreams have come true.

Very recently we dreamed that $1,000,000 worth of lawn mowers could be sold during a time when snow was on the ground and this dream, too, is about to come true.

The getting of plus business, the being ahead of time is always dependent on the sixth sense-on vision, imagination and above all, planning. So, be ahead of the times and the future will catch up to you.

When we take vision and imagination and wed them in marriage they are bound to give birth to planning, and here comes the real physical task for creating from our minds a tangible reality; however, these are nothing more than three spoken words and unless we put then into physical action we do nothing more than exercise our vocal chords.

Research:

Research? Let us now take from our mental storehouse the fact that the bulk of business is done on only a handful of items, from a handful of vendors in only a handful of hours of the week. We must now find out which are the items that are only a handful. This we arrive at through research on proven sales-producing products, and on our intuitive sense pertaining to new, untried products. However, don't permit the word "research" to scare you.

There is research on a grand scale, in an expensive way, over a long period of time, and there is research in a small way that costs nothing and takes only a few moments. As an example, how many did we buy? How many do we have left? We know our sales for a given period of time. We must realize that it is research that gives birth to vision. Once we know a fact that comes about through research we then have vision. We can foresee, we can look into the future with a reasonably good eye. To have vision we must first analyze and know what competition and we ourselves have done and what we're doing.

It is the customer's wants that give birth to imagination and this, too, comes through research or observation. The businessman without observation is an automobile without wheels. We know what the customer purchased yesterday, we know what the customer is purchasing today; therefore, we have a pretty good idea of what the customer will purchase tomorrow. To this knowledge we apply our creative sixth sense for the functions of buying, selling and merchandising.

We Don't Know Our Own Strength:

We just don't know our own strength. Man does not have power any more than an electric cord has current. Power flows through man just as current flows through an electric cord. Most often when we can't perform a given task it's because we believe we can't do it. Very often the power to perform must be drawn our of us by others,

Being Competitive in the Present Times:

There is one proven barometer that measures the degree of competiveness. In my opinion this barometer is advertising expenditures. The more advertising dollars spend the greater is the competitive times. I feel that this 1957 year we are in is more competitive than at any time, mainly because advertising expenditures will soar this year to a record-smashing ten and a half billion dollars ($10,500,000,000), while the economy as a whole has trouble just inching ahead. The top question that will be facing many advertisers before long is: "Are we spending too much, or not enough?"

My personal feelings are that it is not a question as to whether we will spend too much or not enough. I feel that whether we are spending a little or lot we are not spending wisely. Through negligence and recklessness we are not receiving just sales returns for dollar spent, and the reasons are very simply. We do not apply the full measure of our sixth sense-of vision, imagination and planning-to the advertising dollar spent. I feel that industry spends a lot of time deciding on an advertising budget and then stops short when it comes to planning how this budgeted advertising expenditure should be used.

Let's take Goldblatt's as an example: When we buy advertising we do not buy lineage, square inches, full pages or space. We buy dollar sales returns for a dollar spend, regardless of media or size. We are primarily concerned with an advertising percentage cost rather than a dollar cost. We have no dollar limit nor do we budget a dollar expenditure. We do, however, budget an advertising percentage cost and we do limit this percentage, and even this percentage varies depending on the item in question and the time of the year. Just what must we do to get maximum sales returns for a dollar spend?

We must visualize the running of an ad far enough in advance, we must apply our imagination and we proceed to make dummy layouts. From many layouts we choose the one we feel will produce greatest sales returns. We then toy around with captions, copy, composition, illustrations, of course the article itself too, as to whether it's timely. The price, as to whether it's competitive, and all this, mind you, we do-or should be doing-sufficiently in advance so that when we rech the deadline we have achieved maximum perfection. But all of this truly only a small part of the necessary requisites for producing worthy sales per dollar spent.

After all is said and done, advertising is still an intangible element because sales returns must still be dependent on the manner in which we back up and ad. Is our quantity large enough? Do we have the article properly trained and have we created within them a "wantmanship" for wanting to sell the article? Were they sufficiently enthused by the contests and the prizes that we offer for those producing greatest or largest sales? Do we have the proper copy in the sign? Have we been creative and original in all of these elements?

Accordingly, a well-planned backup on a wanted advertised item invariably produces satisfactory sales returns except, of course, if an act of God interferes and a blizzard or an electric rain storm take place. Since I am talking to members of the Executive Advertising Club of Chicago I take it for granted that your greatest interest is advertising and that what you have to sell is advertising space. I feel that those of you that sell advertising space have a real problem on your hands.

Instead of selling linage, square inches or full pages, state selling your customers that which they are interested in, that which they want. They want sales. Sell then ideas and show them how to do more business. This automatically will produce a plus advertising business for you.

The Sixth Sense in Action:

The sixth sense in action. After all, what is manufacturing, buying and selling of not vision, imagination and planning? Why should the playing with electric toy trains be restricted to boys and their dads? Why shouldn't the little girls and their mothers enjoy this privilege?

The Lionel Company, makers of toy electric trains, has lifted the dividing curtain on this subject. For this Christmas you will see Lionel electric trains with a pink frosting locomotive, a buttercup yellow boxcar, a robin's egg blue boxcar, a lilac hopper and a sky-blue caboose. These will be in beautiful pastel colors and a brand-new market will open for the female customer. This company just had to have vision and imagination, and they had to plan such a selling program. That is how all items are created.

A Budgeted Sixth Sense:

Now what have we got? A budgeted sixth sense, and we will never be any bigger or better than our budget and, likewise, we will never be any bigger or better than we think or feel we are.

This nation's business and its being competitive in a country of free enterprise has always grown from the beginning of time, is growing and will continue to grow, because we Americans have and use a creative sixth sense.

Louis Goldblatt

To Get, You Gotta Give or Give and Take

by Louis Goldblatt

Executive Vice President Secretary and Treasurer,

Director of Merchandising Goldblatt Department Stores

Chicago, IL

AN ADDRESS BEFORE THE 15TH ANNUAL
MANAGEMENT SEMINAR FOR SMALLER BUSINESS
AT THE DOWNTOWN COLLEGE OF THE UNIVERSITY OF CHICAGO
ON FEBRUARY 26, 1962

Reproduced through the courtesy of the Chicago Tribune

When I first accepted the invitation to speak to you tonight, I realized to difficult task ahead of me because the subject I was asked to speak to you on was entitled: "What Major Retail Outlets Expect From a Manufacturer and His Product."

In my own opinion, any retail outlet, be it major or minor, has no right to expect anything from a manufacturer and his product without realizing that the manufacturer expects something from the retailer in return. Therefore, in order to get going on this subject, I had to change the title to read: "To Get, You Gotta Give," or "Give and Take."

Any business, be it resource or retailer, such as is represented here tonight, must be dependent on many important elements of "Give" and "Take."

The three principal requisites a business must first be concerned with are–past history, present trend, and, future budgeting. These three requisites shape our future merchandising and promoting performances.

We already know what the past is. It is plainly recorded in history. We already know what the future holds, so we are prepare a budget. A budget composed of "Gives" and "Takes." The quality of our budgeting is dependent on the merchandising techniques we apply to our buying, selling, and promoting functions.

A business, like a human being, lives on hopes and desires. A business, like a human being, sets itself a goal; makes a pledge; takes a vow. In business terms, we call these acts budgets.

A budget when finally created, is composed of a series of statistical figures such as sales, inventory, stock turns, merchandise margin, advertising expenditure, operating cost, net profits, etc. I choose here to call these various elements by such names that usually do not appear on a budget sheet. Accordingly, I will refer to them as "Prime Resources," "Ordinary Resources," "The Retailer," "Advertising," "Display," "Salesmanship," and "Mental Attitude."

You will observe I have two kinds of resources–A Prime Resource, (the long range lasting type), and Ordinary Resource, (the short range, hit and run type), as part of these budgets.

For every ordinary resource that we can convert into a prime resource, we automatically enhance our wishes, goals, vows, pledges, and budgets. In simple words, we improve our merchandising and promoting job.

The word "merchandising" comes from the Latin word "Mercor," which means, to buy and sell. The word "Promote" comes from two Latin words–"Pro," meaning move. Together they mean "forward move." In buying and selling, and in moving forward, our budgeting must have the proper mix of elements.

The Prime Resource Element

Not so many years ago, the expression "caveat emptor" was common–"customers beware." The manufacturer primarily made his goods with the sole intention of selling them to the retailer. The retailer in turn depended solely on his salesmanship in selling his goods to the consumer. Today, the successful manufacturer or vendor, creates his product with the consumer as his sole concern. His primary objective is to give the consumer all that her money can buy, and, the most serviceable product he knows how to make. To do this, he engages in research, laboratory testing, experience, and know-how. When he has finally created the best possible product, he sells it directly to the consumer, through his national advertising program. Then, to further complement his already successful accomplishment, he stands behind each purchase of his product by guaranteeing the consumer's complete satisfaction.

Today, unlike the custom of not so many years ago, this prime resource also protects the consumer by properly labelling his products. Today's products now plainly show the contents and describe the ingredients, whether they pertain to style, color, shape, size, or durability. The resource provides this information on his product's label, in addition to conforming with such provisions as may be required by the Federal Food, Drug and Cosmetic Act, Trade Practice Act, F.T.C., The National Bureau of Standards, Wool Products Labeling Act, Advertising Standards Committee, Name of Woods Code, Better Business Bureau, The Federal Hazardous Substances and Products Labeling Act (That just went into effect three weeks ago), and many more,

I can remember a number of years ago, when the only way to determine the quality of a pound of grass seed was by the price, unless we sent the seed to the laboratory to learn what ingredients it contained. Then, our helpless customers could only take our word for it. Today, when a customer buys a package of grass seed, she knows the percentage of red top, blue grass, white clover, timothy, inert matter, etc. It is printed right on the package.

I can also remember that in the past, when we opened a sack of feathers, or a pillow, we would blow into it so that we could have a better idea as to what portion of the feathers was goose, duck, turkey, or chicken-whether it was part feathers and part down, or, all feathers, or all down.

In those days, feathers frequently weren't even washed. Today, there is a National Association of Bedding Manufacturers, organized by the manufacturers themselves. They constantly make purchases in retail stores, and send them to the laboratories to see whether or not the contents are properly labeled, and if all feathers are washed and sterilized. They do their own policing, thereby protecting the consumer from paying for something they don't get. This in turn automatically protects the retailer.

The progress towards educating the consumer through information contained on products-be they the wood content in a sweater, the filling in a mattress, or the ingredients of a vitamin tablet, has helped to a great degree in placing vendor and retailer relationship on a more harmonious level.

In this way too, the consumer has been educated as to what she has a right to get for her money, and, she has continued to buy, when she has found the product serviceable and satisfactory. Accordingly, as far as the retailer is concerned, this resource has already performed a pre-selling job.

The prime resource knows that if his product is sound, and, if it is what the consumer wants, the consumer will buy it-provided of course, that he supplies the retailer with the necessary sales policy and incentives for feeling the same way about the product.

In this manner, a prime resource never stops perfecting his product. He continues to pour more effort and money into further bettering his product, and the consumer continues to enjoy a better, more luxurious and easier way of life, through the use of these constantly improved products.

In the very recent years, the prime resource has taken on additional responsibilities other than the mere manufacturing of a product. He has now added a series of services to the retailer, as for example the following: he has a back-up inventory stock so that the retailer can operate with a minimum inventory and still get delivery on reorders fast: thereby giving the retailer the opportunity for greater return on investment, through inventory turnover.

He has stepped up his efforts for more efficient inspection functions at the manufacturing level, assuring the retailer of uniform and perfect quality goods. He has designed selling fixtures and signs, and in some cases even provides them gratis to the retailer. He has also improved his packaging, for better self-selling. He has added a personnel payroll, for the purpose of visiting the retailer more frequently, in order to give aid towards producing maximum sales on his product.

The Retailer Element

The average retailer who buys from prime resources no longer depends solely on his own salesmanship. He no longer requires laboratory testing equipment to check up on his resources. He merely requires the ability to be a top retail distributor of merchandise to the consumer. To do that, old ways of selling have been replaced by modern methods. The average large retail distributor functions in the following manner in distributing his resources' goods to the consumer:

He requires a system of basic stocks, unit controls and selling trend statistics. These systems tell him what the customer wants, when she wants it, and how much she wants. Based on these systems, the retailer's buyers purchase their requirements through information compiled by clerical personnel and machines, not by their personal whims, moods, likes, or dislikes, Through these systems, the retailer no longer needs to be a genius or a master-mind. His most important requirements now are to purchase from top prime resources and, to promote the goods he purchases.

Allow me to portray the workings of Goldblatts in both the buying and selling fields. In most cases, when we buy from top prime resources, we automatically become an important retail distributor of nationally known branded items. Our success in doing a good sales job on this kind of merchandise depends upon how we back up the selling program as laid down by the prime resources.

We make use of their national advertising in the newspapers, magazines, radio and television. Our presentation of the product to our customers requires effective display on our selling floors. Most often our displays include window back-up plus store-wide displays. We orient our personnel with all the facts pertaining to the products through a series of meetings bulletins. Very often we make the selling of the item a game, through the means of prizes and contests. We include all our stores on such a program at one time thereby creating maximum impact on the consumer. Of course all of this is done only if we have certain incentives.

Just what incentives do we retailers look for when we take on a resource's product? We are concerned with the reorder business on the item, not just a hit-and-run, sell-and-forget event. The item must produce a good turnover and, produce good investment returns. We must be fully sold on the item. We must know that our customers will get their money's worth; that they will be pleased with their purchase, and, as a result, will continue to ship in our stores.

No, I did not leave out the Very important incentive...the item we take on must be profitable. With all these incentives, we build a stronger bond between our customers and our prime resource.

Of course this in itself is not the complete story of what is required to retail a resource's products successfully. We must also provide our customers with the necessary conveniences, and with courteous service. Naturally, we must also have a powerful and loyal team of employees who receive every known employee benefit and consideration.

Allow me to further elaborate on Goldblatt's buying habits and our relationship with our prime resources. There is one salient signpost the retailer has today that he has had from the beginning of time...the one that has not changed even to this day. For years, the retailers, ourselves included, were concerned with this one question-"will we make our day?" That seemed to be our one and only measuring rod. Strange as it may seem, past history, plus present trend statistics, permit us to plan future sales budgets that come very close to actual sales. We know that if we do nothing more for a given day's sales than we did for the corresponding day a year ago, we can expect nothing better than to equal our sales figures of a year ago.

The ever common expressions in the retail business are, "will you make your day?", "did you make your day?", and, "what percentage did you increase or decrease?"

Life is a game, play to win!

We have attacked this age old sales attitude with counterphrases. Now we say, "what did you buy?" and, "how much did you buy?" and, "from whom did you buy?" You have often heard the proverb, :as ye sow, so shall ye reap." To paraphrase it in the retailing business, it's "As ye buy, so shall ye sell", or, "As ye sell, so shall ye buy."

Some years back we launched a program known as Goldblatt's vendor relationship policy. We listed all the resources with whom we do business by department. We then began the tedious and herculean task of breaking down our findings into a series of statistical figures. We wanted to know which resources produced a profit for us; which were responsible for our markdowns. We wanted to know suck things as what our advertising cots were by resource; what percentage of total square footage in a given department was devoted to a resource's products; what percentage of a department's total business was done by each, and what our rate of stock turn was on the products of each resource. Most important, we wanted to know exactly what percentage of each department's total purchases were made from each resource.

After this information had been compiled, we sifted out all the resources which proved to be prime and these became an important part of our company.

Just as we rate the ability of our buyers in the course of the year, and review their showings periodically, we now rate and review these prime resources with whom we do business.

In recent years we made great strides in furthering our resource relationship policy. At the close of last year, we found that our company had purchased merchandise from 8,364 resources. We found that only 493 prime resources, or less than 6% of all with whom we do business, accounted for 53% of our total purchases for the year.

Our objective is to increase the number of prime resources with whom we do business. It is our further objective to reduce the number of resources which are nothing more than ordinary.

The average layman sees a chain of department stores, like ours, doing $117,000,000 worth of business annually and sees thousands upon thousands of items. The impression he gets is that we sell quantities of each of these many items. That is not true. We do not sell all the items we carry in quantity. There are some items, and only relatively few of them, that we sell in suck huge quantities that they make the thousands of other items we carry look as if they are standing still. It is our guess that 30% of a retailer's inventory produces 70% of his sales, and very often even accounts for 85% of his profits.

For example in our men's furnishing department, which consists of shirts, ties, belts, hats, jewelry, sweaters, pajamas and robes, and where we purchase from 198 resources, yet in this classification of goods, one resource, Phillips-Van Heusen Company, or 1/2 of 1% of all resources this department buys from, does 20% of the square footage nor does it account for 20% of the markdowns in this department. Its rate of inventory turnover is far greater than many other items in this department. This prime resource contributes a greater share to our profit picture than many other classifications of goods combined. We buy this brand from a resource whose product's performance, and whose program for merchandising is classified as a prime resource.

The Phillips-Van Heusen Company made a man's shirt and they made it most excellently. They created a consumer demand because of their knowhow , based upon many years of experience and research. They have given it every known king of laboratory test.

After putting it on the market, they sold it to the consumer through a good job of national advertising. Then, they protected their policy program of distribution which included the necessary incentives from the retailer. Them, they virtually took the customer by the arm and brought her into our store so that all we had to do was display it.

Since our display was effective, and we carried it in the colors, sizes, and styles the customer wanted, through our systems of unit control; had it when the customer wanted it, and conformed with the Philips-Van Heusen Company's policy for merchandising this item, we of course did a top retail distributing job on the product.

No salesperson stood at the counter and used any high-pressure salesmanship in selling a Van Heusen shirt to the customer. It was the customer who demanded the Van Heusen shirt. All we did was take her money, ring up the sale, and wrap her package.

This prime resource and his retailers work harmoniously thereby giving this prime resource the necessary tools for further perfecting his product in the interest of bettering the American consumer's way of life.

The prime resource and the retailer are partners. If two partners do not get along, a business cannot grow. A top prime resource is the top retailer's teacher. The top retailer is the material upon which the top prime resource works. If the one does not value his teacher...if the other does not love his material, them, despite their individual abilities and capacities, they cannot build a growing business, or produce a satisfactory net profit.

It is important that a resource and retailer work very closely. It is important that they be concerned with each other's success and, that there be a constant give and take attitude between them. Both together, purchase the future with the present. Both their futures-the resource's and the retailer's, will always be dependent on what they both do together today.

The Advertising Element

Take Goldblatts for example. Our advertising expenditure last year was slightly under 41/2 million dollars. This sizeable sum was spent in such medic as metropolitan, community, suburban, foreign, and our own shopping newspapers; also radio, television, billboards, telephone, direct mail, etc. I spending this large sum of money for advertising we did not aim to buy linage, space, pages, circulation, or media. Instead it was our objective to purchase the greatest amount of sales return per advertising dollar spent.

Buying advertising differs considerably from buying merchandise. When we purchase a product, we want to know what it is made of, how well it will serve us, are we buying it at a fair price. However, when we purchase advertising, we are concerned with its end result...dollar sales returns. We are good buyers of advertising, only when we purchase a low advertising percentage cost. The greater the seals returns, the lower the advertising percentage cost "Advertising is like the banking business-you never take our more than you put in.

Again the element of "Give" and "Take" comes into play. We must deal with prime advertising media, and in order to get from then a low advertising percentage cost, we must give them a timely, wanted item, attractively priced. We must give the proper copy, composition, and illustration. There is no such think as a perfect ad. There is always one that could be even better, and produce even more sales.

The Display Element

The important element of display or item presentation; very often referred to as self-selection, was the very beginning of self-service. I can remember, some fifty years ago, when my brother Maurice was a salesclerk at Iversons Department Store on Milwaukee Avenue. After working many hours and late into the evening, he would come home and right after dinner, would practice show-card writing. He was preparing himself for a future day when he would be in business for himself. He felt that the most important thing necessary to succeed in business is to know how to display merchandise on a table, how to trim a window, and how to paint a sign.

Forty-eight years ago, my brothers Maurice and Nathan, with their total savings of five hundred dollars, opened up for business. Their ages were 22 and 20. With the after-school help of their two younger brothers, Louis and Joel, their ages 10 and 7, they started off a business that was to grow into the present Goldblatt Bros. Department

Stores that will this year number a chain of thirty (30) stores.

For several years after we were in business, my brother Maurice made all the signs and did all the display work. Today of course we have machines that make signs, and we employ professional interior and exterior display personnel. Signs must have informative copy. The sign on the item must be, not only the silent, buy salient salesperson to our customer. The item on display must stop, tempt our customer, and produce and impulse sale. We may be selling the product that a prime resource produced, buy we will sell much more if we display if effectively. We may spend the money for advertising, and it will produce a certain sales return, buy, the percentage of advertising cost will be lower for the same advertising dollar expenditure if we do a plus business on this advertised item through our display efforts.

I remember how my brothers and I got up at the crack of dawn on cold wintry days to climb a step ladder and pin to the awning outside of our store, underwear, blankets, aprons, etc. Around midnight we would again climb the ladders to take down the stiff, frozen garments. Was it more important then, than it is now, to display our wares? Of course it is much easier now. At least we don't wind up with frost-bitten fingers. The retailer generally must give, and make more use of his display tools, if he is to get more vendor cooperation and sales.

The Salesmanship Element

Just what does what word salesmanship mean? The dictionary defines this word as follows: "The art of selling, or especially successful selling methods." I feel that all selling personnel possess the art of selling and have the ability to apply especially successful selling methods. What the greatest majority don't have is "Wantmanship." What they know and have the ability to do is one thing but whether they want to do it is something entirely different. We need to give "Wantmanship" To salesmanship.

There is nothing wrong with our sales personnel of today. Whatever may be wrong is so because of poor supervision, interest, direction and training. The resource knows how his product was manufactured. The retailer too knows all its virtues. The advertisements in many cases rave about the product. Very often, the display indicates the product's many good features...but, too often, the sales personnel are kept in the dark of the romance connected with the manufacturing and distributing of this product. It is important for the them to be informed about a product's features. Sales personnel need a personal interest in the selling of the product.

This very often is done through prizes and contests, meetings, lectures, and training programs. It is also necessary that selling personnel get the maximum of employee benefits. For them to be interested in their work, they must be happy in their work. They too must see a future for themselves. They must want to sell the item. Their desires rest in their employer's hands. An employee will get nor more from his employee than he gives. The mere giving of a salary is not the total requisite. The employer must give of himself. He must be concerned and interested in his employee's welfare. An interested salesperson will make an added sale; will produce a greater transaction; will sell something to the customer in addition to what she came in to buy, and plus sales of this type represent a still greater net profit, since rent, light, heat, power, and other such expenses remain stationary regardless of sales volume. It takes and added push on the part of the salesperson to step up his or her selling efforts, but that added push requires "Wantmanship," which the heads of business have not instilled in sufficient measure.

The Mental Attitude Element

In preparing a budget of give and take, very much has to do with the mental attitude. Thus far, I have talked about the elements that make up a budget, which I have referred to as prime resources, ordinary resources, the retailer, advertising, display, and salesmanship. This entire list of elements, when put together, produces a past history; produces a present trend, and finally produces a future performance. All these elements are derived from the mother element-"Mental attitude."

Very rarely do we humans ever accomplish more than we set out to accomplish. Very rare also is a business better than it had planned to be. It seems we are creatures of habit. It appears that our minds are cluttered with last-year-itis. We have the tendency of planning to do what we did last year. In projecting a budget we analyze last year's results and our present trend. If we project an improvement over our previous performance, usually it is merely a trifle. Mainly, this is because we do not know our own ability, our own skill, talents, and strength. If I were to ask any one of you to place your ankles on the arm of a chair and the back of your neck on the arm of another chair, with nothing supporting you between your ankles and neck, you would say that you couldn't do it. You truly believe you cannot do it. Yet, if you were hypnotized and put in that position, you not only would find that you had done it buy could even do so with 200 pounds of weight on your stomach.

Subconsciously we very often are powerful and strong. Consciously we do not do a certain thing because our mental attitude tells us we can't...we think small, and as a result, produce small. A business looks at its last year's record. Last year on a given day it did X amount of business. This year it projects a budget to do the same amount of business with possibly a small increase or decrease, and it actually will produce what the budget calls for.

If we were told that we must produce a 20% sales increase...that it was a matter of life or death, I'm positive we would come through with our 20% increase. Mainly, I'm finding fault with the businessman's method of budgeting in that it lacks the proper mental attitude element, which in turn comprises all the elements of give and take that I have thus far portrayed.

For budget to be sound, every small part of this budget must be sound in itself. Actually, we get no more of a future than we earn. IN simple words, we purchase the future with the present. A budget in itself does not produce a successful future performance. The future will never be any better than what we are doing about it today, nor will it be any better than the quality of our mental attitude today.

Give and Take

In conclusion, we begin and end with a give and take function. These are the things a retailer must give:

(1) He must give a permanent home to a prime resource's line of goods, rather than to have his item scattered and mingled among competitive inferior products.

(2) He must back up this goods with effective displays.

(3) He must protect a prime resource's line against competitive lines, and cannot prostitute these products by discontinuing it one day, and adding it back to his stock the next.

(4) His percentage of our-of-stocks on a prime resource's products should be at the very lowest minimum.

(5) The retailer should adhere to the prime resource's selling policy.

(6) He should promote various intervals throughout the year a prime resource's products so as to keep them constantly alive and before the consumer.

(7) He should place purchase orders with the prime resource far enough in advance and at a time when the prime resource prefers it.

(8) He should improve his purchases with the prime resources each year to a new high, and he should never stop growing.

(9) A retailer's account must be profitable to a prime resource, because if he doesn't give them a profit, he won't get a profit.

(10) He must at all time live up to his promises.

If we do this kind of giving, then, these are the things we take:

Life is a game, play to win!

(1) Deliveries must be prompt, and as per the date on the purchase order. A resource who would ship in advance of a delivery date, or later than the delivery date calls for, would have no right to call himself anything buy an ordinary resource. He would also be an ordinary resource if he shipped a larger quantity than what the purchase order calls for, or if he would substitute what a retailer had purchased in either size, style, color, or quality.

(2) A prime resource's product must have a uniform quality standard. If and when this quality standard deviated, then of course he is an ordinary resource.

(3) A retailer expects and should get promotional cooperation rather than be romanced into purchasing a line of goods, and then be dropped or forgotten.

(4) A retailer expects representatives from a prime resource to call on him often and at regular intervals, so that he may be constantly kept on his toes in selling successfully a resource's products.

(5) A retailer wants to and expects to buy proven items-consumer preference type items.

(6) The retailer further expects display and advertising aids from the resource.

(7) On occasion, the retailer wants and expects prizes and contests for stimulating plus sales on a resource's products.

(8) A retailer wants a good return for investment which comes about through a good inventory turnover, This is accomplished through a daily procedure of placing reorders. A prime resource makes this request possible by having an in-stock inventory so that he can deliver fast and often.

(9) A retailer wants to make a profit on the prime resources and this is accomplished when a prime resource has a proper distribution system that protects his retailers from both the retailer's and the resource's competitors.

(10) A retailer expects a resource's promises to be lived up to.

The United States has moved into a period of intense competition from abroad and right here at home. Goods are more abundant than ever. The greatest requisite for being competitive, for doing more business, for attracting more customers, lies in the art of giving. Gibe the customers the values they want. Give the employees of yourselves. Give the resources cooperation. Then, you will get from the customer, from the employee, and from the resources, what you want. You gotta give, to get!